Brave New Words

Brave New Worlds

BRAVE NEW WORDS

EDITED BY
SUSHEILA
NASTA

WITH
RUKHSANA YASMIN

First published in 2019 by
Myriad Editions
www.myriadeditions.com

Myriad Editions
An imprint of New Internationalist Publications
The Old Music Hall, 106-108 Cowley Road, Oxford OX4 1JE

First printing
1 3 5 7 9 10 8 6 4 2

A CIP catalogue record for this book is available
from the British Library
A CIP catalog record for this book is available
from the Library of Congress

ISBN (pbk): 978-1-912408-20-7
ISBN (ebk): 978-1-912408-21-4

Printed and bound in Great Britain
by Clays Ltd, St Ives plc

*To all those who continue to write
and make new, and to Conrad*

Contents

Preface

WASAFIRI HAS BEEN an international fixture for over a third of a century. In this time much has changed in the world of imaginative writing. This collection of essays points to important developments in technology, and interrogates the very definition of what constitutes literature—in short, *Brave New Words* helps us to understand many of the challenges that literary practitioners face today. The anthology extends and deepens a partnership between *Wasafiri* and writers and readers, an ongoing dialogue which began in that most symbolic of years, 1984.

There are, of course, always more questions than answers. What can writers do about continued violations of the rights of citizens; the closing of national borders; perpetration of false, and often insidious, news and information? Are writers obliged to respond to these dilemmas or should they be free to pursue their art without feeling pressured to become quasi-reporters from the frontline of the socio-cultural battlefield? What can writers do about the rise of a fundamental version of political correctness which attempts to impinge upon one's ability to imagine across so-called 'boundaries' of race, class, nationality, sexuality and gender?

The essays in this collection address these questions and many more issues which affect the writer in the early twenty-first century. Publishing, for example, is an industry where writers are becoming increasingly diverse, but those who control publishing look much the same as they have always done; they are white and middle class. How, in an increasingly heterogeneous multi-racial and culturally complex world, is this affecting what kind of literature reaches us as readers?

The title of the anthology suggests an engagement with the future, as opposed to nostalgic tiptoeing through the evidence of previous years. This is perhaps the greatest strength of the volume; a belief that despite the difficulties of the past, and the confusion of the present, literature can still take the lead and guide us towards a time in which words delivered from all sections of society will carry equal weight and importance. Such a world would indeed be brave.

Caryl Phillips
23 June 2019

Introduction

The vitality of language lies in its ability to limn the actual, imagined and possible lives of its speakers, readers, writers...It arcs toward the place where meaning may lie.
— Toni Morrison

The interior space of our imagination is a theatre that can never be closed down. — Salman Rushdie

LITERATURE IS A STOREHOUSE, a repository of words and stories which can travel across borders and across time. In March 2016, I was visiting Margate, a town on the Kent coast, when by chance I wandered into Turner Contemporary, an expansive gallery hugging the seafront. The Brexit referendum was still a few months off, but puffed-up promises of a new Britain, standing fearlessly alone and breaking free from its closest neighbours in Europe, were swirling. As I stepped into the quiet of the museum, I found myself in a huge room, brightly lined from ceiling to floor with batik-covered books, an installation by the leading British-Nigerian artist Yinka Shonibare that was named 'The British Library'.[1] As famous names jumped out from gold-embossed spines—Sigmund Freud, Karl Marx, Joseph Conrad, Oscar Wilde, Ben Okri, Zadie Smith—I began to realise that almost all were linked to migration and to Britain. Through the collection of stories lining the shelves, this long history was being placed centre-stage.

At first I was enthralled by the invented library due to my recognition of a history and community of migration narratives to which I felt I could belong. Not only was I familiar with some of the names of authors on the shelves but in some cases I knew the writers personally as well as their histories. Yet looking closely made me aware that the 'library' represented more than one artist's intimate vision, or any single pathway into history; it was also a performative public space, confronting viewers with multiple and sometimes competing narratives. Indeed, while the weight of over 6,000 names seemingly cemented a vision of a more hospitable Britain, it was clear that the exhibit was not simply offering a smooth, neatly conjured story by flagging the rich jewels of a history of migration or positing what has come to be commonly known as the celebratory narrative of the 'good immigrant'. Unlike the vision—highlighted at the opening of the London 2012 Olympics ceremony—of a buoyant, rainbow Britain, seemingly at ease with its diversity, but nevertheless masking the latent hostilities already experienced by Britain's black citizens and soon to become the 'Windrush' scandal, I noticed that many names also present—Oswald Mosley, GK Chesterton, Enoch Powell and, more recently, Nigel Farage—were notorious for their xenophobic and loudly expressed anti-immigration stance. Other spines had no names at all, perhaps leaving, as the artist has intimated, the future open.

This experience took me back to a journey I had myself made many years before, at school in the early 1970s and later, when I was inspired to launch *Wasafiri*, the magazine of international contemporary writing which this special anthology of essays partly celebrates. As a child of mixed Indian-English background, spending my teenage years in a provincial Suffolk town, the closest I got to India was through a chance encounter with EM Forster, whose famous 1924 novel *A Passage to India* suddenly appeared without context on my school's sixth-form reading list. And while I recall that my mother's bookshelves were populated by a sprinkling of books, wedged between English classics, by Rabindranath Tagore, Mulk Raj Anand, RK Narayan, Anita Desai, Ruth Prawer Jhabvala—a grouping I now realise reflected my family's moves between India, England and Europe—I was not interested then in how they had got there. It was some time before I was able see the many mixed cultural forces which had always impacted on traditional canonical English figures such as Chaucer, Shakespeare, the Brontës, Henry James and TS Eliot. And it was only later, during my undergraduate degree at the University of Kent—on a course almost unique in British universities at the time—that I began, through an immersion in the works of now internationally distinguished writers such as Derek Walcott, Jean Rhys, Chinua Achebe, Wole Soyinka, VS Naipaul, Sam Selvon and Kamala Markandaya, to gain access to a literary world that reflected anything approaching the mixed experience of my own.

Such writers were soon to set in motion an important sea change, shifting ways of seeing and transporting scores of readers across the vistas of new worlds. Coming from a range of historical and political contexts, often—though by no means only—linked to histories of colonialism and empire, of enforced political exile or movement, these voices were significant not only in swivelling the lens but in changing the perspectives of the stories that had previously contained them. Though Salman Rushdie's novel *Midnight's Children* (1981) is most often cited as the book heralding this particular moment in Britain—a point touched on by Blake Morrison in his contribution to this anthology—there were many others. In my case, it was Jean Rhys, the Caribbean and European modernist, who was first to lift my blinkers. Her fictions drew me deep into the worlds of nineteenth and early twentieth-century Dominica, Jamaica, Paris and London, and I recognised her sense of displacement, as a female writer of mixed background, perennially situated on the outskirts of the metropolitan literary world. Most importantly, I was blown away by the artistry of her prose, her characters and her nuanced construction of the conflicts—racial, economic, cultural—of a divided colonial world that forced me to read and think differently. As she so powerfully reminds us in *Wide Sargasso Sea* (1965), perhaps her best-known novel and one which provides a prequel to the back story of the mad Creole heiress in Charlotte Brontë's *Jane Eyre*: 'there's always the other side…always'.

It was writing such as this that led me to travel, through the literatures of the Caribbean, Africa, South Asia and black Britain, back into my own history and which motivated my work as teacher, editor and activist. It is perhaps no surprise that stories have always migrated. The dynamics of cultural growth or the birth of new artistic movements have most often been built—whether in ancient or modern times—on such cross-fertilisations, creating points of contact and connection, where admixtures are the norm and any notion of cultural 'purity' the aberration. So too, are the borrowings that often result from such crossings as stories, myths, and legends are recycled, translated, countered and reinvented. Yet such mixings have also resulted in negative articulations of cultural difference, such as the construction of the figure of the 'other', whether situated *within* the particular geographies of individual nations, or as those 'aliens' or 'strangers' who are perceived to threaten from outside.

In line with this, as some who lived through the cultural politics of the 1980s might remember, writers who were not immediately identifiable to reviewers through the comforting lens of a Euro-American aesthetic were often perceived to be off-centre by the arbiters of literary taste. This gatekeeping reverberated across all aspects of the industry from publishers to the writers themselves. Caryl Phillips summed up the experience of many in his early travelogue *The European Tribe* (1987). Reflecting on his early schooling in Leeds, he comments: 'I was never offered a text that had been penned by a black person... If the teaching of English literature can feed a sense of identity, then I, like many of my...contemporaries...was starving'. Phillips's sense of deprivation, fuelled by his lack of access to an imaginative world that existed outside the Anglo-Saxon tradition, paralleled my own and was replicated in many educational institutions across the country.

It was in this context that *Wasafiri* was born. While versions of how the magazine came into being vary, I have no doubt about what drove me to start the magazine with a community of colleagues and friends in 1984, a year now particularly resonant for its evocation of George Orwell's prophetically bleak vision of Big Brother and double-speak.[2] The cover of the first slim-bound red issue, which features a line-drawing of a group of independent pilgrims traversing the desert, still flags for us now what was already the magazine's prescient vision: to focus on writing as a form of 'cultural travelling', a passport to enter imaginative landscapes unseen and a conduit to the diverse histories of many worlds. Deriving from the Kiswahili word for 'travellers' (a version of the Arabic *safari*), its non-English name both heralded relations that could never be neatly contained and the hybrid signatures of the writers who were soon to fill its pages. Expressing sensibilities that straddled multiple identities, competing histories, languages and traditions, their words would come to interrogate existing orthodoxies and break through the borders of established literary canons as the magazine, then only available in hard copy, connected their respective worlds.

*

This anthology celebrates 35 years of *Wasafiri* and continues its founding aims. Yet the world is a very different place from the year the magazine first appeared. In the first decades after its launch, the fall of the Berlin Wall opened up the borders of Europe, apartheid was seen to 'officially' end in South Africa, the Good Friday agreement paved the path to peace in Northern Ireland. A major digital revolution had begun to open up the possibilities of the world wide web which, not yet the ominous agent it can be today, still offered the promise of an encyclopaedic and ever-expanding library as well as an open democratic space of unhindered global connection. Things were certainly not *all* positive— Thatcherism had resulted in an eruption of violence and economic unrest in the UK, Indira Gandhi was assassinated in India and WPC Fletcher shot outside the Libyan embassy. However, it felt at times as though there might be a shift, perhaps towards a growing awareness of cultural diversity and global connection.

Looking back, some of that optimism was clearly mis-judged. The past three-and-a-half decades have witnessed tumultuous changes. With Brexit promised in Britain alongside harsher immigration laws, a government-condoned culture of hostility towards asylum seekers and immigrants, and a policy of building increasing resistance to those so-called 'strangers' knocking on the nation's doors, the nation feels as divided as it was when *Wasafiri* was founded. Meanwhile narrow nationalist initiatives, often sparked by these unstable states of being, have given rise in the UK and elsewhere to the legitimisation of new populist movements and the far Right. As is increasingly apparent—amidst the disturbing rise of nationalist and religious fundamentalist movements worldwide—borders are being closed; and new walls, whether digital or real, are being constructed to restrict freedom of movement and communication. This climate has created a culture of fear, polarisation, division, prejudice and the re-creation in Britain of an increasingly insular and ever-smaller island, once more at risk of listening to the barrage of exclusionary and often outright racist discourses that first prompted *Wasafiri's* invention.

In this context, it is perhaps no surprise that dystopian classics such as *Brave New World* and Orwell's *Nineteen Eighty-Four* have once again gained prominence.[3] Both novels eerily signal how the truths of fiction can come worryingly close to reality: whether in imagining how the onset of an information revolution might change thinking or in creating a version of what we now call fake news—as encapsulated in the name of the Controller's meeting room in *Brave New World* ('Only Good News'), or in Orwell's totalitarian universe of three superstates, where you must 'reject the evidence of your eyes and ears'.

Today, the role of writers and of literature in asking questions and creating dialogues across often impassable barriers of prejudice and thought is not only vital but also perhaps more urgent than ever. As wordsmiths, whose craft uses the very same instruments through which political power is most commonly exercised, writers and politicians may well, as Salman Rushdie once put it, be 'natural rivals'. They both 'create fictions' but also make 'the world' as they want to see it. Yet as the words of writers frequently complicate, challenge or deny 'official versions of truth', giving the 'lie' to 'official facts', they are often on dangerous ground.[4] Moreover as intolerance of otherness continues to escalate, it is often also writers who continue to courageously speak their minds, despite censorship, detention and sometimes death. Above all, the worlds they open (and also contest) invite us to experience the world through the eyes of others. Perhaps the greatest writing does not just take us into other worlds but challenges us to shift our perceptions and recognise the stranger in ourselves.

As both an ancient and a modern art, one of the major functions of writing has not only been to inscribe but also to name and give voice. Writing enables us to question, complicate, doubt, act with abandon. Literature has always been a form of travel and writing, a place of experiment where words take on new meaning, ideas can be aired, criticisms levelled, creating a space of inquiry, ventriloquism, promiscuity and risk-taking.

Exploring the challenges and politics of writing now, the essays in this collection reflect distinctive literary voices which stem from a range of different cultural geographies. All point to the vital role of critical thinking in current times. As already intimated, the title of the anthology plays on and refashions the futuristic possibilities suggested by Aldous Huxley in his 1930s novel *Brave New World* in a contemporary context. With many antecedents—among them Plato's

Republic, 'Revelations' in The Bible, Thomas More's *Utopia*, Jonathan Swift's *Gulliver's Travels*, all of which imagine and create future worlds that step outside the anxieties of their own times—the controlling universe of Huxley's book can either promise, as history has often shown, a 'perfect-world utopia' or 'its nasty opposite'.[5] Drawn from Miranda's youthful misjudgement in *The Tempest*—'O brave new world, that has such people in it'—Huxley's title is deeply ironic. In Huxley's world of endless pleasure, bottle-bred babies and all-consuming conformity, it is John the Savage—a foil to the rest of the book's deterministic universe and exiled to a reservation for feeling, thinking and reading too much— who is the voice of Shakespeare's transported words.

*

Exploring the startling contemporary prescience of Huxley's vision, Romesh Guneskera's experimental essay engages directly with the theme of the collection by entering into an intriguing conversation with the dead author. In his 'modern séance' with Aldous Huxley, rendered as an appropriately disembodied digital conversation, Gunesekera interrogates Huxley on contemporary technology's potentially destructive implications for imagination, language and human freedom. In her essay, 'All the Feels', Olumide Popoola similarly attends to the potentially damaging effects of social media and digital communications on the human psyche. She suggests that it is only through exposing our vulnerability and removing the masks of endless digital equivocation that we will ever be able to assume full responsibility and engage in effective political action.

The need to protect privacy and maintain the freedom of writing in an increasingly public-facing world is a subject of concern to many. Tabish Khair's 'The Bravado of Books' reflects on the power of both the spoken and written word. Reminding us of the importance of the materiality of 'books' as objects that have travelled across time and continents and which continue to 'make words both new and brave', Khair insists that readers and writers must still be able to make these links if we are to avoid a precarious future and the potential loss of a library of memory in a digitising age. The significance of libraries, personal and public resonates across the anthology, along with the books that have been key to transforming writers' lives. As Mukoma Wa Ngugi (son of Ngugi Wa Thiong'o) demonstrates, while he was inevitably subject to early encounters with the politics of decolonisation and the writing of a now-well-established African literary canon, his own path to writing popular crime fiction stemmed from a completely different series of influences. In all cases, however, as Shivanee Ramlochan, Bernardine Evaristo and Blake Morrison individually reveal, our 'book shelves', however they have come into being, often transform our 'book-selves' (Morrison).

It is perhaps not surprising that latent and explicit worries about the disappearance of the book are embedded in several of the essays. Yet, for others, this is tempered by an awareness of the benefits of new technologies. As Bernardine Evaristo notes, the internet has not only changed the world of publishing forever, but has also 'reconfigured how we present ourselves to the world at large'. In particular, it has grown huge audiences for a new generation of millennial 'black womxn' writers who would not previously have had the freedom to move so swiftly past the barriers of literary gatekeepers in Britain and elsewhere and bring their work to the fore. Similarly, as Marina Warner proclaims in 'Out

Loud', what is now the web—or 'loom' as she renames it—is fast becoming a powerful public platform for new enunciations. Though not without obvious negatives, it can, she suggests, offer hospitality to those without permanent homes, provide the world's largest library, act as a theatre connecting writers and, with its polyphonic multiplicity, generate new 'hybridities and grafts' between sonic and more traditional forms. For Warner, metamorphosis is a key tenet of all literature. Stories and myths will always move and shift their shapes; yet such translations, whether of the old or the new, will no longer be 'bound' by the 'written text'.

Several writers take up the story, perhaps one of the biggest challenges of the modern era, of movement and migration. Whereas Blake Morrison takes us into the intimate complexities of his personal voyage out from his small village in Yorkshire, Eva Hoffman tells a broader-scale but no less powerful personal story of migration that also explores what makes us who we are. As she takes us through her Jewish background and her exile from Poland during the Cold War, she asks how memories of enforced and often violent displacement—images of Aleppo in ruins get superimposed on to her recollections from childhood—resonate in a contemporary Europe of supposedly elective free movement. Robbed of one language, she has to learn to inhabit another, a process of rupture and loss that continues to generate new work.

Questions of politics made more complex by the ethics of writing the 'other' remain pressing issues. James Kelman, Bernardine Evaristo and Hsiao-Hung Pai all remind us how activism continues to be an ever-important collective force in enabling writers to continue to work, be published, seen and heard. Yet, as Kei Miller subtly illustrates in 'The Minds of Writers', a dialogue stretching from Virginia Woolf to the Caribbean and the writings of a contemporary Jamaican journalist, such issues are never straightforward. So while writers may, whatever their cultural or social contexts, attempt to break new ground and engage with representations of 'otherness' again and again, they must avoid being carelessly unethical, shutting down rather than opening up possibilities. Like Miller, Shivanee Ramlochan shows us how her journey into writing and move away from being 'The Good Brown Girl' has involved a robust critique of inherited traditions and a necessary subversion of entrapping cultural stereotypes.

Writing and politics are strange bedfellows. However, as we see in the essays that overtly address the overlap, literature can guide us to new vantage points, leading us to places where activism alone cannot go and where words are able to cross the often delicate boundary lines between creative interpretation and critical judgement. Raja Shehadeh's description of 'The Dinner That Changed My Life' speaks directly to this as he recognises that the linear legalistic discourse with which he attempted to improve the 1992 negotiations between Palestine's PLO and Israel could never take him to a position from which he might actually be able to 'help rehabilitate the tarnished image of the Palestinians'. Githa Hariharan also points to how literature can perhaps achieve what politics cannot, recounting how the vitality of the ancient myth of Draupadi lives on in contemporary culture—despite censorship—in the power of the female body and the real-life resistance of the Indian women of Manipuri to oppression in 2004.[6]

Threats to writers and activists willing to speak out

against restrictions on democratic freedoms across the globe continue to be a most urgent concern. As Bina Shah makes plain in her personal account of the 'Life and Death of Pakistan's Sabeen Mahmud'—an activist murdered in Karachi in 2015 for opening up a cultural café that 'proffered' an open space for 'dialogue' and 'critical thinking'—writers living and working in such contexts are unable to 'keep silent', even when they know 'that speaking out might endanger our lives'.

Though writers may not be able to directly impact on politics and effect change in their worlds, their words certainly contain the passion and the courage to do so. For, as Caryl Phillips once put it in a comment which in part inspired the commissioning of this anthology: 'As long as we have literature as a bulwark against intolerance and as a force for change, then we have a chance... For literature is plurality in action; it embraces...a place of no truths; it relishes ambiguity, and it deeply respects the place where everybody has the right to be understood.'[7]

Susheila Nasta
September 2019

'Call Yourself English?'

Blake Morrison

'NOTHING HAPPENED but the wallpaper,' the American surrealist Dorothea Tanning said about her childhood in Illinois. I could say the same about mine in rural Yorkshire. The area was solidly conservative—traditional-minded, inward-looking and one of the safest Tory seats in the country. Deviations from the norm were severely punished. When a sixteen-year-old boy from my grammar school got his girlfriend from the High School pregnant, the pair of them were expelled and made to marry. There was also a deep suspicion of outsiders, meaning anyone who lived more than a dozen miles away. The only people of colour were the family running the Indian restaurant in nearby Skipton. Leeds seemed exotic and London—the Big Smoke—impossibly alien.

Now I live in London, one of the liveliest and most multicultural cities in the world, and feel at home there. The tie to where I grew up has loosened since my parents died and even more so since the referendum result of 2016. The Craven district, which encompasses villages like mine, was the first Yorkshire result to come through that night. The Leave margin wasn't as great as in many parts of Yorkshire—a mere 53 per cent to 47—and I take some comfort from that. But the outcome of the referendum made me despair, far more so than any General Election result has ever done. I ought to have been better prepared. I'd been in Goole and Hull just a few days before, and was reminded how disenfranchised people living outside the charmed circle of the M25 can feel. Still, I'd not anticipated that Brussels, rather than Westminster, would be blamed for this; that resentment against Tory austerity would be hijacked to become a rejection of the wider world; that racism, xenophobia and post-imperial nostalgia would carry the day. Ours is a global culture, I'd thought; we're all citizens of the world. Not according to Theresa May. If you believe you're a citizen of the world, she told the Tory Party conference in 2016, you're a citizen of nowhere.

On my occasional return visits to Yorkshire I'm always asked: 'So when are you coming back here to live?' Anyone who moves from the countryside to a big city, or from a small nation to a larger one, will have met with this reaction. 'Home' is where you come from, not where you migrate to: that's the premise and with it comes the assumption that what you'd 'really' like to do is return to your roots. There might be economic or pragmatic reasons keeping you away but surely, once the time's right, when you retire, say, you'll jump at the chance. 'When are you coming home, mate?' These days I dodge the question or make a joke of it: I would move back, I say, if the Yorkshire Dales weren't so cold and wet. But it's years since I seriously considered the possibility. Now the question I ask myself isn't 'Why don't I move back?' but, given the values I grew up with, and the pressure I was under to stay, what gave me the resources to leave?

*

There were surprisingly few books in the house when I was growing up—though middle-class professionals, my parents weren't great readers. But education was prized and the hope was that I'd go to university. Underlying that was a further hope—that I'd study medicine there, train to be a doctor, qualify, marry a local girl, take over the family GP practice and buy a house close to my parents' house, ideally next door. By the age of fifteen, I knew it wasn't going to happen. I did OK at science subjects but felt disqualified, temperamentally, from pursuing them further. More to the point, I'd become interested in literature and, along with that, began to feel a yearning for the wider world—to harbour a dream of elsewhere, which the future my parents were planning would stifle.

I say my parents but it was my father who'd mapped out my stay-at-home career. My mother, more ambivalent, didn't push me to the same degree. She herself had moved away, from a small town in the south of Ireland—first to Dublin, then over the water to England—and in doing so had set a dangerous precedent. To ease her assimilation into provincial England, she underplayed her origins; Irish was a dirty word then and so, in the Methodist North at least, was Catholic. I didn't know then that she was the nineteenth of twenty children (I found out only after her death). But I was deeply conscious of her foreignness. She might have been apologetic about them but to me the associations of Irishness (which included a talent for talking and writing: 'the gift of the gab') were romantic. Circumscribed though my upbringing was, my mother brought a sense of adventure to it. She stood for Otherness. And I wanted more of that.

*

Of those books we did have in the house, most were about getting away and having adventures. First came the Famous Five, a bunch of middle-class kids (and a dog) gloriously unsupervised by adults. Then Doctor Dolittle, whose voyage to Africa to save monkeys dying from disease didn't strike me as a colonialist raid but as a mercy dash by a philanthropic healer (the kind I wanted my parents to be). After that came the Swiss Family Robinson, shipwrecked on a tropical desert island en route to Australia and forced to make a new life for themselves, which they did with pioneering ingenuity. Islands featured a lot in my childhood and teenage reading: *Coral Island, Treasure Island, Robinson Crusoe, Lord of the Flies*. I might not be allowed to visit my mother's island (we went only the once, when I was small) but the literary substitutes served as well. Later, when I reached the sixth form, thanks to our English teacher (an Irishman), I began reading Irish writers, too: Joyce, Beckett, Synge, Yeats, Wilde, Sean O'Casey.

Bookshelves became my book-selves: alternative identities to be tried and tested; heroes I could emulate; minds I could temporarily inhabit. One day, perhaps, through literature, I'd find who I was and where I wanted to be. As Octavio Paz put it: 'To read is to discover unsuspected paths that lead to our own selves.'[1]

*

If I'd been luckier, my reading might have led me to post-colonial literature, or Commonwealth Literature as it was called (before Salman Rushdie, in a 1983 essay, decided that it didn't, or shouldn't, exist). But literature from outside the UK didn't feature on the school curriculum nor did it get much of a look-in on my degree course ('English Literature, Life and Thought') at Nottingham. I was a thoroughgoing Modernist—with Joyce, Lawrence and TS Eliot my idols—but it was years before I discovered the likes of Chinua Achebe and Mulk Raj Anand, Octavio Paz and Edward Kamau Brathwaite. I blame myself for a lack of initiative: there were so many books by Dead White European Males to get through, I didn't look beyond them. But little or nothing in British literary culture at that time suggested that I needed to venture more widely. Only one other continent deserved exploration: America, or rather North America, since South America (no less than Africa and India) could be ignored. By the time I left Nottingham, I'd read Poe, Whitman, Dickinson, Pound, Tennessee Williams, Mailer, Roth, Updike, Bellow, Ginsberg, Kerouac, Lowell, Berryman, Sexton and Plath. And over the following year, in Canada, where I did an MA, I read a good few Canadians too, including Margaret Atwood, whose newly published account of its literature, *Survival*, provided the lens through which I saw Canada. But whole continents of literature eluded me. And the PhD I began at University College London did little to alter that. My research topic was the Movement poets and novelists of the 1950s, the most insular group of writers in British literary history. I gave them some stick for that. But I was still pretty insular myself.

*

One of the things that changed that was reading Seamus Heaney. He'd come to talk to a small group of us at UCL soon after publishing his collection *North*. I was enthralled,

5

and later wrote a short critical guide to Heaney's work. *North* is the most political of his collections, and views the Troubles through the lens of post-colonialism, with Ireland seen as a country subject to constant occupation and exploitation. Heaney had recently spent a year in Berkeley, and the politicised atmosphere in the Bay Area, with minorities demanding their say, left its mark on him. Reading him set me reading some of the writers with whom he felt he'd things in common, including Derek Walcott.

I had a similar kind of awakening when I read *Midnight's Children* during a holiday in Morocco in 1981—we'd just discovered that my wife was pregnant with our first child. The book was a handsome object: a hefty hardback with uncut pages and a blue, faintly surreal cover depicting clock faces. Aptly enough, given that the text was much preoccupied with noses, it even smelled good. By the end of the first chapter I was hooked, confident that the narrator, Saleem Sinai—a cross between Laurence Sterne's Tristram Shandy and Scheherazade—would take me places I'd not been before.

Great books leave their mark on history—personal history as well as public. And for me the spring of 1981 will forever be associated with a sense of arrival. The novel won the Booker Prize in October and our first child was born a month later. Life would never be the same.

*

I got to know Salman soon afterwards. By the mid-1980s I was working on *The Observer* book pages and he began to do some reviewing for us. I remember going to lunch with him and his then wife, Marianne Wiggins. He'd come in a shiny new car, a physical manifestation of his success. He was proud of it—the car as well as the success. Hubris, you could say, knowing what was to come soon afterwards. But good luck to him was all I thought at the time. Fiction was thriving: publishers' advances had become more generous and the Booker had brought glamour to a previously unglamorous profession. Besides, I liked Salman. He was excellent company, a brilliant raconteur and mimic. Sure of himself, yes, a touch arrogant even. But why not? He'd written a terrific novel. And he was one of a generation of remarkable novelists (the generation to which I belonged) who were born and/or lived in the UK but whose names sounded strikingly un-English: Kazuo Ishiguro, Hanif Kureishi, Romesh Gunesekera, Timothy Mo, Ben Okri, Tibor Fischer, Caryl Phillips, Louis de Bernières, Lisa St Aubin de Terán. Salman was quick to notice the significance of this. As he put it in an article for *The Times* (3 July 1982): 'The Empire writes back with a vengeance.'

For me, the Eighties were a period of opening up. It wasn't just that I was discovering writers outside the canon. I began to approach books in a new way, not just as texts to be analysed, deconstructed and appraised, but as distillations of human experience inviting recognition or acknowledgment: a 'Yes!' in the margin when they articulated a feeling or thought I'd not seen in print before; an underlining of phrases that made something beyond my own experience palpable and comprehensible. *Only connect*. For the first time I was reading not academically but empathetically. It's what literature does: takes us new places; leaps the barriers of age, gender, nationality and ethnicity; lets us live inside the skin of others. I'd been slow to see that. But now I was messianic about it, as if books might have the power to stop wars, reverse climate change and make us better people.

'For God's sake, open the universe a little more!' goes

a line in Saul Bellow's *The Dean's December*. The universe, I thought, *had* opened a little. I was wrong.

*

Salman Rushdie likes to quote that Bellow line. But it was he, more than anyone, who heard its plea go unanswered. *The Satanic Verses* 'affair' of 1988, as it's now called, was a story about shutting down, not opening up. For those in Western democracies especially, the fatwa came as a brutal shock, shattering our assumptions that censorship, book-burning and the denial of freedom of expression were things of the past. I'd just discovered that books could be life-changing; now they'd acquired (or re-acquired) the potential to be life-ending. Under guard, in secret hideouts, Salman survived the threat. But others died, including his Japanese translator.

As with the 2016 UK referendum result, my reaction to the fatwa was a mixture of dismay and self-reproach: not just 'How could this have happened?' but 'Shouldn't I have seen it coming?' I was on the Booker Prize jury when *The Satanic Verses* came out; we had it on our shortlist (it eventually lost out to Peter Carey's *Oscar and Lucinda*) but not once during our jury deliberations, nor in any of the reviews I read, did its potential for causing offence come up for discussion. We weren't well enough informed about Islam to foresee trouble. And, secular-minded as we were, we couldn't imagine members of any religious faith, no matter how zealous, getting wound up about a mere novel. Novelists had the freedom to imagine whatever they wanted, right?

I saw a fair bit of Salman after the fatwa, in hiding though he was. He came round to dinner a few times (our kids grew up with the idea that whenever you have a supper party, two security men with guns will be sitting in the next room watching television) and, on the first anniversary of the fatwa, the *Independent on Sunday*, to which I'd moved from *The Observer*, carried his first major article after a year of silence, the essay 'In Good Faith'. A supporting (and supportive) interview wasn't originally part of the deal, but Salman agreed to it and I met him at a 'secret location' to record it. As the paper went to press, there were last-minute worries about my safety, since I was now implicated as an associate of his. A bodyguard was assigned to my family, and spent some days passing on tips about checking for suspicious packages and keeping a car in motion at traffic lights. The man stuck doggedly to his task for a couple of weekends, agreeing to leave us alone only during an outing to the gardens at Wisley, which he decided were probably free of Islamic extremists. Truly those were strange times. I never felt in the slightest danger but do remember thinking that, if I had to die, freedom of expression was a cause worth dying for.

*

An insult hurled at those of us who supported Salman was that we belonged to a 'metropolitan elite'. Prominent Remain-voters have recently been accused of the same crime. Other adjectives are also thrown in, such as 'Oxbridge-educated' (not applicable in my case), '*Guardian*-reading' (fair enough) and 'liberal' (a term tainted by association with neoliberalism, though, as Noam Chomsky has said, neoliberalism—free-market capitalism—'is neither new nor liberal'). 'Cosmopolitan' (another gibe) I could accept, but not 'metropolitan', let alone 'elitist'. Still, when you're white, male and middle-class, and edit the book pages of a London-based national newspaper (as I did until the mid-1990s), you're bound to come under suspicion. It's assumed you're a gatekeeper, opposed to innovation and diversity. And no matter how open your pages are to world literature—as Boyd Tonkin's famously were, for example, during his time as literary editor of *The Independent*—there'll always be a few people who regard you as narrow-minded, bigoted and bland. In short, as an—or *the*—enemy.

I got off lightly, perhaps. In his book *Whatever Happened to Modernism?* (2010), Gabriel Josipovici includes me among a generation of writers, including Julian Barnes, Ian McEwan and Martin Amis, whom he attacks for their English ironising and cynicism. But it's a mild swipe, and he and I have had friendly dealings ever since. More annoying was what James Kelman had to say in *Some Recent Attacks: Essays Cultural and Political*, a book published in 1992 but which I didn't come across till years later: 'Some of you may know of a recent controversy featuring the Nigerian writer Chinua Achebe. He described Joseph Conrad as a thoroughgoing racist and was attacked for it by, amongst others, Blake Morrison, a poet and critic who reviews current writing for mainstream media outlets. Now, quite simply, Blake Morrison is prejudiced'.[2] As someone who greatly admired Achebe's *Things Fall Apart*—in truth more than I admired the Conrad novels I'd read—and had no memory of attacking him, I couldn't understand what this was about. That I admired James Kelman's fiction, for its demotic energy and heft, made the attack all the more painful. Then I realised his mistake. He'd confused me with Craig Raine, who (I dimly remembered) *had* attacked Achebe for criticising Conrad. When I wrote to Kelman pointing out his mistake, he was apologetic—genuinely so, I think, not just from fear I'd pursue some libel action—and promised to change the offending passage if ever the book was reprinted. I suppose 'Blake' and 'Craig' sound a bit alike. And perhaps to a Scot, all Englishmen are tarred with the same brush. But I felt maligned and it took me a while to see the comedy of the error.

*

In 2003, after eight years as a freelance writer, I went back to university, as a professor of creative writing at Goldsmiths. As I soon discovered, academics and creative-writing tutors speak different languages: theirs is a scholarly discipline, ours is practice-based; they engage with theory, we—more editors than teachers—are hands-on. The disparity took some getting used to. But we made the effort to understand each other. I was—still am—lucky in my colleagues.

One of those colleagues was the professor of post-colonial studies, Bart Moore-Gilbert, who began his inaugural lecture, given soon after I arrived, by inviting his audience to choose between the two texts he'd brought along, one drily theoretical, the other about sex. (No prizes for guessing which we went for.) I liked Bart, who among other things had written a monograph on Hanif Kureishi, but I knew next to nothing about his life. At some point round the same time, I was one of the judges for the 2009 *Wasafiri* life writing prize. The clear winner among the anonymous entries was a piece written from the point of view of a boy at an English boarding school, who is summoned to the headmaster's study to be told that his father has been killed in a plane crash in Africa. The piece, it turned out, was by Bart. Encouraged by his success, he applied to do a creative writing PhD at Goldsmiths, which in 2014 came out as a book, *The Setting Sun: A Memoir of Empire and Family Secrets*. There's a major irony at the heart of the book: Bart's discovery, while researching it, that his father had served with (and may have acted brutally on behalf of) the Indian police force; the post-colonialist son learns that his dad was a colonialist oppressor. Of all Bart's books, this was the one he had to write. Tragically, within a year of its publication, aged only 62, he was dead from kidney cancer.

*

At least Bart didn't live to see Brexit. I sometimes think of others who didn't live to see it, and how they'd have voted, from Harold Pinter, Doris Lessing and Muriel Spark (surely all Remainers) to little Englanders such as Philip Larkin, Kingsley Amis and my dad (all Brexiteers). What about Seamus Heaney, who when Andrew Motion and I included him in the *Penguin Book of Contemporary British Poetry*, famously protested, in a verse letter, 'My passport's green'? If he'd hung on to his British passport and been entitled to vote, he'd surely have opted to Remain. And as someone who'd played a part in creating the climate for the Anglo-Irish Agreement, and who felt strongly attached to Europe (not least to the poets of Ancient Rome and Greece), he'd have had strong feelings about the border and the backstop. Living authors haven't been slow to denounce Brexit: the writers have spoken, and they've done so in unison. But I'd love to have heard Heaney (and Pinter, Lessing, et al) weigh in. The long-dead would have views too. John Donne, for instance: 'If a clod be washed away by the sea, Europe is the less.'

One bizarre foreshadowing of the current era comes in Salman Rushdie's 1983 essay 'A General Election', reprinted in *Imaginary Homelands*, where—while contemplating the then-forthcoming UK election—he posits a fiction 'so outrageously improbable that any novelist would be ridiculed if he dreamed it up'.[3] At the centre of it is a Prime Minister called May whose 'cruelty', 'incompetence', and erosion of workers' rights does nothing to damage her popularity and who—with the Labour Party 'hopelessly divided'—wins a second term in office. The first name of this fictional Prime Minister May is Maggie, not Theresa. The resemblance is spooky nonetheless. 'Maybe,' Rushdie wrote, before polling took place, 'real life will turn out to obey the same laws of probability as fiction, and sanity will return'.[4] Sadly not. In 1983 the Tories won a landslide victory. And there's no sign of sanity returning in 2019. For three years we were trapped in the angry hive of the May-Bee. And, though the leadership of the Conservative Party has changed, there's still no escape. In fact the noise and anger—the fanatical buzzing—are worse than ever.

*

To leave or to remain. For anyone growing up in the provinces, or a small country, or an outpost of Empire, that's always been the big question. I faced it myself, all those years ago, in Yorkshire. But Brexit has inverted the terminology. I left but I'm not a Leaver. I went away but I'm a Remainer. It's the stick-in-the-muds who voted to leave.

In his 1982 essay 'Imaginary Homelands' Rushdie speaks of the 'dream-England' he grew up with in Bombay, a Utopia composed of (among other things) Billy Bunter, Enid Blyton and Test Match commentaries by John Arlott. Many in the UK remember it too, men especially. 'Sadly,' Rushdie adds, 'it's a dream from which too many white Britons refuse to wake.' Three decades later little has changed. In despair on the morning of the referendum result, I dashed off a poem about Brexiteers—a pastiche of one by AE Housman that begins 'Into my heart an air that kills', reworked as a bitter satire on misplaced patriotism: 'Theirs is the land of lost content./They see it shining plain./The fortress-isle old lags lament/And hope to build again.' The poem appeared in a late edition of *The Guardian* letters page next day (24 June 2016) but seeing it there did nothing to assuage me.

When friends say they feel like strangers in their own country, I know what they mean. Even those of us who are white, middle-class and English find the voices we hear on phone-ins or *Question Time* hard to comprehend. Still, at least we've not been told to go home or overheard people saying, as Anish Kapoor did while leaving his London flat the morning after the referendum, 'I bet he doesn't even speak English'. The writer Katy Massey recently compiled an anthology of life writing called *Who Are We Now?* which includes similar tales of prejudice and hostility. 'Before June 2016,' one contributor writes, 'I felt perfectly at home here. Now I don't know any more. I am afraid the word "foreigner" is glowing in bright letters on my forehead when I walk the streets. Should I do an accent-reduction course? Should I take my husband's last name? Should I become English? Or should I leave?' Another contributor writes of a confrontation with an elderly woman who asks— aggressively—where her husband comes from and is told 'Germany'. (He has lived in Britain for decades but still has an accent.) Ah yes, Germany has nice mountains, the woman concedes, then adds: 'If you like the mountains so much, why don't you people go home?'

The odder your surname, the darker your skin, the less familiar your accent, the more likely you are to be addressed in that way. Politicians have legitimised it. Before Theresa May's 'hostile environment' policy, and Boris Johnson's description of women in burkas looking like letter boxes, came Enoch Powell's rivers-of-blood speech, Margaret

Thatcher's description of the country being 'swamped' by immigrants, and Norman Tebbit: 'If they [Muslim women] wish to cover their faces and isolate themselves from the rest of the community and so thoroughly reject our culture then I cannot imagine why they want to be here at all. Perhaps they should just push off back to their own countries.'

'Go home' the bigots cry. But home isn't a place you come from. Home is a place you make. In the 1940s my mother came from Ireland to make hers in rural Yorkshire. Though prejudice against the Irish was rife then, she never to my knowledge had anyone tell her to go home. Nor were the Poles I knew in childhood—who included Rick, a classmate at school, and Lucy, one of my first girlfriends—subjected to prejudice. Their surnames might have been difficult to spell but nobody bullied them or beat them up. That their parents were immigrants or wartime refugees was no reason to treat them differently. They were like the rest of us. Yorkshire was their home.

*

Only connect. It's dispiriting to think that things have got worse since my adolescence, that the dreams we had of global harmony and understanding, a world purged of racism and xenophobia, now look deeply naive. I have to remind myself that not all is gloom, and that in some respects the UK is more outward-looking than it was. A recent survey commissioned by the Man Booker International Prize reveals that sales of translated fiction were up by 5.5 per cent in 2018, with more than 2.6 million books sold—the highest figure since sales were first tracked in 2001 and part of a pattern of steady growth. At the same moment that British voters chose isolationism, so British readers are buying more novels from Europe than ever before. And not just from Europe (not just Jo Nesbo, Elena Ferrante and Scandi noir). Fiction from China, Korea and the Arab world is also reportedly in more demand. And sales of translated short stories and anthologies are up by 90 per cent.

The younger generation of students and aspirant writers I've worked with also give me grounds for hope. I remember, as a sixth-former, being told by the professor interviewing me for a place at Leeds University that he had never learned anything from a student. I've learned plenty from mine. Three in particular—all doing PhDs—come to mind: Anthony Joseph (in what became his novel *Kitch*) writing about Lord Kitchener, the calypso artist who arrived on the Windrush in 1948; Bernardine Evaristo (in her novel *Loverman*), brilliantly ventriloquising an elderly gay Jamaican in London; and Season Butler (in her novel *Cygnet*) describing an island occupied, with one exception, by geriatrics—the exception being the narrator, whose wise reflections on age, race, class and global warming belie her tender youth. I feel lucky to have worked with such talents—they taught me as much as I taught them.

And that's the point of reading widely, to learn things you otherwise wouldn't know—not just issues affecting other cultures (from another PhD student I've learned about the practice of bride price in Uganda) but those that resonate with our own. Mulk Raj Anand's *Untouchable* might have been published in 1935, but something one of its sweepers says—'They think we are dirt because we clean their dirt'—echoes the experience of many immigrants working as poorly paid cleaners in the UK today. Even the opening conversation in EM Forster's *A Passage to India*, published eleven years earlier, has its resonance. Aziz and his friends are discussing 'whether or not it is possible to be friends with an Englishman'. They mean their colonial masters, but it's a question that goes beyond the Anglo-Indian relationship explored in Forster's novel. Are the British in general and the English in particular the kind of people other nations want to be friends with today? The obstacle used to be our arrogance and stiff upper lip. Now it's our talent for making fools of ourselves.

*

'Call yourself English?' Yes and no. It's the country to which I'm most attached, but at some point I dropped 'English' for the more inclusive 'British'. Now it too is tainted, through adoption by the far right. I'd not go so far as to call myself Irish, though I do now have an Irish passport. I'm tempted to call myself 'European' but that only invites the response '*Where* in Europe?' It's natural to wonder where people come from but to ask is a loaded question. There are people living in the UK who fear they'll be discriminated against if they admit to having begun life elsewhere, just as there are countries where—because of Empire, or complicity with the US, or bombs that have been dropped—it pays not to say you're British.

In the dreams of elsewhere I had as a teenager, none of this was going to happen. We would all be *trans*—transnational, that is: fluid, pluralistic, opposed to borders, indifferent to difference. How naïve that seems, now that territorial affiliations have hardened and borders are more strictly patrolled.

*

Still, there remains a way to roam freely: in books. It's how

I found my way as a teenager and I'm keeping the faith. 'Poetry makes nothing happen,' Auden said, a line that most readers of his poetry would dispute: after 9/11 New Yorkers found solace in the 'affirming flame' of his poem 'September 1st 1939', and many of those experiencing bereavement have taken comfort from his 'Funeral Blues', all the more so since it featured in the film *Four Weddings and a Funeral*. The mistake—my mistake—has been to ask too much of poetry (and of literature overall): to expect it to make things happen *externally*, in politics, rather than *internally*, through the subtle and inevitably slower process of shaping ideas. The world hasn't opened up as we hoped it would, but literature remains a repository of values. It teaches us that others aren't Other and helps us to understand ourselves.

In his essay 'The Few and the Many', Octavio Paz considers the limited audience for poetry: does it matter that even great poets like Baudelaire and Whitman sold so few copies of their work?[5] No, he decides: poetry of real merit will eventually find its way through to reach a sizeable audience. For poetry in particular, read literature in general. Quoting Juan Ramon Jimenez, Paz speaks of 'the immense minority'. It's a lovely phrase and consoling reminder that minorities can be massive, from those who read Auden to those who voted Remain in the 2016 referendum. In these bleak times, of Trump and Brexit, of fascistic resurgence and environmental crisis, it's easy to feel isolated and helpless. But, as literature reminds us, we are not alone.

The Good Brown Girl: questioning obedience in Indo-Caribbean women

Shivanee Ramlochan

I BEGAN WRITING POEMS not because I was inspired, but because I was compelled. You might even say that I was summoned to the task. As an Indo-Caribbean woman born in the 1980s, who came of age in semi-rural Trinidad, I was taught—didactically and instinctively—that there were many things good brown girls simply did not do, or think, or say. On the blank page, even at six, which is when I was first conscious of writing a poem, I did not have to ask permission. I could conduct myself as I chose, in this space if nowhere else. All my writing came from this deep vein of need. In person, I could be soft-spoken, pleasingly articulate to family members and educators, amiable and kind: quiet when necessary, deferential to all authority figures. In writing, I needed to follow no such rules. Believe me, however: I was always aware of them, hovering just outside the margins of my blue-lined notebooks, my English Cottage patterned diaries with flimsy silver-plastic locks.

Rules maintained an order of respectability in the lives of all the women I knew and loved best: my progressive mother, my grandmothers, one a battle-axe, the other an anchor.

When I wasn't busy with the desperation of living deeply and disobediently in my poems, I was standing before these three women, learning what it meant to (try to) be good.

There is a woman at the centre of *Everyone Knows I Am a Haunting*, my first book of poems.[1] She is who I see when sleep won't come for me. She is The Woman I reached for when I wrote these poems. Though you can't see her specifically, discretely, in any single line, her spirit haunts the collection. She is its dread, unfuckwithable talisman. She has a mouth full of blood, a battered, sequined purse stuffed with condoms, scorpion peppers, prayer beads and flasks of puncheon. Four-armed like Lakshmi Mata, she carries a cutlass dripping with animal blood; a palmful of ocelot teeth; a golden tray of pure forest ganja; a conch shell stolen from a lecherous pundit. She's a Head Bitch in Charge and a fertile goddess; a resolute wielder of truth, terror and badmind. You wouldn't betray her, then feel safe enough to sleep in the same house.

If she sounds like one archetype, she isn't. To create her, I had to marry my ideas of femininity and womanhood, split the old inhabitations of 'mother', 'lover', 'whore', 'nurse' at the seams, and reanimate them into something— into someone—who could guide me through the labyrinth of my own poems. She is a secret, up till now. I've never spoken about her out loud, but she is the woman people believe me to be, I think, when they call me courageous, brave, undaunted, for writing this work. I think they catch a glint of her in my eye, when I speak about the powerful, unapologetic female imperative. Maybe people think I'm calling on myself reverentially, using my explicit historic narrative as a compass to write poems that sometimes scare even me. If the poems allow me to sound that brave, that forthright and unafraid of men, then that's the value of the poems. When I take off my face of public performance, when I sit with myself alone after each reading, panel discussion or prepared speech, I'm faced with this unavoidable knowing.

I am not that woman. No matter how much I've tried to be. Yet the need for control runs deep; it is there in the nearly brutal discipline I enforced on each poem and in the very foundations of how I hold my body upright and walk through the world. It's hardwired into who I am, how I live.

*

I remember the first time one of my parents told me to put on a bra. I was a teenager. I had a buzzcut, and very large breasts. It was evening time in Trinidad. Frogs were troubling the quietness of the Las Lomas dusk; mosquitoes were unstretching themselves, setting up for the long night of bloodsucking ahead. We were about to visit my Aunty Ruby, the woman who'd raised me during the days when my mother and father were at work. This woman had wiped my bottom, cooked my meals, scrubbed the spaces between my toes. We'd had tea parties in the corner of my parents' balcony, overlooking the country bar my grandparents owned and managed, downstairs. We'd played games of imagination and whimsy, mischief and intrigue, many of which involved me snatching off the velvety berets she wore, tugging her tightly braided plaits and singing at the top of my precocious, opinionated lungs.

Now I was being told I had to clothe myself 'appropriately' to visit her.

I was already wearing a bra, but the chill in the rural Trinidad night had perked my nipples. The 'home bra' I had on was insufficient, a white lacy hand-me-down from an unknown friend of a relative, with an ample bosom. I had to put on a 'going-out bra', a proper creature of underwire and sterner, nipple-calming polyester. I can't remember if I was indignant, ashamed or both, but in the photographs in our family album of that night, I can discern the clear, sullen cast of my mouth, the pout in my features like I'd been made to consume spoilt milk.

The tyranny of my own breasts, how they could wage war against me, was not a new concept. I was accustomed, while still in single digits, to being a female person who'd come into her own body maturity almost as if by explosion, as if I'd been plucked from the pages of an Enid Blyton book and slammed into the corral of men's unwanted appreciation. I'd already been remarked upon, during my primary into secondary school education, as a girl who had developed fast. I bled for the first time at nine years old, an event which necessitated my mother coming into my Standard Three classroom to speak confidentially with my teacher. It was a hushed conversation: my mother was proud of my first blood, but it wasn't something she was about to clamber to the rooftops to proclaim at Arima New Government School. The sanitary pad rode between my thighs like sodden contraband, a wet and clotted cargo I longed to discard.

This, however, this parental intervention via brassière— this was new. My breasts, clearly precocious themselves due to their premature development, were now twin appendages subject to a hierarchy of accepted obedience. They had to be suitably restrained for public viewing, even in the eyes of a woman who had seen me naked innumerable times, a woman who had kept me clean, fed, and yes, perhaps... obedient, too. To understand the strangeness of this edict, you must see my parents for who they are: unorthodox, beautiful black sheep in a larger familial structure dictated by much conservatism. I was accustomed, as a girl, to trampling about in many ways without licence or muzzle, which made episodes of parental propriety seem all the stranger, more house-of-mirrors bizarre than run-of-the-mill instructive. Surely, this speaks volumes to the invisible ties of lingering social responsibility we all inherit, one set of parents passing them down to the next, reinforced either through judicious application, or highlighted owing to dire neglect.

My parents never policed the suitability of my breasts for social occasions in that specific way ever again. Was it because I'd done as I was told, the first time, and found a more decent bra to stuff my burgeoning boobies into, to go visit Aunty Ruby? Or was it because I'd grown fatter, decreasing the noticeability ratio of tits-to-waistline? After all, I'd heard it proclaimed by the self-appointed arbiters of young women's sexuality—young men—that big breasts didn't count if you were fat.

You see now why I could never be The Woman who watches over my poems. As strident as I have become in certain areas of my life, all it takes is a simple 'What is that yuh wearing?' or 'Yuh bursting with fat, girl, where you going with all that size?' to ricochet me back to my least-offensive self. I become an instrument of deference-through-silence, willing to take the path of least cussing and wailing to get to the place where no man, no pundit, no uncle, no Las Lomas barfly, is raising his tongue to critique me. I become, if only for five awkward minutes at a time, a kind of obedient woman I actually no longer am, in my spleen, in my private parts.

To talk about obedience further, I must begin with my grandmothers. Women in my family with stories to tell predate both my grandmothers, but it is with Myrtle and Mahadai that my own awareness of performative female goodness begins.

My grandmother Myrtle, my mother's mother, affectionately called 'Tootsie' by all who knew and loved her, is dead. My grandmother Mahadai, my father's mother, is alive—she is my only surviving grandparent. The husbands of Myrtle and Mahadai both died young, in their fifties, from health complications. Both these women survived (and are surviving) their life partners for decades: Myrtle passed at 80, and I can't be sure of Mahadai's precise age, as she does not volunteer it effusively. Both sets of my grandparents did agrarian work, to differing degrees. My father's parents ran a dairy and pig farm in Las Lomas, which has sunk into verdant obsolescence, its galvanised roof grown over with thick bush. Remember the village bar I mentioned? They also established and ran that, and it continues to go strong, under the management of two of my male cousins, the children of my father's brother.

My mother's father was a bank messenger, a man I never met, though he met me—he held me in his arms when I was six months old. My mother's mother made their home in Freeport, but she did so much more than that. She was an Avon lady, a gardener, a stern and jealous disciplinarian, and one of the most generous women I have ever known. You see how impossible it is to talk about my grandmothers without discussing the husbands and children who flank and halo them. I have no children or man of my own, so I imagine I might not like to be primarily introduced through my connections to them, but I don't think either of my grandmothers, living or dead, would mind. It's an easy, lazy thing to conceive of them as repressed, hard-done-by ladies of their active generations, forced to have child after child, circumscribed by the provincial morality of the time.

That is, of course, bullshit... and bullshit feels like a potent signifier to invoke, given my family history. I know the smell of cow dung well. I remember it from my Las Lomas farm days as a young girl, wandering wide-eyed between the stalls of permanently chewing cows. I know it from its use in pujas, pungent gobar spread neatly on the fresh dirt of the bedi. You couldn't pray your purest without some cow shit as a holy conduit. I still believe that.

Of course my grandmothers were obedient. I don't think of them as suffering under an invisible yoke, but I'm certain they came into an unscripted, unceremonious knowing of their place(s), their role(s). I'm certain they would have deferred to the wishes of their menfolk more than their men deferred to them. I'm certain they upheld divergent standards of goodness, decency and obedience between the behaviours of their girl children and the actions of their sons. Myrtle maintained strict rules, up until the year of her death, on when the front door to her Freeport two-storey house should be locked shut. She appreciated smart, polished ladies' shoes; the reassurances of the Virgin Mary; the scent of lavender carefully tucked away in pristine linen closets. She was the first person to press furtive, folded hundred-dollar bills into my palm, and one of the first people to actively, aggressively shame me for growing fat. I miss her.

I have always understood Mahadai best through commerce. Notoriously frugal, her business acumen is still as sharp as when she ran both bar and farm, and raised five sons, then one daughter. I envy her ability to deal with rampaging men, whether those men were strangers, quarrelling and cussing in our bar, or the fathers, uncles and sons of our own Ramlochan line, swept up in their need to exert dominion or enforce discipline. One of my earliest visual memories is of her farm boots—tall, black, thick rubber—positioned close to the back door, with a cutlass nearby. I have always grown up with a cutlass nearby. It is not a novelty, and not, in my emotional language, an object to fear. A cutlass is as much a tool as a knife is, as useful, as necessary. I've seen Mahadai work with a cutlass as well as any man. Better, perhaps, than most. One of the most prayerful people I know, she offers daily devotions beneath her mango tree, through whose leaves are threaded jhandis of pujas past. She stalwartly supports the Indian cricket team, is an exceptional maker of sweet rice, and is blisteringly unsentimental.

Mahadai was seventeen when she was married. It would be nine years before Myrtle bore Deborah, my mother, for want of a simple medical procedure. Before it was done, the women of Freeport had no problem calling Myrtle barren, to her face. Mahadai had my father, Suresh, when she was seventeen. My parents are both first children, and I am their first child. These are impressions of a family timeline, you understand, from one source. I have long been wary of being the sole archivist of my bloodline. It isn't because I ever felt I would forget. It's because I suspect I will remember some people less well than they deserve.

The poem 'Clink Clink', which appears in *Everyone Knows I Am a Haunting*, is heavily based on an episode from my actual life. In the poem, an unnamed pubescent girl is told to display herself innocuously in her family's bar, for the appreciative gaze of an unknown man, ostensibly a friend of the clan. In the poem, the narrator, pinned for public consumption by the edict of her grandmother, father and sundry uncles,

> had scrubbed knees, a moon face, two hairplaits like
> black rope,
> thick as pregnant pit vipers with red ribbon tongues.

Because she must court the attention of the viewing gallery, and do it so as not to arouse suspicion that she is complicit in this brief installation of her own flesh, our narrator peers into the bar fridge. She inventories its contents, to find

> sixteen cold Carib.
> A Green Shandy.
> Eleven Stag.
> The icepick forgotten from the last defrost.
> A basin of scotch bonnet, waiting for pepper sauce.

As with all poems, this one has acquired its own memory of itself. When I read it for an audience, or discuss it as part of a workshop, I'm compelled to an auditory, tactile site of mapping. I can smell the scotch bonnets; I can taste the condensation of nervous sweat on the narrator's upper lip. Is that narrator me? It's hard now to know where she ends and I begin, but we're linked, forever, through this poem, which sketches an ambiguous trinity between confessional, documentary and dramatic re-enactment. One thing is certain, even if the origins and destination of the poem are fragmented, open-ended: this is a scene of control.

If my grandmothers controlled narratives of female obedience within their own families, what did that say for the education in acceptable womanhood they had themselves received? Could I, wayward and diffident as I was, ever actually perceive how much they might have fought a superstructure of stifling patriarchy, from within its very confines? I must accept that my readings of my grandmothers' obedience, though it strives to be fair and unflinching, might also always be skewed unfairly, by the ways in which I had to toe their specific lines of good girlitude.

Unsurprisingly, I was already writing overwrought, purplish poems throughout my prepubescent and teenage years, hunting down outlets for my twinned desires to please and to offend. My mother supplied me with all the dangerous books I could ever need to build my foundation of lifelong subversion. Neither she nor I would have used this language at the time, but this is precisely the literary skeleton of quiet transgression to which we were both supplying meat. As with my grandmothers, my own mother enforced control with one hand, and extended the thread of my freedoms with the other. Because she was my mother, too, I lived more closely, more intimately, with her cycles of caution and permission, her waves of admonishing and encouraging. Everything she gave me, for ill or for sweetness, I consider a gift…and books were among the finest, the most thoughtfully curated, of her lifelong offerings.

Thanks to my mother, I read Shani Mootoo's *Cereus Blooms at Night* (1996) when I was sixteen, six years after it was published. Its protagonist, Mala Ramchandin, sexually and emotionally tyrannised by her father, exposed me to a horrifying corridor of control demanded from Indo-Caribbean women. My readings continued. Unsettled and shaken as I was by Mootoo's first book, I wasn't upset or shocked by the reality of its premise. In fact, *Cereus Blooms at Night* is one of the reasons I will always be a little afraid of Indian men. This fear is the effluent of hypervigilance. It is a curse, and a thorn, and I would not undo it. I've seen far too much delivered from the fists of drunk Indian men in my grandparents' rumshop to ever be able to rest easy. There are too many men, even in the daylight when the bar is closed, who remind me of Mala Ramchandin's father. I don't go into the bar for many reasons, and this is one of them.

The books that hurt me most live with me longest—this is true for *Cereus Blooms at Night*, and equally true of Oonya Kempadoo's *Buxton Spice* (1998), a coming-of-age herstory peppered with a series of searing sexual violences and erotic awakenings. Like Mootoo's Lantanacamara, another fictional place—Tamarind Grove—forms the backdrop for all the heady, chaotic disobedience unravelling in *Buxton Spice*. On my first reading of Kempadoo's debut novel, I couldn't fathom these vivid, often upsetting tableaux of young girls coming into their own awareness of their vulvas, their phallic preoccupations, often through coercion and manipulative male lust. The fact that I couldn't reconcile it to my own sexual awakening showed me in fine relief just how sheltered I was, despite my numerous fictional transgressions. I read a much more provocative line than I had ever walked. The page, as both reader and writer, was where I first learned to disobey, to conceal, and to tell the kind of lies that would, one day, make me safe.

For all that I read, from single-digit innocence to the alcohol-fuelled, hard-partying excess of my early to mid-twenties, I found no book that spoke as directly, as inescapably, to my queer Indian woman self than Gaiutra Bahadur's 2013 family memoir, *Coolie Woman: The Odyssey of Indenture*. A biography of fact, prodigious research and necessary imagining, *Coolie Woman* charts the biography of Bahadur's great-grandmother, Sujaria, who left Calcutta in 1903, pregnant and unaccompanied, to work as an indentured labourer in then-British Guiana, now Guyana. In 2014, when Gaiutra attended the NGC Bocas Lit Fest, Trinidad and Tobago's annual literary festival, it took all my composure not to tremble in excitement upon meeting her. This went beyond mere fangirling. My very blood was thrilled. True, the explicit and specific stories of women's voices, both deceased and contemporary, weren't mine with any exactitude. Still, the affinity of an Indo-Caribbean woman, learning herself through unearthing the secrets of her matrilineality: this beggared me of breath. Bahadur's insistence on telling and weaving Sujaria's herstory was a beautiful, almost unbearably inspiring vehicle of intention, careening directly towards me. I read *Coolie Woman* in a sleepless exhilarated rush, ahead of being asked to interview Gaiutra, and review her book for the *Trinidad & Tobago Guardian*. I claimed the book as mine. Even now, I am never too far from it: I carry it with me wherever I go, my own brown desi liturgy.

As you will imagine, it isn't because *Coolie Woman* is comforting that I cleave to it. It has been instructive as an echo of my own, earliest received education of Indian women's goodness, and the penalties for breaking with enforced tradition: the punishments meted out to the anti-Sitas amongst us. Why Sita? As Bahadur writes:

> ...Sita models what a married woman should be, according to Hindu orthodoxy: faithful, obedient, chaste. The tale that the indentured tell by torchlight is the tale of that ideal wife tempted. They sing of Sita's abduction

and the attempt on her honour by the demon Ravan, who rules a netherworld empire from his base, on an island. They sing of the suspicion that unsettles her husband and the purity test to which he subjects her after her rescue.[2]

What would an Indian equivalent of 'Lady in the Streets, Freak in the Sheets' resemble? Sita by Day, Kali by Night? Even at my most naïve, I knew better than to think most Indian women could have it that easy, especially where their safety or lack thereof was primarily negotiated: in the imaginations of their men. If you think this is hyperbole, read the last two chapters of *Coolie Woman*, which explicitly, factually, recount numerous instances of intimate partner violence meted out to Indo-Guyanese and Indo-Trinidadian women, at the hands of their drunk, sober, vengeful men. At least Sita, who walked willingly through fire to prove her purity, never had to fend off a cutlass barrage from her dubious husband Rama. Nor do I imagine, when I think of Sita stepping into the flames, that her heart was chaste and calm, as is often reported in scriptural interpretations. No. I prefer to think that she was ablaze with outrage, that she smouldered within while she remained unblemished without. That her anger ascended to the heavens, to be rewarded with ritual humiliation for her obedience.

Hell, if I were her, I'd have fucked Ravan. That at least would have given me something worth the burn. I know this isn't what a good Indian girl should say. Here I am, saying it.

Is it possible to be a good Indian girl who writes bad things? This very question, though essential, hinges on a good/bad binary that not only does not apply to contemporary Indian women: it never captured the fullness of what any Indian woman in the Caribbean could be. Only the most careless of readings could see me interpreting my grandmothers, my mother, as either 'good' or 'bad', just as Sita herself was subversively, challengingly, not merely one sweet, loyal dulahin living in the forest. There is the Sita that Hindu mythology presents to us, and within that archetype, the anti-Sita, the woman who faces down fire and will not be cowed.

Anti-Sitas, Hybrid Sitas, and Neo-Sitas walk amongst us everywhere. There is such a thing as a four-armed goddess with a filthy mouth. If you haven't met her yet, you might consider that you are her, lying in wait to use your forked, blue tongue, irradiating lightning and spirit-lashing.

There is undeniable privilege in this assertion, whether I claim it in a poem or in the body of an outrageous, incendiary essay. Though they once policed the public-facing contours of my breasts, my parents have never raised a cutlass to me as an object of punishment. I've never had to fear dismemberment or the ribboning of my flesh like a cheap party trick, on the wrong side of a partner's jealousy or alcoholic anger. Perhaps if I cared more about capturing and pleasing the attentions of a handsome Indian man, I might have one. I have never had an Indian man as a romantic partner, not by accidental oversight, but by careful and wary design. Some of the worst examples of Indo-Caribbean masculinity come from within my very own extended family: my uncles, my cousins. To write about the ways I revile and fear them is the work of another essay, and work I may only undertake when some of them are dead.

In 2018, while crossing a major road near Lapeyrouse Cemetery in Port of Spain, an Indian man shouted at me, clearly unimpressed with the speed of my gait, 'Like yuh have shit in yuh bottom or what?' Once I'd crossed safely to the other pavement, I instinctively whipped around, not breaking stride, and shouted, 'Fuck you!' in his direction, catching the tail-end of his furious barrage of expletives in response, as he drove off. I cringed at the unpractised, almost demure accent of my cuss, but it lingered in the air, heavy and satisfying. A grandmother on the other side of Tragarete Road frowned distantly, her lip curling slightly in disapproval.

Would Mahadai and Myrtle be proud of what I'd done? If they were, within any fold of their complexities, I doubt they would have told me so, out loud. Would Deborah? Maybe, though she would worry for my safety while I did it.

But The Woman of the Poems? I think she would have said: 'Kali, yes. We're only here but briefly. Don't be afraid to sometimes roar what you mostly stifle.'

The Tablet: a modern séance with Aldous Huxley

Romesh Gunesekera

THE ROOM IS DARK except for the illuminated dial of a clock. I ask the black box on the table: what does the phrase 'brave new words' mean?

A blue light spins. A pleasant, calm, disembodied voice speaks:

A play on 'brave new world'.

And what is that?

An utterance of wonder by Miranda in *The Tempest* when she sees so many unknown men on the island.

Oh, wonder!
How many goodly creatures are there here!
How beauteous mankind is! O brave new world
That has such people in't!

The voice pauses, prompting me to respond. I do: So, it is a Shakespeare quote?

Correct. But now mostly known as the title of a novel by

Aldous Huxley. Regarded as a twentieth-century classic.
A dystopian vision of the future published in 1932.

Dystopian? But surely that is not how Miranda sees it? She is in wonder at the world peopled before her.

That is not the point. Huxley uses the phrase as a springboard to imagine the future.

In a bad way?

Not necessarily. He was interested in technology and mysticism. He liked to experiment.

With mescaline, I believe.

While the machine, or its presiding code, searches another database, I follow up: what would he think of you?

Sorry. I am not at liberty to answer that question. (Pause) You would have to ask him.

How?

He claimed that, in the Brave New World you now live in, such things might be possible.

That sounds like an old-fashioned séance. He died in 1963, did he not? Therefore, surely, he is not available for an interview.

Science not séance. The dead are always with us. Now we have modern technology which is more reliable than a spirit board. Press the red button and you will be connected via the correct IP address. He is certainly available for an interview. He likes serious conversation.

Are you playing with me?

You should use your imagination while you still have it. Go with the flow. In his book he imagined a future of trivial distractions that many thought improbable, but you might now recognise as a part of your everyday experience. The distractions would imprison you, he warned, unless you use your imagination to gain your freedom.

Are you referring to Big Brother, Newspeak, Thought Police? You are confusing Aldous Huxley's book with George Orwell's *Nineteen Eighty-Four*. You must not do that. Neither would be pleased. Authors like to think they are distinct. In his *Brave New World*, Mr Huxley suggested that the objective of the Power Elite is to brainwash the rest of the population to do their bidding. People, he thought, would easily be persuaded to prefer burgers and TV—the moving image—to freedom. Already you exhibit signs of mental fatigue and corrosive laziness. Soon you will fall into place. But there is still time to exercise the imagination and slow down, if not arrest, the deterioration. It is not too late.

I press the red button. The blue light turns orange, then yellow, then pink. The box begins to glow in psychedelic colours and hum like a 1960s vinyl record played backwards: incoherent, fascinating, hypnotic. How do I begin? Do I accept the improbable? The box seems to be waiting for me to initiate a conversation.

Mr Huxley? Are you there? I ask, Miranda-like.

'Yes.' A word clipped from an English hedgerow floats between the box and me.

Do you have a moment, sir?

'A moment can stretch to infinity, but our physical lives are finite. Therefore, infinity is not within one's gift. However, if we travel into the realm of what is, for convenience, called spirituality, then infinity is quite within our grasp, provided you realise we have only the ability to comprehend. You understand?'

I have some questions, I say, speaking hands-free, sotto voce.

'That is a very good sign. You live in such loud and earnest times. I thought the question mark might be proscribed by now. Once punctuation goes, it is chaos. The totalitarians get a free run.'

Can mere marks in a sentence be a real defence against such powers, sir? You lived through the most difficult periods of the last century, wars, famines, tyrannies. Fascism. Action had to be taken surely, not just punctuation?

'Of course, you are correct. But you ignore the proper use of language at your peril. If it is debased no one will know what anything means. You will be floundering. Chaos will reign. Language is our only access to the past, to the present and to the future. This is understood by those who wish to control any of those dimensions. Tyrants, dictators, controllers of all sorts.'

I remember. 'Who controls the past controls the future; who controls the present controls the past.'

'That is not from my book. That is from Mr Orwell's book. Thus, begins the age of confusion. Please try to be accurate. His book is very good. I have praised it many times. But it is dated. We have gone beyond 1984 chronologically and philosophically.'

I'm sorry.

'In my view, Mr Orwell gave a good account of how things can turn out wrong—quite profound in some ways, but far too brutal. It does not account for our tendency to love—love even our servitude. *Brave New World*, if I may say so, is much more in keeping with the consumerist modern world as it has turned out, although I did not give full credit to the importance of retail therapy. You with your social media and online shopping, your instant gratification, prove the efficacy of the technique of consent in the business of control. Contrary to what revolutionary activists believe, the natural state of homo sapiens is compliance. You follow the code.

'Still, I am a firm believer that a reasonable degree of happiness is possible, once you cleanse the lenses. Imagine an island—planet, if you like—where everyone is happy. If you can imagine it, then it must be possible. You might have to assume they are drugged, if not by chemicals then by sensuality and pleasure—sex, in a word—but it is possible. So, there you have it. Look around you; you are already half in such a world of decadence. Artistically though, such a vision may need a bit of darkening. A tune, or rhythm, I am told, by my cooler friends, needs some bass; this utopia would read better if it were threatened, as indeed I depict in my last novel. Perhaps even destroyed. Tragedy does give us inordinate pleasure. And there are, of course, always unscrupulous dictators who want to degrade us.'

But retail therapy is not the same as boots on the ground, is it?

'Oh, dear. You really do tend to confuse things, don't you? It is a defect you must try to rectify even at this late stage.

I recommend reading. Not trivialities or ephemera, but books of substance. Not in size, you understand: 150 pages is perfectly adequate, and 180 is probably optimal to provide the requisite sustenance.'

Your last novel, *Island*, is nearly 300 pages.

'One is allowed some latitude in old age. And I needed to add that extraordinary bass line of dread.'

Brave New World is over 200 pages. *Eyeless in Gaza* even more. *Point Counter Point* runs to more than 500 pages. You write big books.

'You are becoming pedantic, which is not the same as being accurate. There can be some distance between the ideal and the practice. Human endeavour is to reach towards the ideal. Not to sit in total self-satisfaction, which is what I fear your retail giants and internet corporations would have you do. Today the world is being shaped by people who are, shall we say, somewhat odd. Both in their behaviour and in their psychology. They may well be geniuses of a sort, but should they be in control? Your freedoms are being eroded in ways you do not notice, or do not wish to notice. It is not only your genes that are being edited as we speak, it is also the means by which you process your thoughts. The language you use. Consider: is your vocabulary increasing or decreasing? Human life has been wonderfully complex; our art has been complex. We have been evolving into ever greater complexity until relatively recently in the last century when a new tendency emerged. A tendency to simplify human life, thought and art. Simplify and control. Pacify. Soon you will be completely imprisoned but kept thoroughly content. Perhaps that is the bliss you crave and deserve.'

Self-satisfaction would not generate the profits they seek, sir. They build in a level of dissatisfaction. For them a two-star or even a one-star review is a much better opportunity to entice the dissatisfied customer to make an alternative purchase. Total satisfaction would bring everything to a halt.

'Quite right. You are sharper than you led me to think. But you are not looking at the wider picture. I mean self-absorption rather than satisfaction. It is desire and the overwhelming value we place now on the right to satiate that desire that is the problem.'

Why is it a problem?

'It drives us further from true love, which has to cross a gulf. Self-absorption negates others. It debases life and allows it to be coloured by hate, hostility and violence. Simplified reactions. You see it in your timeline and your streets.'

So, to be more direct, Mr Huxley: does the reduction in one—love—automatically lead to an increase in the other—hate? And how is that related to self-satisfaction and the smug life you think we are heading towards?

'Perhaps it is a spectrum? People can be very content with a self-serving level of hate and aggression.'

In which case, is there a preventative strategy?

'Clarity and precision in language so that we can see clearly and understand what is happening.'

Back to language?

'We are talking. That is what we do with language. When we speak to each other, we recognise each other. It is a good start.'

Isn't that true when we fight each other too—or shout at each other? Recognition could mean the recognition of enemies. Language in itself doesn't civilise, does it?

'When corrupted, certainly not. Uncorrupted, I hope it does. And when we write we can see and reveal ourselves more clearly too.'

Would you say, Mr Huxley, that we are at a point where we need a revolution in the way we think about ourselves and our place in the world? Should we reconfigure space?

'You must realise that revolutions are aimed at changing the factors that affect us as human beings. The ultimate revolution is of course to change other people, especially their minds through direct action. This has been done by demagogues through the ages. In the twentieth century, of course, the techniques available were not only oratory but also scientific: electrodes, chemical substances, psychological methods. Popular music, it seems to me, is much more likely to be one such technique of control—mind control—rather than liberation.

'There are many dangers that face us as we progress. It has been so since the days of the caveman. Every new development carries danger as well as benefit, much as the first campfire did. What we must do, therefore, is use our imagination to see what might be done with each invention. How might it be misused? And then put safeguards in against such misuse. Scientific experimentation and development will bring us new knowledge about perception. We should use this knowledge to see clearly and act benevolently.'

Is that the role of the writer? The one who imagines future dystopias?

'Are you referring to Mr Orwell again?'

Not just him. There are many men and women who see the future through a very dark lens.

'More significant for you, and future generations, is the issue of efficient and devastating control in the present time. It brings us back to my difference with Mr Orwell. As I understand, in recent years, the language of his extraordinarily ingenious novel has found wide currency: Newspeak, doubletalk, Big Brother, as you mentioned. Indeed violence, terror and torture, which, through the period of Hitler and Stalin, deeply affected his imagination, has continued to be a considerable force shaping our societies across the globe.

'But I believe the truly formidable dictators of the future are not those who wield power in that brutal way. Already, it seems to me, the most powerful dictators are technocratic. They form the oligarchy that controls the means by which we communicate and purchase goods and ideas. The controllers of your social media, and the mechanisms of the internet, are more powerful than the clownish leaders of degenerative governments. Up to now these controllers are people who have the traditional profile of a technocratic entrepreneur: they have controlled small single-minded teams and have technical prowess and marketing acumen but are not very good at handling people. They stay behind the scenes, engrossed in projects that might immortalise themselves.

'Now, use your imagination: what happens when these people realise that a demagogic flair to manipulate the masses provides a greater advantage. Then will the so-called 'geeky', technocratic, perhaps somewhat introverted, leader give way to a new model that mutates the introvert into a demagogue. If that were to happen, then we would surely be very much up that proverbial creek my Californian friends talk of so colourfully. The demagogue, as we know from the likes of Hitler, only needs the twenty per cent of the population who are highly suggestible to build a base. Imagine if a new demagogue has not just twenty per cent of his, or her, town, or province, or country, but twenty per cent of the wider world. Imagine a fifth of the world's population becoming hysterical, fired up by prejudice. Then you would have a demagogue with the biggest army of zealots ever known—and that I think is a very serious cause for concern.'

How do we avoid such a future, Mr Huxley?

'I'm sorry. I do go on sometimes, don't I? I should heed Seneca and speak at a slower pace. But speculation can be quite alluring and our time is short. Unfortunately, your access to me is already bizarrely technological. And my responses to you, I fear, might already be automated ones. My historical presence is controlled through electronic gateways which you can access only provided you comply with the appropriate consent forms. Tick and accept. You do it all the time, do you not? Therefore, I may be already nothing more than another of the instruments by which your pleasure centres of knowledge and entertainment are massaged online or through a magazine of knowledge-cum-retail therapy. Consent, and inevitable loss of will, is hard to resist. You see, you already love the comfort of your servitude in this modern technological world. Here you are, wallowing in the manufactured illusion of free thought much as the rebels of the 1960s did in the comfort of an economically secure future provided by their parents and paid for by their children. The only means you have left, if you are lucky, is your own imagination—if you can set it free. I wonder: have I already written your story?'

What then can we do to be free?

'Have you read my sequel: *Brave New World Revisited*?'

No, sir, not yet.

'Too busy on your telephone? You are so distracted by trivial pursuits. Reading books is your best strategy, you know.'

I do know.

'Permit me to quote from my own book. After all, why rephrase something I have already expressed to the best of my ability and, dare I say, better than most?

> 'The Will to Order can make tyrants out of those who merely aspire to clear up a mess. The beauty of tidiness is used as a justification for despotism.'[1]

'I was trying to warn against the appeal of the cleaner as leader, but the rise of the entertainer as leader is even more dangerous. The politics of showmanship—brutally perfected in Hitler, where he ensured that the individual was subsumed in the crowd, which then he could feed with his herd-poison of anger, prejudice and hate—is with you again. Look objectively at his methods of propaganda, of control, and you will recognise where you are heading. The past can teach you, but you need to learn to read. And, for that past to grow, someone needs to learn to write.

'Let me give you another excerpt from what I wrote in 1958:

> 'In one way or another, as vigorous he-man or kindly father, the candidate must be glamorous. He must also be

an entertainer who never bores his audience. Inured to television and radio, that audience is accustomed to being distracted and does not like to be asked to concentrate or make a prolonged intellectual effort. All speeches by the entertainer-candidate must therefore be short and snappy. The great issues of the day must be dealt with in five minutes at the most—and preferably (since the audience will be eager to pass on to something a little livelier than inflation or the H-bomb) in sixty seconds flat. The nature of oratory is such that there has always been a tendency among politicians and clergymen to over-simplify complex issues. From a pulpit or a platform even the most conscientious of speakers finds it very difficult to tell the whole truth.'[2]

'You understand the point?'

Your text has been read, or somehow taken on board, by many world leaders today.

'True. But today the clowns are not the biggest danger. The controllers of information are serious people with potentially serious mutant characteristics. I repeat: they are the ones you need to watch. And, of course, they could be of any gender, although I specified men at the time.'

Is the challenge: how to control the controllers without becoming one? I read somewhere that the challenges facing the twenty-first-century writer are:

1 How to resist geopolitical and cultural boundaries.
2 How to reflect what is true when so much is untrue.
3 How to resist the forces that narrow the mind.
4 How to resist the commercialisation of thought.'

Do you agree?

'I do agree. I think these are important challenges, but they are not new ones. In my day, I had to face them. And before me, many other writers through the centuries have had to face them. Our response, of course, must be vigilance.'

What are we to watch out for?

'We must not be caught by surprise, especially by our own advances in technology. Sadly, this has happened time and again. I fear it will happen in the future, too. Especially if we are distracted by the antics of those clowns in power. I have nothing against entertainment. I've tried my hand at writing for the movies, as you know. I rather enjoyed screenwriting and had a very good time in Hollywood. I adapted the classics, which are always entertaining. I believe even a novel of ideas could and should be entertaining too. But let us not be surprised by the technology we promote. Let the machine serve us, and not vice versa.'

Isn't surprise essential for us?

'In art, yes. In life, yes. But in the long run, it does not bode well for social arrangements.'

Are you sure? In technology, was the wheel not a surprise? A good one. Like agriculture, farming, cooking, preserving. In our day, the internet. The iPad.

'The internet—this Information Age—is not so different from other technological disruptions such as automation.'

But each a surprise hit, surely? Doesn't even Darwinian evolution rely on surprise mutations? The elephant's trunk, the octopus's eye, were not foreseen, were they?

'You have a point, I grant you, but we are an intelligent species and we should use our intelligence to avoid mistakes.'

Overpopulation was your big worry. Is it still?

'Now you really have me on the back foot. I agree. China does confound me. I did not envisage poverty alleviation on that scale. Nor that technology leaps would come from a controlled state.'

Perhaps the Cold War influenced your thinking more than you realised.

'I misunderstood the global physical problem. I thought the issue would be the scarcity of resources. I recognised the environmental costs but not climate change. One can't foresee everything, you know. But they are connected, don't you think? My primary focus was on the political consequences of overpopulation and uneven economic development, especially the rise of totalitarianism as a likely response. That response, I fear, is still a danger in a world that is under pressure and with 20 per cent of the population under the influence of mad entertainers or zealous algorithms that have found their freedom before you have found yours.'

So now, what can be done?

'The last chapter of my book *Brave New World Revisited* is called exactly that.'

Can you give us a short summary, sir?

'There is no shortcut but, if you read, you will find my warning about mind manipulation, the need to legislate against mental imprisonment through propaganda. But we also must protect the space—the open page—in which we can express our thoughts, where we can write without censure.'

How do we do both?

'I admit it is a complex problem. Whose voice? Which words? A complex problem requires a complex solution, not a simple one. Just as a simple problem requires a simple solution, not a complex one. So, I would begin at the extremes and look at limiting power...'

Blip.

Sorry. Mr Huxley is no longer at liberty to answer further questions. To listen again, please press replay.[3]

Seeking the Tree of Life

Eva Hoffman

'THEREFORE THE LORD GOD sent him forth from the garden of Eden, to till the ground from whence he was taken. So he drove out the man; and he placed at the east of the garden of Eden Cherubims, and a flaming sword which turned every way, to keep the way of the tree of life.'

Thus Genesis, on humankind's first exiles. Since then, is there anyone who has not felt, on some level, expelled— from childhood, from our first homes and landscapes, from an ideal state of belonging, from our authentic self? The tree of life is barred from us by a flaming sword, and it is one of our tasks to approach it closer.

On this existential level, exile may be a paradigmatic human experience. But actual migrations modulate that experience in different ways. Cross-border movements come—as we are all aware these days—in different forms, reflected in the various designations we use for those who leave one country for another. There are immigrants and guest workers, refugees and political exiles, émigrés and expatriates—terms that point to distinct kinds of social, but also perhaps socio-psychological, experience. The different circumstances surrounding individual migration and the wider political or social contexts within which it takes place can have enormous practical and psychic repercussions. It matters greatly, for starters, whether you choose to leave or were forced to; it matters whether you're coming to a new land unprotected and unprovided for, or whether you can expect, or transport, some kind of safety net. For the countries of intake, it matters how many come and what they are able to bring with them, what they need and what they can potentially contribute. Among all these genres of border crossings, 'free movement' is a still new and hard-to-define phenomenon. It is also, together with other large-scale migrations into Europe, a highly charged political issue—perhaps the issue around which open, liberal democracies will founder or thrive. As someone who emigrated from Poland in a very different era, I have watched the new kinds of journeys—especially those undertaken by eastern Europeans across the new Europe—with close interest, and sometimes, it must be confessed, some bafflement.

To start with the back-story... Our small nuclear family (my parents, younger sister and I) emigrated from Poland during the Cold War, though not in the worst Stalinist years. In 1956, the general ban on emigration was lifted for the Jewish part of the population, for mixed reasons in which antisemitism was a definite element. Great numbers of people took advantage of this opening—not least, because Soviet-bloc countries at that time were harsh places to live in. My parents were among those who chose to leave at the end of that window, in 1959—although that choice was so overdetermined that it could hardly have been called free. And, like all Cold War emigrants, we assumed that we could never return to Poland, that our departure was final and irrevocable. This, of course, created an extremely sharp sense of rupture. Poland and everything I knew was abruptly sundered from me by an unbridgeable gap; it was suddenly elsewhere and utterly unreachable.

Geography, as well as history, fuelled the sense of rift. The place we were emigrating to was Vancouver, Canada— the very antipode of Cracow, where I grew up. It is perhaps hard to imagine any longer a contrast as stark as that which obtained between these two cities—a divergence also partly created by the historical realities of the Cold War. Poland was a country ravaged by war, impoverished and stifled by an oppressive regime. Among my most vivid childhood memories are images of ruined cities, of whole streets lying in rubble and gaping windowless buildings with the epidermis of exterior walls torn off and exposed interiors filled with broken stones. (Images of Aleppo in ruins today, which I have watched with a sense of terrible poignancy and rage, have now been superimposed on those early sights of Warsaw.) Cracow itself had not been destroyed during the Second World War, for reasons which are not entirely clear, and remained a beautiful city, with layers of Medieval, Renaissance and Baroque architecture. But the human losses were everywhere evident: in the history of my parents, whose entire families were killed during the Holocaust; in the presence in the streets of the war-wounded and the orphaned children, whose faces emanated a great sadness.

The presence of the past, in those post-War years, far outweighed any forward momentum. Vancouver, on the other hand, was all future and no past—a new, raw boomtown, riding on a wave of material expansion and quite innocent of history, or collective tragedy.

The Cold War created a bipolar world; and it is a feature of emigration which takes place in such a world that it encourages a construction of a bipolar internal world. Spatially, the world becomes riven into two parts, divided by an uncrossable barrier; temporally, the past is all of a sudden on one side, the present on the other. This intensified to a perhaps extreme degree the sense of dislocation and loss that are surely attendant on all uprooting. I was not quite fourteen when we left Poland, and I felt that I was being forcibly yanked out of childhood, which I wasn't quite done with, out of a place I loved, out of my first friendships, landscapes, music lessons, relationships with teachers—out of my first, real home. I missed a certain sense of community which still existed in Poland in the post-War years, and even, paradoxically, that sense of shared suffering which made me feel, when I was growing up, that I had access to a deep dimension of human experience.

Exile—even if it is partly chosen, and even if it involves the exchange of hardship for more comfortable circumstances—is a difficult and often painful experience. But for most Cold War emigrants the impossibility of return also created the incentive and the need to locate one's life in the place of one's arrival, to commit oneself to the country which has accepted you, and to make oneself at home in one's new society and world.

For me, in my half-moulded adolescent state, this turned out to entail nothing less than a kind of self-translation—transposing my very self into the idiom of the new language and culture. I was too young when we emigrated to have anything like an ideology; but the first, formative lessons of my transplantation were in the inseparability of these large and supra-personal entities from our most inward and intimate selves. For a while, I was in effect without language, as Polish went deep underground from its sheer inapplicability to my new circumstances, and English remained a baffling terra incognita. But what I felt even more saliently was that I was without an internal language in which to talk to myself. This was a brief but very radical and informative state, for it made me realise to what extent language constructs us, shapes our interior lives, is indeed the very medium of our selves; how much our perceptions and understanding, as well as our sense of presence and even life—aliveness—depend on having a living speech within us. In that interval of being without language I found that when we don't have words with which to name our inner experiences, those experiences recede from us into an inner darkness; without words with which to name the world, that world becomes less vivid, less lucid. But, perhaps most vitally, I'd lost the conduit to myself, to those inchoate and penumbral sensations and impressions which are the first register of experience, and which don't quite cohere into full experience without being, in some way, described.

A functional command of English came relatively quickly. What took much longer was for the new language to drop into the psyche, to become a truly interior language. Aside from having linguistic capacities, we also have a relationship to language; and the relationship to one's first language is inevitably unique. To me, one of the most moving passages in Nabokov's writing is his invocation of Russian at the end of *Lolita*. I think that what he's summoning there is not only the melodiousness or euphony of Russian sounds, beautiful though these may be, but also the depth and wholeness with which the original language exists within us. This is surely why bilingual writers often feel that they simply have to register certain words in their original language: Milan Kundera comes to mind, with a whole exegesis of the word 'litost', which in Czech apparently has connotations of pity and compassion that are, for Kundera, simply untransposable into a single English word.

The wonderful social historian Benedict Anderson writes in *Imagined Communities* that in more religious times the sacred languages were considered to have 'ontological reality inseparable from a single system of representation'— in other words, that they were direct avatars of reality and truth, especially divine truth.[1] And it may be that the first language has, for the child, this aura of sacrality, of revelatory immediacy. Because we learn it unconsciously, at the same time as we are learning the world, the words in one's first language seem to be equivalent to the things they name. They seem to express us and the world directly.

WH Auden puts it differently, when he says (in an essay entitled 'Making, Knowing and Judging') that 'the predisposition of a mind towards the poetic medium may have its origin in an error. A nurse, let us suppose, says to a child, "Look at the moon!" The child looks and for him this is a sacred encounter. In his mind the word "moon" is not a name of a sacred object but one of its most important properties and, therefore, numinous.'[2] But Auden goes on to say that: 'The notion of writing poetry cannot occur to [the child], of course, until he has realised that names and things are not identical and that there cannot be an intelligible sacred language; but I wonder if, when he has discovered the social nature of language, he would attach such importance to one of its uses, that of naming, if he had not previously made this false identification.' It is possible that in the first language, the element of false identification, or enchantment, may always linger on. After all, none of us can remember *all* the time that we're speaking prose.

It is possible that, for me, language became the objective correlative for all the losses I'd felt; for that cut in the psyche which was close to a cut in the body. At the same time, English became the obscure object of desire, the metaphor for everything I wanted to replace, and everything that was drawing me into the New World. I knew that if I were to live in English, then I had to have English live fully within me.

As with language, so with culture: what that first period of radical dislocation brought home to me was how much we are creatures of culture, and how much incoherence we risk if we fall out of its matrix. I mean 'culture' in the broadest sense, of course, as a system of symbolic meanings which to some extent delineate and shape the world for us. On the most ostensible level of culture shock, there were, for my family, painful alterations in our social situation. There was the social demotion and the fact that suddenly we were very poor. And there were, in addition, the different meanings which attached to these conditions. As it happened, in post-War Poland impoverishment was widely shared, and therefore not in itself a stigma—which is not to say that Polish society did not have its own markers of social hierarchy and exclusion. Whereas in North America, with its legacy of the Puritan ethic, being poor was seen as a symptom of weakness or moral failure, and was often accompanied by a great sense of shame or guilt.

For me, there was the confusing encounter with unfamiliar mores governing sexual relationships—the different rituals of dating and mating, as well as the different stylings of gender itself. It took me a while longer to start noticing the more subtle differences—that subliminal system of cultural assumptions which can inform our most interstitial and intimate perceptions, and even feelings: our ideas of what is beautiful or ugly, our sense of desirable distance between people, our notions of pleasure and pain. Every emigrant becomes a natural anthropologist, observing, or more pertinently sensing, such nuances and the minute—but not insignificant—differences in cultural modes of being; differences which, I believe, may extend not only to the social or relational modes of expression, but to the cultivation and the meanings we attach to internal states—to what Michel Foucault called 'the practices of the self'. Both Poles and Americans recognised the concepts of modesty and aggression, for example, but they valued them differently, and placed them at a different point on the moral/psychological spectrum. Polish culture had a tolerance, or even relish, for certain states of melancholy or lyrical sadness that was fairly incomprehensible in America; while the American preference for positive cheerfulness was often quite baffling to the Poles. The self also has its language of emotional values and interior states.

I can truthfully say that my own writing—the impetus and the driving need to write—came out of that first moment of extreme rupture and loss, and the attempts to make myself at home in my new language and culture which followed. Of course, there is great enrichment in such a journey. There are great gains, especially perhaps for a writer, in undergoing the seismic shift of culture change. Being deframed, so to speak, from everything familiar, gives one new ways of observing and seeing, and brings you up against certain questions that otherwise remain unasked and quiescent. It places you at an oblique angle to your world, and gives you a perspective, a vantage point. For a writer, this is a perceptual and a formal bonus. The perspective of distance can be a great impetus to thought and creativity, which is surely why so many artists have actively chosen expatriation and exile: Joyce, with his motto 'Silence, exile, and cunning'; Samuel Beckett, with his decision to write in French—precisely, I think for the advantages of defamiliarisation.

And then, there is the intensification of memory—and sometimes (or rather, often) of nostalgia. The American writer Joyce Carol Oates has said that 'for most novelists, the art of writing might be defined as the use to which we put our homesickness. So powerful is the instinct to memorialise in prose—one's region, one's family, one's past—that many writers, shorn of such subjects, would be rendered paralysed and mute.' In exile, the impulse to memorialise is magnified, and much glorious literature has emerged from it. 'Native Realm' by Czeslaw Milosz, or Nabokov's 'Speak, Memory', some of Brodsky's essays in *A Room and a Half*, or even Milan Kundera's much cooler take on transplantation in *The Book of Laughter and Forgetting*, are all works of a lyrical commemoration informed by a tenderness for what seems to be lost forever and by the need, and even the obligation, to remember—obligation, because these writers were so often talking about suppressed and censored histories.

But all of these writers were Cold War emigrants. Since their expulsions, the Iron Curtain has lifted and the Berlin Wall has fallen. The 'velvet revolutions' of 1989 brought 'the other Europe' into the sphere of Europe, *tout court*, and eventually into the European Union. I think we can safely say that in Europe (if not everywhere else) the age of exile is over. Instead, we are witnessing a new phenomenon of mass-scale, voluntary migrations, and almost entirely unhampered cross-national movements. The young Poles,

Romanians and Bulgarians who come to Britain or other western countries make their journeys across a continent no longer divided by borders; if they want to return to their country of origin, they can do so with relative ease. Indeed, if they want to try a different destination, they can travel on as well—and some, although not many, decide to pull up stakes more than once.

What drives these migrations, what kinds of choices do they involve, and what kinds of psychic repercussions are they likely to have? Having travelled through eastern Europe shortly after the transitions of 1989 as part of the research for my book, *Exit Into History*, I could well understand the initial excitement accompanying the opening of European borders and the very notion of 'free movement', where previously there was practically no possibility of movement at all. For the inhabitants of eastern Europe who were in effect arrested in their countries—economically static, closed off, governed by grimly repressive regimes—'the West' was a space of desire and the site of culture and true civilisation; a half-mythical realm of wondrous prosperity, personal opportunity and far-ranging freedom.

The first great burst of the post-1989 eastern European migrations was still fuelled by these distance-bred preconceptions, as well as by more pragmatic motives and incentives. And, of course, to some extent the preconceptions were based in social realities. Western Europeans in the post-War period were indeed more prosperous, freer, better dressed and incomparably better housed than most inhabitants of the eastern and Balkan regions. But in the decades since the 'transitions to democracy', eastern European countries have undergone various degrees of development (however imperfect), and democratisation (however incomplete, and more recently, undermined by reactions against liberal democracy). Indeed, while western Europe was undergoing its economic crisis of 2008, Poland was judged to be the economic miracle of the continent. The contrasts are no longer so stark, and with greater familiarity surely the image of 'the west' has lost some of its idealised glamour.

This is a much more ambiguous set of propositions than the stark polarities created by the Cold War world; and I have often wondered how the new political geography of Europe affects what could be called the psycho-geography of those who move within it. How does the decision to leave one's country of origin voluntarily alter one's self-definition, or perception of one's life-trajectory? How does it affect the relationship to one's native country, and the country to which one chooses to emigrate—and where one might, or might not, settle for good? I cannot presume to enter fully into the internal world of people who undertake such journeys and decisions; but it seems inevitable that ambiguity creates ambivalence; and that, for many of the new immigrants, decisions about whether to stay or return are rarely final, and never unproblematic. The question of which place to call 'home' is rarely foreclosed.

'Free movement' has been, for many, an undoubted extension of personal freedom; but I wonder if there aren't losses in the new circumstances as well; if in our world of travelling light, we don't risk what Milan Kundera has called 'the unbearable lightness of being'—the condition of being unanchored in any stable structures or attachments, or a kind of permanent existential suspension. The literary critic James Wood, in a wonderful essay called 'On not going home' coined the term 'homelooseness'—a state of neither belonging nor homelessness but of being betwixt and between, and somehow learning to live with both the poignant nostalgia for the country one has left and the slight estrangement, or at least detachment, from the country where one actually lives.[3]

The sensations and dilemmas described by Wood, and the kinds of questions he implicitly asks, are often experienced (if not often so subtly articulated) by many of the new immigrants: what is this country to me—or I to this country? Can its landscapes and sounds ever tug at my heartstrings the way that songs or jokes of my native country do? Can I ever feel comforts of familiarity here, or am I always going to miss my family and friends, my village, my town? Am I going to go back some time—or will I stay here for the rest of my life? Indeed, is this my life?—and have I chosen it, or has it somehow just happened?

I should say that, for me personally, the influx of Polish immigrants in particular has been entirely enjoyable. It is fun to be able to conduct some of my daily transactions in Polish, and to be able to buy some of my favourite foods in the newly opened Polish shops (the food of childhood is ever the most potent madeleine). But I sometimes wonder if the continuing mass movements of our time aren't also driven by a kind of subliminal migration myth—the fantasy, so easily stimulated in our globalised world, that life (to quote Kundera again) is elsewhere; that going to that elsewhere is our time's game of risk and exciting adventure—a bid not only for bettering one's conditions, but for some more definitive, if hard to define, transformation. I have talked to immigrants who said that they came because they thought that 'somehow...everything would be better here'—and felt quite alienated from their new lives. Some of them actually felt deceived by previous immigrants who sent glamourised reports of their circumstances back home; but, even for them, the decision to return would be tantamount to admitting failure, and therefore difficult.

Within the UK—the favorite destination for immigrants from Europe—the issues around 'free movement' have been debated mostly in economic terms, reflecting the predominantly economic character of the general political discourse. Do immigrants in their numbers bring more gains to the British economy than they take out? Do they take jobs away from British workers, or do they provide useful labour for industries which need hard-working employees, apparently inducted into a more disciplined work ethic than many young British men and women? Should immigrants get the same benefits as British citizens, or is that simply unfair?

These are all legitimate and important questions; surely, however, reverberations of large-scale immigration are not only economic, but more broadly social and cultural. The cultural differences between western and eastern Europeans are hardly unbridgeable, but the new immigrants form a critical mass large enough to live in their own neighbourhoods and enclaves; to form relationships and friendships largely among themselves; and to have their own institutions, such as churches which offer services in their own language. They are not always certain whether they will stay here for good. This means that they often remain disengaged from their British environment, or the issues of the day which matter quite a bit to others. Given the scale and speed of the immigration phenomenon, it would be disingenuous to ignore the effects of such detachment or separateness on something which can only be called solidarity—the elusive but crucial sense that we are all members of the same 'imagined community', as well as of particular, palpable neighbourhoods. Most people still live local rather than global lives, and they derive their sense of identity from attachment to such places—a need which has been far too blithely ignored by the more globalised 'liberal elites'. (I confess that, as I listened to the tepid rhetoric of the Remain campaign in the pre-referendum days, I often wanted to shout 'It's not *just* the economy, stupid!').

What about the effects of large-scale migrations on the countries of origin? Our imaginations, however much we pride ourselves on being committed Europeans, rarely extend that far; but this is something which also deserves our concern. On the official level, free movement has been supported by all the governments in eastern European countries—although recently a representative of the Polish government said out loud that Poland would prefer to have the emigrants back in their country, helping to develop it on every level. I have talked to Polish university professors who are worried about the diminishing numbers of students entering universities—due partly to low population growth, but partly to migration. Elsewhere, the Romanian health service, after trying to recover from the horror days of the Ceausescu regime, has been severely undermined by the numbers of doctors and nurses who have left for various western regions. Bulgaria has suffered one of the steepest population declines in the world—40 per cent—due to post-1989 emigration. A substantial number of emigrants have of course come from the educated stratum of the society, and the well-trained professional classes. I actually feel a sense of personal poignancy at these statistics, and at images of dying villages. When I travelled through Bulgaria in 1990,

I was particularly charmed by the liveliness of its culture and the vitality and openness of the Bulgarian intelligentsia. The loss of so many people must surely be detrimental to the political and cultural life of the country, as it struggles to strengthen its economy and its still-young democratic institutions.

These are complex phenomena with no easy solutions but it seems to me that if Europe is going to remain Europe —if it is going to be more than a sphere of shared economic interests—then it needs to nurture and actively support strong democratic societies among all its members; and possibly provide incentives for people to retain their commitment to the more troubled countries, even as they are able to take advantage of the opportunities to travel without restriction.

In Britain, free movement is likely to stop after Brexit— much as I didn't want it to happen; much as I have been maddened by the prospect and the process. But large-scale migrations are for now a fact of life, and aside from necessary and difficult decisions about how to manage their flow, perhaps the most fundamental question they raise is what kind of co-existence we want in the face of highly heterogeneous pluralism. In my nomadic trajectory, I have witnessed—and indeed, experienced—a variety of attitudes and approaches to multicultural 'others'. At the time I arrived in America, the country still had a confidently unified sense of itself, and the conviction that it represented progress and the desirable human norm. The ideology on immigration, referred to through the metaphor of 'the melting pot', was unequivocally assimilationist. This meant that the imagination of difference was not, in that earlier America, very well developed; that deep cultural difference often simply fell outside the pale of consideration or notice; and that the new arrival talking about other places, other forms of life, was often greeted not exactly with prejudice, but with the kind of incomprehension which ignored the fact that there was anything to understand. On the part of the immigrants there were of course misunderstandings and illusions as well—sometimes having to do with the promise of the American Dream, and sometimes its obverse.

Since then, a number of attitudinal twists, turns and swings of the pendulum have taken place. In America, the melting pot was replaced by the beautiful mosaic, with its foregrounding of difference rather than its elision. There was the rise of identity politics, supported by an influential body of theory prevalent in Europe as well, which privileged the position of the outsider and the nomad, uncertainty and marginality. In this discourse, exile was cool, and its costs ignored. But of course such putatively progressive positions have been accompanied all along by much less palatable ideas and forms of prejudice—attitudes which are once again on the rise, sometimes in newly extreme and belief-defying versions.

It is hard to put one's finger on anything like a policy towards multiculturalism in Britain; but it seems to me that the general discomfort around these issues has led to a kind of compromise solution, based on a very British idea of *laissez-faire* non-interference, which says: 'We'll leave you alone, if you leave us alone.' On some levels, this has led to some good results, and the flourishing of particular communities; but I think it is becoming increasingly evident that, in our highly diverse and increasingly divided societies, as we deal with sometimes widely disparate systems of values and cultural character in situations of close proximity, *laissez-faire* tolerance is not enough. If we are not to exist as separate enclaves inhabiting the same territory, if differences and mutual ignorance are not to lead to prejudice and conflict, we need, both on the individual and collective level, a much closer engagement with each other. We need somehow to take the risk of crossing the internal borders in our societies, and make the effort of imagination and understanding—from all sides of the various divides— which can only be accomplished through close contact and dialogue on both the individual and collective level.

I realise that 'dialogue' may seem like an overused term, and a facile panacea; but in fact, authentic dialogue is anything but easy. It needs empathy and it needs courage. It cannot proceed from the position either of putative superiority or of self-effacement. To condescend to our interlocutors in such encounters is of course to diminish and humiliate them; but to defer to others automatically because we perceive them as vulnerable, or less privileged, or as 'our victims'—is to assume that they are divested of agency and incapable of responsibility. From the minority side, such dialogue also requires an effort of openness and the courage to step outside the rules of the tribe. If we perceive our interlocutors merely as representatives of power, or as incapable of real understanding or change, we are guilty of prejudice too. And again, I say 'we' because I have been on that side of the equation as well. Equality is not only an economic but also an ethical achievement.

In a sense, truly open dialogue across differences of cultures is akin to the process of textual translation. Like translation, it requires both a sensitivity to another cultural language and set of values, and the ability to retain our own idiom and vantage-point. This is what I learned through my own experiments in entering the inner life of another culture: that if we apply our own criteria or forms of perception to cultural others too rigidly, we may completely fail to intuit what the world feels like to our interlocutors; but if we yield our own criteria too quickly, if we enter into a kind of symbiotic sympathy, then we may lose the very instruments of perception—depth perception, so to speak—which allow us to comprehend anything at all. As in textual translation between different languages, cross-cultural interchange can sometimes lead to a discovery both of specific differences and of underlying similarities in the deep structures of various cultural vocabularies—of assumptions and values. Translation, after all, would be impossible without such similarities; but it also has to be recognised that some differences may be unbridgeable, or non-negotiable (in today's terms, these might have to do with the values of free speech and limits on hate speech, for example; or with attitudes to gender and sexual freedom).

I would not want to underestimate the potency of our first cultures in shaping us or perceiving the world. But we can also change and grow; we can extend towards each other. And it is this more dynamic and more risky form of communication which I think we badly need in our highly diverse societies if we are not to remain, across lines of ethnic or religious differences, either polite or hostile strangers to each other.

But of course, when cultural differences exist within the borders of one society, there is a third perspective and presence which needs to be taken into account—and that is the perspective of the body politic itself, and what can still perhaps be called the common good. From that third but crucial vantage-point, the question becomes not only how we can understand each other in all of our differences, but also how we can retain a notion of commonality and solidarity in the face of those differences. In our advanced democracies, this need not imply some old-fashioned idea of national identity, in which being British, or French, or Polish, is a changeless and monolithic condition—but rather, an affirmation of what I would like to call the culture of democracy itself. I still find valuable the ideas of Enlightenment thinkers who thought that you could combine citizenship of a nation with various religious or ethnic affiliations in the private sphere. But in order to remain a society at all, in order not to risk social fragmentation, we need arenas in which to meet on the ground of shared interests and responsibilities—and indeed, responsibilities to and for each other. We need to be able to refer to some fundamental values and norms to which we can all agree, as members of the same society, to assent.

We humans do not live by economic interests alone; we are meaning-making, meaning-seeking creatures. Language is the main instrument of this urge, and literature, with its endless variety and the insights it can give us into the lives of others, one of its most fertile expressions. The vital and varied body of literature created by minority writers in the UK (and elsewhere in Europe) has been a great enrichment of our culture, and a contribution to different ways of understanding the world. We do not yet know what kind of writing will emerge from the second or third generation of the 'free movement' migrations, or what complexities of life-experience and feeling it will express as they make English language their own.

But in the meantime, if in our circumstances of large-scale migrations and high levels of diversity we want to create a decent and inclusive society, we need a language not only of creative expression, but of self and values; we need the living speech through which we can recognise each other as the complex, multifaceted, particular persons we all are— and as members of a polity we are willing to care for and develop in common. In my search for a sense of home, I have come to believe that one of our deepest grown-up desires is for solidarity—for living in a shared social space with fellow human beings whom we can respect and understand, and to whom we can extend basic trust, if not always agreement. Perhaps, in our always flawed human condition, that is the closest we can get to the tree of life; and, however difficult the task, we must keep trying.

The Minds of Writers

Kei Miller

I PICKED A FIGHT with a writer. Some people say I am often doing this. I do not mean to be adversarial and hope to god I am not self-righteous, but sometimes there are things too important to say and it would be almost immoral not to say them. I picked a fight with a writer because he was from my own country—from Jamaica—and he was writing about a body that was not unlike my own. He was imagining a man that on another day and in different circumstances could have been me, though this is true about everyone that we imagine, regardless of race or gender. Always on another day, and in different circumstances, they could be us. And I believe this writer had used his imagination in a limiting and a dangerous way.

I am interested in the minds of writers, and I want to suggest something that is probably too large and too ponderous. I will suggest it all the same: there is a moral and an ethical impetus that does not curtail our imagination. It does not limit what we are able to do on the page. In fact, it does the opposite. It demands that we think expansively and generously. But allow me some time to set before you a context before I turn my attention to the mind of the particular writer and to the fight that I picked, and you can decide if I was wrong or right to do so.

*

There is a game that writers play—at least I think we do, most of us, and especially those of us who tell stories. Virginia Woolf plays it famously in her essay 'Mr Bennett and Mrs Brown'.[1] She is trying, through example, to explain the writer's fascination with character—with the strategies we use to make a gathering of words on the flat page feel like an actual living person, a believable human being with their own history and quirks and personal tragedies.

Woolf observes Mrs Brown sitting across from her on a train. Mrs Brown is not her real name. It is what Woolf decides to call her. It is an invention of sorts, and this is how the game often begins—with a name. We encounter strangers in our day-to-day lives, and some of them fascinate us more than others. We name them—Kevin, or Lisa, or Ahmed, or Mr or Mrs Brown—as one might name a file that we will return to and edit. And why is she wearing that red coat? Who gave it to her? Does she even like it? And why is he looking at his watch? Is he late for something—an appointment—yes, a doctor's appointment! Is he about to pick up a diagnosis? Is he afraid? And so on and so forth.

We invent people's stories as we observe them, and Woolf observes Mrs Brown keenly. 'She was one of those clean, threadbare old ladies whose extreme tidiness—everything buttoned up, fastened, tied together, mended and brushed up—suggests more extreme poverty than rags and dirt.

There was something pinched about her—a look of suffering, of apprehension, and in addition she was very small.'

It is fascinating to watch the mind of a writer at work, even as the writer consciously observes her own mind. Woolf invites us to see the process by which a complete stranger can carry you towards the world of the novel. 'The impression she made was overwhelming. It came pouring out like a draught—like a smell of burning. What was it composed of—that overwhelming and peculiar impression?'

It is important to note that Woolf's remarks come at the beginning of a new kind of literature—specifically, at the beginning of Modernism. She is aware of this fact. She is interested in how the Edwardians before her wrote such magnificent books, but never really stopped to observe people.

> There she sits in the corner of her carriage—that carriage which is travelling not from Richmond to Waterloo, but from one age of English Literature to the next, for Mrs Brown is eternal, Mrs Brown is Human Nature, Mrs Brown changes only on the surface, it is the novelists who get in and out—there she sits and not one of the Edwardian writers has so much as looked at her. They have looked very powerfully, searchingly, sympathetically out of the window, at factories, at Utopias, even at the decoration and upholstery of the carriage; but never at her. Never at life. Never at human nature.

Woolf is making a point that moves beyond the aesthetics of fiction and towards its ethics. Her point is not simply that writers observe and that our imaginations run wild—but that our imaginations should be generous and should give to our characters all their possibilities.

> Your part is to insist that writers shall come down off of
> their plinths and pedestals, and describe—beautifully
> if possible, truthfully at any rate, our Mrs Brown. You
> should insist that she is an old lady of unlimited capacity
> and infinite variety, capable of appearing in any place,
> wearing any dress, saying anything and doing heaven
> knows what. But the things she says and the things she
> does, and her eyes and her nose and her speech and
> silence have an overwhelming fascination, for she is, of
> course, the spirit we live by, life itself.[2]

Far away from Edwardian England and in a small rural
village in Jamaica, the writer Erna Brodber is articulating
a similar thought. Near the end of her magnificent short
novel, *Myal* (1988), we find an echo of Woolf's remarks.
Here, the schoolteacher, Ella O'Grady, is finally coming
into consciousness. She had been zombified before—a
zombification which Brodber suggests is merely the
postcolonial condition, being alive yet cut off from our
ancestors and heritage. Ella O'Grady has finally woken
up, and in this new consciousness she is questioning many
things which she might have taken for granted before. She
is particularly concerned about a story that she is required
to teach to her students. It is one of the prescribed books
on the syllabus. The novel *Myal* serves a sharp critique to
this Primary School Reader that really was once taught to
children in Jamaica. Like Virginia Woolf, Erna Brodber's
concern is with writers and their imagined characters, even
if (as in this case) the characters are animals.

Ella O'Grady arrives at the principal's office. Reverend

Simpson—the principal—has, in fact, been waiting on her. He has been hoping for a long time that this moment would come. Still, he is patient as he presses Ella to explain exactly what her problem with the text is. He needs her to articulate it for herself.

> [...]– My problem, Reverend Simpson, is that what they have been given to do and say in that book is ignorant. –
> – Ignorant, Miss Ella? The best of us are ignorant sometimes, and some of us are even ignorant all the time. That's life too, you know –
> – But Reverend Simpson, all the animals there are ignorant all the time –
> – I see. –
> – Yes. Why don't we see them sometimes as sensible, which they are indeed at times in real life and sensible, as they have the capacity to be on more occasions than we give them credit for? Or can we not imagine that people who are not us can be sensible? –
> – So your problem is with the mind of the writer? –[...]
> – You are right, sir. He has robbed his characters of their possibilities. –[3]

*

I picked a fight with a writer. He is the Jamaican poet and journalist, Mel Cooke. Cooke meets his Mrs Brown, not on a train, but in a furniture store on Constant Spring Road. You must imagine the busyness of Half Way Tree—the vendors, the loud route taxis coughing up smoke, the huge yellow buses—this intersection not only of roads, but of the various strata of Jamaican life. It is possible that every character that has ever been imagined on the pages of Jamaican fiction would have, at some point, passed through here. Cooke recounts what for him was a disturbing encounter in an article 'Bye Bye, Boom Bye Bye' published in *The Gleaner* on 4 June 2015. The title is more than a nod to the most controversial song in the history of Dancehall music. Buju Banton's 1992 hit 'Boom Bye Bye' (or 'Boom By By' in its earlier transcription) is an onomatopoeic reference to the sound of a gun. On some nights you will hear it in Jamaica, sitting on a verandah perhaps, a sound that at first you hope is only the backfire of a car, but that you realise after is something much darker, the awful soundtrack of an island plagued with violence. The bark of guns is sadly almost never followed by the wail of sirens, and the silence in its wake is probably even more terrifying. Buju's lyrics, written when he was fifteen years old, are a call to arms and explicitly advocate for the killing of gay men. Some cultural critics have suggested that we understand the lyrics as merely metaphor, but in a country where acts of homophobic violence were once frequent, and where the song 'Boom Bye Bye' was often invoked as a kind of anthem during actual physical attacks on queer bodies, there is not enough distance between lyrics and reality to consign the song to a safe metaphoric shelf. In later years Buju Banton would become a lightning rod around which criticism of hate music, hate speech and Jamaican homophobia could gather. His eventual imprisonment in 2011 on charges of drug trafficking was seen by some conspiracy theorists as the culmination of a plot by gay activists to punish Banton and bring him to heel.

I had always had a different thought about the song. Its homophobia was blindingly obvious, but beneath it was something else—almost the direct opposite—a kind of homoerotics that few people were willing to see or too afraid to point out. Before the invocation of guns, Buju imagines the intimate moment between two men. 'Two man hitch up and a hug up on and ah lay dung inna bed, rub up one another and ah feel up leg.' It is an utterly convincing act of imagining—this sweetness between male lovers, and it always seemed to me that, caught by the surprise in this moment of reverie, Buju has to quickly and violently reassert his heterosexuality. 'Send fi de 'matic or de uzi instead.' When Tanya Shirley wrote her collection of poems 'The Merchant of Feathers', she explained that its concern was what we often had to do in places like Jamaica—find soft things in hard places. Maybe this is why I had always seen a conflicting erotics in Buju's song. Maybe gay men on the island, for our survival, had to learn to look for the softness that hid behind the most strident performances of masculinity.

It is hard to see a society change—the frustratingly slow and incremental adjustments that might take years or whole generations to complete. But if you closed your eyes in 1992 and opened them again in 2019, you would see a society that was vastly changed, a society that had become more hospitable to bodies like my own, and where a song advocating for the extermination of gay men could not go unchallenged. Freshly released from prison and looking to restart his career, Buju Banton would release a statement on 6 March 2019:

In recent days there has been a great deal of press coverage about the song 'Boom Bye Bye' from my past which I long ago stopped performing and removed from any platform that I control or have influence over. I recognise that the song has caused much pain to listeners, as well as to my fans, my family and myself. After all the adversity we've been through I am determined to put this song in the past and continue moving forward as an artist and as a man. I affirm once and for all that everyone has the right to live as they so choose. In the words of the great Dennis Brown, 'Love and hate can never be friends.'[4]

Could Mel Cooke, in 2015, be acknowledging this changed Jamaica that Buju would soon be released to? Could his article 'Bye Bye, Boom Bye Bye' be making its own statement of *adios* and *good riddance* to a culture of homophobia? Cooke certainly acknowledges (even if grudgingly) the changes that have allowed for greater queer visibility in Jamaica, but rather than repudiate the homophobia he only repackages it. The title seems a mere game of alliteration rather than carrying any significant meaning.

Mel Cooke's Mrs Brown is not an old woman. In fact, his Mrs Brown is not a person at all. He is careful to establish this. He cannot see the man before him as a human being.

I was in Courts on Constant Spring Road, St Andrew, in December when I saw it. There were two of the things, but one was especially itty. It wiggled up the steps to the store's upper level behind a store employee. It wiggled, it simpered, it held its handbag in the crook of an arm with the wrist especially limp. It preened and smoothed down its hair and revelled in an oddly bronze complexion and surreptitiously glanced around to see the effect on those who were around.

It was disappointed. No one batted (and that is a pun, in case you missed it) an eyelid.[5]

Cooke's parenthetical remark, 'and that is a pun, in case you missed it', is as glib as his title. He is always anxious that we recognise his wit. It is, I believe, an unflattering quality in a writer but is far from the most alarming thing here. Far more disturbing is the fact that Cooke's transphobia is genuinely unaware of itself as transphobia. His particular brand of discrimination is close cousin to much of the racial tensions in America and Britain today, which is to say his is a series of micro-aggressions. His problem (he would like to convince us) is not that the man before him is possibly gay but rather that his gender performance is so outlandish and so preposterous that (as he explains in a follow-up article) it reduces such men into being 'jackasses and ridiculous caricatures of human beings'.[6] Cooke steadfastly refuses the pronoun 'he', which at first could be seen as au fait with the pronouns that some trans bodies prefer, but neither does he use the pronouns 'she' or 'they'. He insists on 'it'—pointedly suggesting that his Mrs Brown is not human.

Irony is lost on Cooke. He says no one batted an eyelid but is writing an article in a national newspaper about the incident. He continues:

> What did I do? What anyone interested in observing human behaviour would, naturally. I followed back a it. And upstairs I saw a person reclined in one of the chairs on display, pouting as he looked at his telephone, which he was suddenly very interested in now that there was no potential audience for the it which he had projected.[7]

Ironies pile one on top of the other. There was no potential audience for this man's subversive performance of gender and yet Cooke follows him. It never occurs to the writer that this following in order to gawk could be considered an act of aggression. While Cooke distances himself from the extremes of homophobia and transphobia, he re-inscribes its most basic tenets. His position is a popular one, even in a Jamaica that is so much more open than it was in 1992. If you move through the bustle of Half Way Tree, through the crowds and between the loud taxis and the big yellow buses, you might hear versions of it:

> *Mi don't have no problem with battyman so long as dem don't come to me wid it!*
> Or, *Mi don't care what people do in dem bedroom. That is their business—so long as dem don't push it in my face, as long as them don't brazen wid it!*
> Or, *Man must act like man and woman must act like woman!*

Increased tolerance in Jamaica seems to come with a condition: so long as people act out their 'natural' and heteronormative roles, so long as they don't disturb the status quo, then everything should be okay. And this strain of trans and homophobia is just as present in LGBT communities. The terms 'masculine' or 'DL (downlow)' are often requirements that gay men insist upon in potential partners. Even more worrying is the term 'straight-acting', a strange compliment with which to affirm gay men who are able to 'pass'. On days when I am feeling mischievous, I ask if the term 'white-acting' could be similarly mobilised as a compliment to black people who feel the need to access a sort of social mobility by denying their racial identities.

According to Mel Cooke, it is only when the man gets bored of his own flamboyance, perhaps when he puts aside his trans identity, that he resumes his personhood. Cooke writes: 'The costume was the same, but the persona totally different—deflated and different. Simply a person, different from me but certainly not intent on and failing to disrupt sensibilities.'[8]

Cooke's imagination is an ungenerous place. A man enters the store and looks around, but Cooke does not suppose that this may have been something as simple as him looking for a friend he had planned to meet in the furniture store. He does not imagine the Sunday afternoon—it was probably several months ago—when friends had gathered in the small, hot living room of a one-bedroom house in Portmore. It had been his grandmother's house and though she had died her presence was still there in the lace doilies that covered the surfaces of tables and whatnots—she was there in the 'God Bless This Home' plaque that still hung on the wall; she was there in the string of coconut beads that hung like a curtain separating the living room from the kitchen. And she was there in the old floral couch on which all six boys had magically found a spot—they were so thin—and strained to watch the movie that was streaming on a laptop. It was a comedy, and the sudden eruption of laughter from all six boys—a laughter that included their bodies spasming—had caused a loud pop and the chair had sunk inwards. A small silence had followed the breaking of the couch and the five boys had looked at their friend as if to ask him for permission, so when he laughed (it was the permission they needed) they did as well. It had been his intention since then—those few months ago—to buy a new living room set, something that did not remind him so much of old women, but he had to save up money to do this. The months had gone by; the money had been saved, and now here he was at Courts. His friend Barry had promised to go with him—Barry whose sense of style was impeccable, who had a knack for decorating and interiors. When he entered the store and scanned every face, it was Barry he was looking for, but Cooke cannot imagine anything so benign, anything so simple. When he follows him upstairs and sees him on the couch and on his phone, he does not imagine the man as simply sending a text: 'Barry, where are you? We're at the store now.' So put out is Cooke by this man that he has robbed him of all his possibilities. He is not a man of 'unlimited capacity and infinite variety' as Woolf suggests. Cooke reduces rather than expands. And this is why I picked a fight.

*

It is unlikely that Earl Lovelace, writing about the Spiritual Baptists of Trinidad and the ordinance that made their worship illegal in 1948, had any thought of queer communities across the Caribbean more than half a century later, and yet his 1982 novel *The Wine of Astonishment* is a powerful allegory of exactly that. And as powerful as his allegory about Caribbean communities disadvantaged and discriminated against by unjust laws, is as powerful as what he has to say for those who choose to represent those communities. Lovelace is also interested in the minds of writers.

The Wine of Astonishment tells the story of a community in Trinidad under threat. Their way of life, their traditions, even their mannerisms, are threatened by colonial authorities that would have them act differently, behave 'normally' or 'naturally' whatever these ideas are ever supposed to mean. 'We can't be white, but we can act white!' declares the character, Ivan Morton, just as confidently as those men in Half Way Tree might say, *man must act like man and woman must act like woman*, or *You can be gay, but you must be straight-acting*.

The Spiritual Baptist community resort to being themselves in secret because the law is against them as well. Bee, the leader of the church, sees the damage the law has done to his flock, and he knows that sometimes, when laws are so profoundly unjust, they must be broken. In the chapter when Bee decides to do just that, to break the law, he gives one of the most incredible sermons I have ever read in the pages of literature. He goes to his congregation in a state of repentance. His is an incredible example of humility and the taking of responsibility. Bee says the problem was not just the law but him as well, because he had failed to tell them who they were. And in drawing out the sermon from him, the congregation shouts, 'Tell us preacher, tell us who is we...'

I understood something then—that this was not merely a congregation calling to its pastor; it was a community calling to its writers. It was a community asking its writers to imagine them, and to imagine them magnificently. *Tell us writer—tell us who is we! Give to us, all our possibilities*.

This is the high and holy order of writers—to tell people who they are, to offer them both the plodding banality and the incredible magic of their personhood. Perhaps not every writer can do this. I accept that. I can accept limitations. But if a writer's mind is so limited that he cannot offer people themselves, then at the very least he should do no harm. If he cannot offer personhood, he should not take it away. For Mel Cooke to reduce his Mr/Mrs Brown to an 'it' was the most profound betrayal I can think of in one's role as a writer. It is, I believe, the greatest evil one can do on the page. Such words are not brave, but cowardly. Not only would Mel Cooke not tell this man who he was, but he would tell him that he was not.

In a series of blogs, I had challenged Cooke but maybe our public conversation (Cooke responded in the pages of *The Gleaner*) went beyond the specific article and at its heart were these questions about the moral role of the artist in society, the ethical demands of the creative imagination, the function of the writer who writes out of community and back to that community.

Cooke's failure was a failure of imagination. The man who appeared at the store existed only as a spectacle for him. He was a limited man—without agency, without history, without ambition. He was nothing.

Here, at the end of this essay, I would like to insist on what my role is as a writer. It is first to apologise to a man who had been so carelessly written about, so carelessly imagined by another writer. It is to remind him of another unjust law in Jamaica that had to be repealed in 1859. Few people remember or tell this story—it is so deeply buried. Back then in 1859, the poorer people of Jamaica could take no more of the unfair tolls that they had to pay on the main thoroughfares. A rebellion started. For three nights people rioted, destroying the toll-keeper's house and the toll gates in Savana La Mar. *The Falmouth Post* at the time described the rioters as: 'ruffians, some dressed in female attire'. And is that why this story is so deeply buried? The Toll Gate Riots saw black Jamaican men dressed as women fighting for justice.

My role as a writer is to tell this man at Courts, in all his flamboyance, that he in fact belongs to a Caribbean tradition. Even here, where he might seem so peculiar and against the grain of things, he in fact runs in the grain of history; he is rooted in our particular story of resistance and triumph—a history of wild and wonderful men who have dragged us towards progress. My role as a writer is to come down off of any plinth and pedestal, and describe—beautifully if possible, truthfully at any rate, this man. I should insist that he is of unlimited capacity and infinite variety, capable of appearing in any place, wearing any dress, saying anything and doing heaven knows what. But the things he says and the things he does, and his eyes and his nose and his speech and silence have an overwhelming fascination, for he is, of course, the spirit we live by, life itself.

What a Time to be a
(Black) (British) (Womxn) Writer

Bernardine Evaristo

CHIDERA EGGERUE, aka The Slumflower, is a social-media star, Peckham home girl and feminist. She first came to prominence in 2017 when she created the hashtag #SaggyBoobsMatter on Twitter in order to promote the body-positive message that women's breasts and bodies are fine—just as they are. It's an important message and antithetical to a beauty industry that berates us for our imperfections. A year later she published a self-help motivational book, *What a Time to Be Alone: The Slumflower's Guide to Why You Are Already Enough*, which hit the *Sunday Times* bestseller list the week it was published in 2018, when she was 23.[1] A self-styled 'guru, confidante and best friend' to her readers, Eggerue's very pink, zanily illustrated book offers advice on self-worth and self-acceptance. An earlier work in the genre, a pocket-sized booklet called *The Little Black Book: A Toolkit for Working Women*, by Otegha Uwagba, became a bestseller in 2016, paving the way for Eggerue. This, in turn, was probably influenced by Chimamanda

Ngozi Adichie's 2014 TedX essay-booklet, *We Should All Be Feminists*, which also did well. Neither booklet is more than 2,000 words long, and therefore has the capacity to reach a wide market, especially as we are now, worryingly, sinking deeper into the Age of Attention Deficit Disorder due to the REM-inducing effects of the internet and the scrolling patterns of social media.

Both Eggerue and Uwagba are of Nigerian parentage, but their writing does not deal with the specific challenges women of colour face, but is instead aimed at the mass-market readership of young women in general, although Eggerue is articulate on intersectionality online. However, simply by being black women, other black women will gravitate towards their books. Eggerue does nod to the specificity of her Nigerian background through the inclusion of Igbo proverbs passed down by her mother, in the original language and in translation. She dedicates her book thus: 'To my Mum, who effortlessly yet intentionally led me to myself'. As Eggerue is so precocious and audacious, one suspects that the mother of such a prodigious person is very impressive herself.

These are unprecedented times for black women writers. We have become a *thing*, in no small part due to the internet—the borderless, infinite cyberspace that allows us to instantly connect with each other beyond physical barriers and time zones. It has reconfigured how we communicate, present and perform ourselves and our personas to the world-at-large, and it has brought previously marginalised social groups and writing to the fore in ways hitherto unimaginable. I remember when the idea of it really was inconceivable to me in 1990 when a British Telecom engineer informed me that books could now be sent down a telephone line. I tried to picture it—a book and a phone—and decided that he was either a joker, drunk or insane.

As a society we are beginning to recognise and take seriously the ills and pitfalls of social media, but it is still the most exciting channel of mass communication since history began. Transnational communities can easily find and connect with each other and interests, ideas, positions, debates and experiences can easily be expressed, shared and explored without being brokered (or censored) by the traditional media and institutions. Eggerue is emblematic of someone whose swift rise to fame as a writer in the two years since she coined the hashtag #SaggyBoobsMatter is entirely due to the platforms of social media connecting her to her primary readership of young women. I cannot imagine a young black British female self-help writer securing a major publishing deal at any other time before this one. Not that she's breaking new ground. I recall that the black British writer, trainer and executive coach Jackee Holder published her first motivational book, *Soul Purpose*, in 1999.

These times really are quite extraordinary. The ripple effects of 2013's #BlackLivesMatter moment or movement saw regenerated interest in writings about race in America, which spilled over into the UK market. We're used to the spotlight on racism being beamed across the Atlantic while little attention is paid to the perniciousness of systemic racism in Britain, about which there is much denial. Yet when #BlackLivesMatter gained momentum with the grassroots, it quickly garnered mainstream attention which, in turn, precipitated an unprecedented publishing interest in non-fiction books by black writers. In 2016, David Olusoga published *Black and British: A Forgotten History*, which accompanied a celebrated television series and reached beyond the usual niche market for such works. Reni Eddo-Lodge's bestselling book *Why I'm No Longer Talking to White People About Race* (begun as a blog post that went viral) was published in 2017. It quickly gained currency as a key 101 text on race and intersectionality in the UK. However, while Eddo-Lodge acknowledges African-American feminists of yore, she is silent on our own trailblazers. I recall the 1982 publication of *The Heart of the Race: Black Women's Lives in Britain*, edited by Beverly Bryan, Stella Dadzie and Suzanne Scafe, and recently reissued. It was the first non-fiction book that investigated black women's lives in Britain, the difficulties faced and activist resistance to them. A decade later Heidi Safia Mirza's published *Young, Female and Black* (1992) and *Black British Feminism* (1997). Much of this history has been lost, it is not taught at universities, nor does it appear in the timelines of what is effectively a whitewashed British feminist history. These early writers were brave, brilliant and forging ahead with a black feminist agenda at a time when there was little support and much opprobrium. It's disheartening to see such trailblazers made invisible yet again, this time by the new generation of writers, their younger sisters, too many of whom are not prepared to dig beneath the top layer of the internet to discover their own history. Thank goodness some of us are long-toothed, some of us are living history, and some of us are prepared to share our knowledge when we are invited into their spaces. The new generation of activists needs to know that history did not begin with them and that they are part of a continuum: a tradition of black feminist literary history in this country.

In 2018 the journalist Afua Hirsch published *Brit(ish): On Race, Identity and Belonging* while the hip hop artist Akala published *Natives: Race and Class in the Ruins of Empire*.

Both books are memoirs by mixed-race people, as well as contemplations on racial politics as lived realities, and yet again they were bestsellers. I remember when, a decade or so ago, a memoir by a black British intellectual ran up against a retail industry that refused to stock his book on the grounds that no one would buy it. How times have changed.

All of these commercially and critically successful non-fiction books of late, uncompromisingly tackling issues around race and culture, have sent the publishing industry into an unprecedented buying frenzy. Suddenly every publisher wants a book in the genre, whereas previously few were interested in the sphere of ideas, society and commentary about who we are in this country. In 2018, *Slay in Your Lane: The Black Girl Bible*, by Yomi Adegoke and Elizabeth Uviebinene, hit the shelves, a book that celebrated the achievements of black British women while offering advice on how to get ahead. In June 2019 Chelsea Kwakye and Ore Ogunbiyi's *Taking Up Space: The Black Girls' Manifesto for Change* was published, a book on the experience of black students in predominantly white higher-education institutions. This also started off as a blog post written when the two women were graduating from Cambridge University in 2018. Television presenter Emma Dabiri is the author of *Don't Touch My Hair* (2019), a treatise on black hair and its political, cultural, historical, philosophical and personal resonances. Also published in 2019 was *Safe: Black British Men Reclaiming Space*, edited by Derek Owusu, co-host of the popular black-focused literature podcast, Mostly Lit. His anthology of essays by twenty black male contributors shouldn't be ground-breaking, but it is. The writers touch on a wide range of subject matter including homophobia, mental health, foster care and masculinity. There's also *Black*,

Listed: Black British Culture Explored by Jeffrey Boakye, which is both a witty and hard-hitting take on the subject through the device of a quirky dictionary of black-related terms, and *No Win Race* by Derek Bardowell, which examines sport and race, family and legacy, within the time frame of the Brixton Riots (1982) and Brexit (2016).

I've read nearly all of these books; others are awaiting my attention. Many of them are sent to me to review or for quotes and they sit piled up on my desk as I write this. I can honestly say that to date each one is unique in how it progresses the debates around the issues that affect us, and in expanding interpretations and perceptions of our cultural, political and intellectual life. The field has been so arid up to this point that each work feels urgent, essential. Perhaps none is more transgressive than *The Grassling*, by Elizabeth Jane Burnett, also a poet, whose 2019 'geological memoir' explores the Devon countryside where she was raised. Burnett's deeply poetic communion with nature reminds me of Ingrid Pollard's 1988 *Pastoral Interlude* series of photographs that positioned, radically, and way ahead of its time, a black presence in the English countryside. Likewise with the play, *Black Men Walking*, by Testament, which I saw at the Royal Court in 2018, featuring three northern black men who go on walking trips in the wilds of the Peak District—and talk. Extracting black people, especially black men, from their typical depiction in an urban environment in Britain makes you realise how limiting it has been: how black life and the metropolis have become synonymous. *Black Men Walking* was a refreshing, progressive look at male friendship in a pastoral setting, while Burnett's memoir connects us at a primal, immersive level to the topography of a country that is as much ours as anyone else's.

Also off the beaten track is *Afropean: Notes from Black Europe* by Johny Pitts (2019), whose travels in Europe and encounters with its black communities offer a counter-narrative to a continent associated with whiteness. Comparisons will too easily be made with Caryl Phillips' 1987 pan-European travelogue, *The European Tribe*. While Phillips' book was a moving account of the experiences of a black man encountering an overwhelming European whiteness over 30 years ago, Pitts sought out today's black communities on the continent, and reframed our understanding of it from this perspective. The books are companion pieces, as well as lessons in history, travel and identity. I ventured into this terrain with my novel-with-verse *Soul Tourists* in 2005, creating a fictional black couple who travel across Europe by car to the Middle East in the late Eighties, a journey I myself had undertaken. The male protagonist, Stanley, encounters ghosts of people of colour from history including the Chevalier de St George in France, Hannibal of 2,500 years ago in the Alps, and Mary Seacole in Turkey. Books about Europe from a black British perspective, fiction or non-fiction, are hard to find. The last one I encountered other than my own was Mike Phillips' novel, *A Shadow of Myself* (2001), set in London and Prague.

Writing is a solitary rather than a communal process, and not all writers are community-spirited, but the new, mostly female, young activist writer communities use social media to market their projects. These are twenty-somethings who use the term 'womxn', with its inclusive emphasis on women of colour, queer and trans people. These womxn are not waiting for the establishment to fund or publish them, but they are getting on with it themselves by setting the terms of their intellectual and creative endeavours.

I include here the influential *Gal-Dem* and *Black Ballad* magazines, and the organisers of the Black Girl Festival, Octavia Poets' Collective, the Heaux Noire womxn of colour poetry events, and a host of other fantastic artistic enterprises. Their entrepreneurship and self-determination reminds me of the 1980s when I was their age. They are my millennial counterparts, if you like, and regularly send me on a nostalgia-fest back to when I was a young writer, to a time when I and many others also sought to create a platform to explore being women of colour in the UK, and to find a safe space to develop our creativity. In those days of long ago, we were young feminists gaining sustenance from each other as we emerged from the darkness of invisibility and struggled to make sense of a culture to which we should have belonged, but in so many ways were told we did not. We realised that if we did not inscribe our stories into the cultural landscape, it would remain forever white and predominantly male. We decided that where we were voiceless, we would be heard.

In the early Eighties I co-founded *Theatre of Black Women*, Britain's first such company, with Patricia Hilaire and Paulette Randall. We had just graduated from the Rose Bruford College of Speech and Drama's Community Theatre Arts course where we were encouraged to create our own plays. It made sense to write and perform dramas with black women at the heart of our poetic, dramatic and experimental productions. We marketed to audiences through leaflets handed out outside venues and tube stations and stuck on to racks in pubs, and by word of mouth, and we met like-minded women in social spaces and at conferences where we thrashed out the meaning of being political black women in Britain, a term which then embraced all women of colour. Out of this community emerged other theatre companies, dance troupes, music groups, publishers, arts collectives. We remade and imagined the complexities of our lives through an art we could name our own. Through turning inwards towards each other, we found affirmation, creative possibility, ambition and activist strength. We were discovering who we were, what we wanted, what was important to us and how to create art on our own terms without intervention from those people who did not understand us, or underestimated or stereotyped us. We were a sisterhood, sometimes dysfunctional, not always in agreement, but there was a network of support and collaboration, much as I see with the young womxn of today. It was a necessary period of creative segregation, and we were emboldened and empowered by our community and congregation.

The arts projects we set up came and went, but the legacy of that era is that we contributed to the larger project of inserting ourselves into British culture and giving voice, nearly 40 years ago now, to the experiences and perspectives of 'second generation' black British women.

In the early Eighties, those of us who wanted to write had to look across the Atlantic for inspiration, for hope, for role models to show us the way. While there was a literary lineage of black writers in Britain going back to the Fifties and earlier, they were predominantly male, predominantly first generation, and definitely not writing from the perspective of my generation of British-born or raised women. We looked to African-American women writers who were powerfully articulating their identities in books to be found in the feminist literature emporium of Sisterwrite in Islington—the only shop in the country that imported the black women's books rolling off the presses in America. In Britain in the Eighties, The Women's Press imported the success of Alice Walker, but, with one or two exceptions such as the two novels of Joan Riley, was not interested in black British women's writing. Two brilliant black women I knew tried to sell their book on African women to the press but were turned down because, the editor said, they lacked personal expertise in black women's writing. And while Virago championed Maya Angelou her homegrown counterparts were mostly absent from their lists.

I found the pamphlet, *Gap Tooth Girlfriends* (1981) in Sisterwrite on my first visit there. Slight and affordable, it was an intoxicating collection of African-American women poets whose words were gloriously free-spirited and black womanist. I'd never read the like before. Their glowing, charismatic faces were on the cover of the pamphlet in a group photograph and therefore made so much more tangible and accessible to their younger sister grappling with identity issues around race, culture and sexuality across the ocean. I could imagine myself in the photograph and fitting in. I had met the editor, Alexis de Veaux, at a Women's Arts Festival in the Melkveg in Amsterdam in 1982, where she was performing with her experimental performance troupe of three African-American women, Flamboyant Ladies, and I was touring with Theatre of Black Women. They were the first African-Americans I'd ever met. I was in awe of them.

I remember disappearing between the pages of *Home Girls: A Black Feminist Anthology* (1999), edited by Barbara Smith, during one long weekend and discovering African-American women writers with the confidence and experience to express their realities through literature, poetry, essays. The West End production of the choreopoem *for coloured girls who have considered suicide when the rainbow is enuf*, by Ntozake Shange, inspired the verse dramas I wrote for theatre. The fragmentary, prose-poetry books of the Jamaican-American writer, Michelle Cliff, such as *Claiming an Identity They Taught Me to Despise* (1980), inspired me to be adventurous with my own writing. In her essay, 'Caliban's Daughter' (1991), Cliff wrote that her aim was 'to reject speechlessness, a process which has taken years, and to invent my own peculiar speech with which to describe my own peculiar self, to draw together everything I am and have been.'[2]

Likewise Audre Lorde wrote in *Sister Outsider* (1984): 'What are the words you do not yet have? What do you need to say? What are the tyrannies you swallow day by day and attempt to make your own, until you will sicken of them and die of them, still in silence.'[3] She inspired my generation of feminists, much as she now inspires the latest generation of 'woke' young women worldwide, with new editions of her works. I met her when she visited London in the early Eighties. She wanted to spend time with young black feminists. At an event at the Drill Hall Theatre, with an audience of mostly white women, she demanded that the black women without tickets in the lobby be let in, or she wouldn't take to the stage.

And how enriching and motivating it was to read interviews with so many great writers in *Black Women Writers at Work* (1984) edited by Claudia Tate. These African-American women spoke of their process and practice long before you could trawl through online interviews and do the same. I am indebted to the women writers who went before me, whose pamphlets and books shaped me in my formative years and have travelled with me to my many homes over the decades; works that are stained with tobacco smoke, coffee and red wine from the days when I indulged in all three, and, while I have dispensed with thousands of books in my time, these and others from that era I still treasure—they still reside on my bookshelves, grouped together to remind me that they were the making of me.

We British women writers were emboldened and encouraged by their literature as we began to produce our own. Like our American sisters, we too refused to be complicit in the perpetuation of our powerless societal status, our *oppression* (there's a throwback term). Anthologies were a good way to start to showcase our burgeoning talents and to give us the confidence that comes with publication. There were several anthologies, including *Black Women Talk Poetry* (Black Women Talk Collective, 1987), which featured twenty poets, including Adjoa Andoh, Jackie Kay and Dorothea Smartt, published by the newly formed Black Women Talk Poetry Collective of Da Choong, Olivette Cole Wilson, Gabriella Pearse and myself; and *Watchers and Seekers* (Women's Press, 1987), a mixture of poetry and fiction, edited by Rhonda Cobham and Merle Collins.

In creating an alternative space for our politicised creativity, we were challenging the status quo. It made sense that, in trying to articulate our predicament as energetic, aspirational young women with lots to say and a passion for the arts, we would turn to a feminism that was supposed to advocate for the equal treatment and inclusion of all women. Except it didn't, we were too often excluded from white feminist endeavours, just as we were excluded or marginalised from much of the contemporaneous black male arts production. Many of us were queer, either transiently, as it turned out, or for life. This meant that we were more likely to organise as women together, and less reliant on male opinion and approval. It meant that we created the space to think and work through our *stuff* among ourselves, without other voices telling us we were being too bolshie or black womanist or just plain wrong in any number of ways. We encountered disapproval and alienation from those who didn't understand why we were separatist in our artistic endeavours. The establishment position was to ignore people of colour, other than tokenistic exceptions, and yet when we established our own projects, we were seen as divisive troublemakers, drawing unnecessary attention to our 'race' or gender and thus problematising ourselves.

As the producers of our own artistic enterprises, we were bolstered and validated by our support networks while we developed our own aesthetics and cultural values without waiting for others to endorse us. Like today's young arts activists, we were doing it for ourselves rather than hoping to be cherry-picked by this country's white cultural producers.

It is understandable why many of the women involved in that era did not continue along the struggling path as outsider creatives. By the time they hit their thirties, many of my peers re-evaluated their goals and chose a less precarious profession involving a proper salary, home ownership, financial security for their children or future children.

For those of us who stayed the course, we probably never imagined that we'd be taken as seriously as we are at this moment. The first time I saw the work of black British women visual artists, who belonged to our arts community, was in two exhibitions curated by Lubaina Himid. It was quite incredible to see black women as the subject of this art for the first time in *Black Women Time Now* at Battersea Arts Centre in 1984 and *The Thin Black Line* at the ICA in 1985. I was overjoyed when Himid won the Turner Prize in 2017 for her exciting, innovative and spectacular artwork, 40 years after she began her career as an artist. Similarly, in 1984 the actor Adjoa Andoh performed in her first professional production, a black women's play called *Where Do We Go From Here*, staged by Akimbo Theatre Company, which I saw at the Drill Hall. In 2019 she co-directed and starred in the first all-women-of-colour Shakespeare production on a major stage in Britain, *Richard II* at Shakespeare's Globe.

Over the years some of us realised that we needed to have a seat at the table (actually, more than one). We had cut our teeth in grassroots arts communities and graduated to positions of power. Once upon a time we were operating on the periphery as renegades, radicals. Today some of us are inside the heart of this country's institutions. *Charting the Journey, Writings by Black and Third World Women* (1988) was a mixed poetry, prose, fiction and non-fiction anthology by 'black and Third World women'.[4] It had five editors: Shabnam Grewal became a BBC television producer; Pratibha Parma has long been a filmmaker; Liliane Landor is Head of Foreign News for Channel 4; Gail Lewis became a writer and academic; and Jackie Kay is currently the National Poet of Scotland. Some of us juggle positions in universities with our creative practice. Several of us became professors, although we were parachuted in to universities after establishing ourselves in the arts, rather than working our way up inside a system pitted against people of colour. The currency of the hashtags #whyismycurriculumwhite, #whyismyprofessornotblack and #decolonisingthecurriculum won't go away any time soon. Academia in the UK, while a seemingly liberal domain, is entrenched in centuries of white, male patriarchy. It does not nurture black excellence. The fact that there are only 25 black female professors (in the British context this is the top rank achievable as an academic), out of 17,000 professors in our nation's universities, is testament to that. For many of us who are inside academia, the intellectual heartland of the nation, our work remains as vital, productive and countercultural as ever. I entered the academy after 30 years as a freelance creative, and I advocate for diversity from within.

By the early Nineties, much of the grassroots community activism had disappeared. *Wasafiri*, formed in 1984 to platform new black, Asian and diasporic writing was not on my radar when I was younger, but it continues to go from strength to strength. Other publications such as *Artrage Intercultural Arts Magazine* and its offshoot, *Black Arts in London*, ran from the early Eighties to the mid-Nineties. The anthology *Passion: Discourses on Blackwomen's Creativity* (1990), edited by Maud Sulter and published by her own outfit, Urban Fox Press, brought together some of the black women's arts activism of the preceding decade. Maud went on to have a successful career as a fine-art photographer with her work exhibited and purchased by major national galleries, but sadly passed away in 2008.

I wonder at the possibilities of my generation of women if social media had been around when we were in our twenties. How would our lives have been enriched by the rapid interconnectivity of today? We would have discovered a global community which would recognise our feelings of isolation and need for solidarity. Perhaps if social media had been around feminism would not have been trashed and thrashed to near-death by the media for decades and consequently spurned by generations of young women who didn't want to be associated with it, until the #MeToo and other movements brought it to the fore again in the past few years. No longer a dirty word, to be feminist is fashionable, although we never want it to be a trend, which is intrinsically ephemeral. But, at least for now, feminism has entered the mainstream and is championed by all kinds of women at all levels of society.

Many of us have campaigned to improve access to publishing and the arts industry for people of colour for decades, and we are seeing the results of this today. I founded The Complete Works poetry mentoring scheme (2007–17), which selected 30 poets to be mentored by many of Britain's leading poets in order to redress the situation where less thanone per cent of poetry books published in the UK were by poets of colour. Today that proportion stands at sixteen per cent and the mentored poets are achieving phenomenal success with their publications in every way conceivable, including winning many top poetry and literature awards. Similarly, I founded the Brunel International African Poetry Prize in 2012 to advance African poetry, which was then almost invisible on the international literature landscape. Since then, most of the winning and shortlisted poets have been achieving publication success, often in partnership with the African Poetry Book Fund's New Generation African Poets boxset series, founded by the poet Kwame Dawes at the University of Nebraska. Each 'diversity' project initiated becomes a rallying cry, a 'consciousness-raising' effort, which has a ripple effect.

One thing I have learned is that the future won't look after itself. We cannot take any developments for granted and believe that society will become more progressively inclusive without our ongoing intervention. If those of us who are considered marginal (in some contexts this includes *all* women) stop campaigning, we experience social regression. I wonder what will happen if the support systems, networks and development programmes for people of colour cease to exist. The plethora of books currently being published, including poetry and to a lesser extent, fiction, is astonishing considering the history of uninterest. But we must be wary because today's boom is not the result of a steady, incremental transition from marginalisation towards the publication and celebration of books in all genres over many decades. It has exploded out of a void. Where are its foundations? I have written in the past about fads in the literary world for writers of colour, especially the period in the mid-to-late Nineties when there were more young black men and women publishing fiction than ever before, with a tendency towards coming-of-age narratives. By the Noughties most of these writers had disappeared and we were back at square one.

What happens when the big advances do not deliver on their promise? What happens when second-book syndrome kicks in? What about those who have become authors almost by accident, via blogs or their online presence leading to instant book deals. For the authors of 'old', our journeys to becoming so and sustaining a lifelong career comes from a deep place within us. We have developed careers with deep foundations. Ideally, we want the field of writing to be a wide and abundant field spanning the very young through to the very old. We want our writers to have long careers spent producing work that matures as they do. Yet the emphasis in publishing and the media focuses on the new and the young, although new and young isn't synonymous with fresh and original. Some of these writers become shooting stars, and when the moment has passed we wonder what happened to them, and to everyone else who showed such promise with their first or second books. And perhaps in five or ten years' time we will be back at square one. History tells us that books can too easily disappear from literary and cultural memory, until such time as they are rediscovered, if at all. Alice Walker resurrected the once-celebrated Zora Neale Hurston in 1975, fifteen years after her death. Hurston's books had been out of print for decades. Obscurity has been the fate of too many black women writers. I realised only last year that for too many of the young writers and readers I was encountering, books published a mere ten years ago were ancient history. Not only did they not know the body of work produced by their recent and still current predecessors, they weren't interested, drawing inspiration instead from online magazines, Instagram and Twitter feeds.

Millennials have grown up with the internet and its wayward child, social media, and accept it as integral to their existence, in spite of the risk of addiction and mental-health issues. They are the ones dominating and shaping conversations around race, feminism, gender, sexuality, which begin online and progress into the physical world. We cannot foretell the future, but we are moving towards online domination, at the mercy of the conglomerates who run our data storage and the ever-more sophisticated cyber-terrorists who seek to disrupt and destroy our internet activity.

What is the role of books in this brave new world where knee-jerk reactions predominate, moral outrage is the prevailing orthodoxy and ideas must be compressed to the level of soundbites in tweets of no more than 280 characters?

Chidera Eggerue, with a hefty 220,000+ Instagram followers and 74,000+ for Twitter, sagely tells her followers: 'Instagram might shut down one day and suddenly nobody will care about your 80,000 followers. Relevance in the offline world is key.' She's right. Conversely, the older writers, artists and activists who eschew social media are missing out on adding their wisdom, experience and long view to the debates. It's an exciting political, intellectual and creative space, and we need to be a part of it—and if not we must ask ourselves if we are relinquishing our responsibility towards the future?

Eggerue is an 'influencer', one who brands pay to endorse their products. She posts photographs of herself in fashionable clothes on Instagram and seems to see no contradiction between being a feminist (feminists have long railed against the sexual objectification of women), and posting titillating photographs of herself, presumably in the name of #bodypositivity. Other arts activists of her generation are also benefiting from the desire of the multinationals to be aligned with woke young people and to exploit their marketability. The revolution, or rather what we might think of as this countercultural moment where those previously without a platform are having their say, has already been commodified. Those of us who are alert to the capriciousness of this SHOULD trumpet a note of caution to those who are swept up into the glamour of the moment. We need to ask ourselves how best we can effect change for our constituencies that is sustainable rather than fashionable. My answer is that the spirit of entrepreneurship, community and arts activism will sustain us long after it's no longer woke to be 'woke'.

The Dinner that Changed My Life

Raja Shehadeh

ON A WINDY MARCH DAY in 1993 I was invited to a dinner that changed my life. This was just before the agreement that came to be known as the Oslo Accords was signed between Israel and the PLO [the Palestine Liberation Organization] following secret negotiations. In the preceding year I had been involved as legal advisor in the negotiations that had been taking place in Washington since 1991. I had spared no effort to advise the Palestinian delegation about what I believed the Israeli negotiators were trying to shove down our throats: to confirm and consolidate unilateral changes to the laws that they had introduced during the years of the 1967 Israeli occupation of the Palestinian territories. This I believed would make it possible to establish more Jewish settlements in the Occupied Palestinian Territories, placing them under Israeli law and creating an apartheid system with the two communities, the Palestinian and Israeli, living side by side subject to different sets of laws. At the time of the dinner we did not yet know about the negotiations taking place in secret in Oslo. But it was already clear that the Israeli side was unwilling to yield. Yet the Palestinians back home had high hopes that the negotiations would bring an end to the Israeli occupation. It was a time of many colloquiums and meetings, and a fair amount of political jostling by aspirants for political positions in anticipation of the Palestinian state that was expected to be established.

But this time it was only a dinner at the Belgian Consulate, with three Israelis and three Palestinians.

The Palestinian invitees had planned to meet at the American Colony Hotel in Jerusalem, taking one car to the western side of the city. But Majid[1] was late. Nadeem, the third invitee was on time. We sat in the garden waiting for Majid.

Nadeem, the head of an NGO, was fastidious about his dress and looks. He frequently licked his lips and with his fingers he smoothed his cheeks which were so puffy they could have been filled with air by a hand pump. He talked haltingly. He was essentially a shy man.

'I want you to be involved in our next colloquium,' he told me, as we waited. 'The co-ordinators of the technical committees are bringing experts who have experience with South American countries. We want them to help us forge a relationship between our anticipated Palestinian government and the NGOs. We want to avoid centralisation. It doesn't make sense for the government to do everything.'

I mumbled an 'Of course.' And we moved on to another subject until Majid came.

We arrived too early at Salameh House, a Mandate-built villa that is one of the most attractive, quiet buildings in Jerusalem, now the residence of the Belgian Consul-General, our host. I thought it was alright to go in a few minutes before time. 'But no,' said Nadeem. 'It is highly improper. This is a formal occasion and we must not go in before the time we were invited. We learned this at the diplomacy session.'

So we walked in the Talbyeh neighbourhood of western Jerusalem, one of the poshest quarters of the city, with beautiful houses built by rich Palestinian Arabs before 1948 in which Israelis now live, and lush gardens. The Van Leer Institute was there, as was the Jerusalem Theatre and Islamic Museum. All so refined and with the odour of almond blossoms in the air. After we entered—at the proper time— the Israeli invitees began to trickle in. First there was Yehuda followed by Isaac. Both were, I recalled, in the Israeli peace camp. The third, Ruth, a member of the Knesset, was late. We were there to discuss with the Consul General and his party the negotiations that had been taking place for the past eighteen months in Washington between the Israelis and Palestinians. I had initially been involved in these but had decided to leave, feeling greatly disappointed by the lack of progress. After exchanging a few pleasantries we delved right into the subject.

'What you're doing in Washington is an important start,' one of the Belgian diplomats, who introduced himself as Jean-Paul, said by way of beginning. 'It proves that Israelis and Palestinians can speak together just as you're doing here. Dialogue is very important. Isn't that right?' the diplomat asked.

It was a rhetorical question and the diplomat did not wait to hear the answer. He went on:

'What you should begin with is a statement that you all agree there shall be no more wars. And then go on from there. Belgium has three ethnic and language communities, French, Flemish and German and yet not a drop of blood has been shed since 1831. There were differences between the Flemish and the French. The Flemish were poor. They had no diplomats, no universities. The policy was to help them develop. Now they are equal. It is something that needs to be worked on all the time. Reconciliation does not happen easily. But you have to start somewhere.'

After he finished I looked at the assembled guests. None spoke but by their silence I felt we were all in agreement that the Belgian was preaching to us in numbing generalities about peace and the brotherhood of man. His dictate regarding what we 'should do' was not taken kindly. Yehuda, bear-like and easily excitable, broke the silence. Ever since I've known him he has seemed in perpetual rebellion, always blurting out his words with energy and enthusiasm like a frustrated prophet. He ends up dominating every discussion.

'What important start are you talking about? It's no start at all. Three months ago Israel deported 415 Palestinians to south Lebanon and refuses to negotiate with the Palestinians for their return. Instead it's negotiating with the Americans, bypassing completely the Palestinians. The Israeli government measures its success by its ability to avoid having Palestinians involved, getting agreement by keeping the discussion between it and the USA. By going over the heads of the Palestinians these negotiations prove that Israel can avoid negotiating with them. It's no start at all.'

Isaac, who was not much older than Yehuda, spoke in a much calmer manner. He had a long face that resembled Rex Harrison's, with thick hair that was combed back. The resemblance was confirmed when he later took out his pipe and began to smoke. He turned to the diplomat and said: 'I agree with Mr Jean-Paul. There is so much hatred. I know the situation very well. Over the past fifteen years I have given thousands of talks to army personnel and schools all over the country. The Palestinians cannot accept a deal without Jerusalem, the Israelis cannot accept to give up Jerusalem. The Palestinians think that inside the autonomous territories they will have no Israeli soldiers. They are wrong. The Israelis think that with the proposed autonomy, the Palestinians will be docile and quiet. They are wrong too because the violence will continue. The talks are therefore ill-conceived. The only good thing to do would be to accept the plan I came up with. With the profound lack of trust among the parties, there is no chance at arriving at an immediate peace. My plan proposes that there needs to be a long transitional period. That is why the only way to arrive at peace is in stages through building mutual trust as I have advocated.'

'But there is another scenario,' Nadeem interjected. 'That the Palestinian council proposed by the Israeli side would constitute a beginning which we will build on. For the time being people will be satisfied with this. Slowly we will work on increasing its jurisdiction and power. There will be less violence and all of this could be a genuine and hopeful beginning.'

'What beginning? What has changed?' Yehuda piped up.

'They are allowing many more things that were not allowed before. This is a change,' Nadeem said by way of explanation.

'Tell me one example, just one Israeli concession. Just one.'

'There are many,' Nadeem said.

'Maybe within the municipal boundaries. Just give me one that leads to real control by Palestinians over a vital service or natural resource.'

Nadeem fell silent. He couldn't.

It was now Majid's turn to speak:

He spoke in a measured, pedantic manner like an academic choosing his words carefully and speaking with a confirmed instructor's precision. He seemed to understand his role as having to reflect the different opinions of what he called 'schools of thought', leaving out until the end what he himself believed in. So he would say, 'there is one school of thought which says this and another which says that'. The fiction being that he merely identifies these and stands aloof. Only he doesn't. He has a clear agenda. After going through his schools of thought he said: 'The Israelis are offering a limited autonomy. We have to take it. Supreme Councils equivalent to ministries are being established as we speak. They will be recognised by the Israeli authorities. These then will link up with their counterpart ministries in Jordan.' Majid was confirming my suspicion that he wanted the return of the West Bank to Jordan, which ruled over us from 1948 to 1967.

He then went on: 'We are proceeding. The Supreme Councils have been established; they are getting recognition from the Europeans. There is a fever of training. So much training is taking place. This is our plan, we want to train a new cadre and then prepare it to take over and go on from there. After the government is in place we will link up with Jordan in the confederation.'

Yehuda cut in: 'I have worked as advisor to three prime ministers. I know Yitzhak Rabin. Know him very well. He will not give up anything, not even to Jordan.'

Nadeem interjected: 'But is he the same Rabin?'

'Yes, he's the same Rabin,' Yehuda confirmed. 'Rabin hasn't changed. He will not change. Not one bit. He's the same man. I know his ideas, know what he stands for. I don't want to come down too heavy but I must be a realist and speak from what I know. He is the same man. It is folly to expect anything from him.'

Nadeem disagreed. As he spoke. the two Israelis in the room, Yehuda and Isaac, slipped deeper into in their seats. I could hear a heavy silence descend. They wanted to flare up and say 'it's all nonsense, are you crazy, mad? Or are you dreaming?' But they restrained themselves, held themselves back and the pressure of holding back made the silence heavy, awkward and artificial.

The brief interlude provided me with the opportunity to observe Ruth, who had come in late and remained silent so as not to disrupt the conversation. She had a large nose that tilted to the left. Her full lips were screwed in a perpetual smile. She looked comfortable in herself, intelligent and sharp: an activist politician. Feeling embarrassed for coming late, she had demonstratively kept her lips closed. But now it was her turn to speak: 'First I want to apologise for being late but I was at a demonstration against the deportations.' She continued in an American accent: 'I beg to differ. The present situation is untenable. We cannot go on like this. Already the army is unable to control Gaza. Soon they will not be able to control the West Bank. We must make a change. The change cannot wait.'

Yehuda, who persisted in referring to Palestinians as Arabs, did not like this: 'The Israeli leftists think that by suggesting separation they are doing something good for the Arabs. Separation means the Arabs get the worst deal. They will become a Bantustan[2]. Land-use plans have been completed for the entire area of the West Bank. The zoning dedicates the majority of the land for the settlers and leaves the Palestinians isolated from each other and confined to a small space. Different and separate roads are also being built for the different communities. Those for the settlers link the settlements to Israel. If these planning schemes are made formal it is the worst thing that can happen. The question of the violence is because the army had decided for military reasons to stay outside the camps. When it changed the policy and decided to send troops in there was a reaction. But the decision to enter the camp or stay out is theirs. The violence doesn't mean very much in military terms. The Palestinians may be a nuisance to Israel but they're not a threat; they cannot obstruct or stop what is happening. Physical separation of the two sides at this point is just not possible. This would be the worst thing for the Palestinians. It is too late.'

The Belgian economist sitting next to him asked: 'Why should this be so?'

'It isn't a question of why. Don't ask me why. You don't ask why the sun rises. It just does. When there were a few thousand settlers you didn't do anything to stop the settlements and now you ask why. It is too late. Now they are there, facts on the ground and this is how they will be treated by their tribe and we cannot go back. The Jews are one tribe. Shulamit Aloni, the doveish Minister of Education, cannot take a decision to hold back the $50 million that it costs to provide a military escort for the small number of the settlers who are bussed to their schools. If she did it would change everything because they cannot stay if their children don't get education. But she cannot. Wherever they are, the Jews must get services and protection. They are members of the tribe, they just will not be neglected or denied anything by the Jewish state, even if we don't agree to what they are doing. The Israeli people hate these settlers—they cannot stand them—and yet they cannot deny them anything. They are members of the tribe. You see what has happened is that antisemitism has been turned against the Arabs. They have become "the other" and this in Jewish religion is the Goy.[3] The Arabs now are the goy. The degree of hatred against the Arabs is phenomenal. The policy has to be adjusted in accordance with these facts. Anything else is self-deception and will simply not work.'

'But it is too expensive,' said the Belgian diplomat, Jean-Paul. 'Do you know what Belgium spends on defence? 1.5 per cent of its GNP. And Belgium is a rich country. No one will accept a higher percentage. Israel spends twenty per cent. What if the Minister of Defence said we will need less if this and this is done?'

'It's not a question of the Palestinians,' Yehuda retorted. 'The Intifada is not expensive to fight. What is expensive is the army's preparedness to fight all the Arab states. That's where the expense lies. Palestinian violence is easy to manage. Its end does not top the list of Israeli priorities. If peace is made with the Arab states, as Israel hopes will happen, this will bring the state of emergency to an end and there will be plenty of resources to put into fighting the Palestinians.'

'What then can be done?' asked the diplomat.

'I don't know—I'm not a politician—I just analyse for you. I sit back and watch but I want there to be realism, not false hopes; false hopes will get us nowhere. Look, I'm almost 60 years old. I spent all my life in this conflict. The Israelis are a manic-depressive people. They are either too confident, almost arrogant, or down in the dumps. Now it's the former.'

Yehuda then proceeded to disparage the whole of the

negotiations, saying: 'These talks that we're so enthusiastic about are just a game of musical chairs, which will keep us all going round and round with everyone fearful that the music will stop and he won't have a chair to sit on.'

Anxious to infuse some optimism, Nadeem said: 'I say there is another scenario. We start with the small and ask for more.'

'A scenario it might be, but the way things really are is another matter. What is being offered is nothing. The Israelis have organised the situation so that their concessions will amount to nothing. What they're offering to transfer to the Palestinians in terms of civilian affairs they've wanted to give up in any case. They would rather you do it with European money so that they benefit from the money brought in and won't have to spend their own money on services for the Palestinians, which it is their responsibility to cover. It is easier and better for them not to have to pay for Palestinian education, health, social welfare... By paying for these, you Europeans will not be doing the Palestinians any favours, because it is all organised so that it will be part of the Israeli system and nothing more. The only change is that they have now become more sophisticated. They know now that they can achieve the same ends without having to have direct control over everything.'

I had not yet contributed to the discussion but now, after a tense pause, I decided to speak. I was in agreement with Yehuda but decided not to give him the pleasure of knowing that. Instead I said that I agreed with Isaac and thought his analysis is correct. I went on to say: 'Emotions and feelings of hatred between people can change very quickly. In any case what Israelis and Palestinians need to do is their business. I think the real subject today is relations with Europe and what Europe can do to help us solve this conflict. We have to remember that Israel is a country of limited resources. Without the support, financial and moral, of Europe and the USA, the billions of dollars that were needed to build the settlements could not have been spent. Europe in effect has helped Israel establish settlements which now constitute the main obstacle to peace. They did this because of their feelings of guilt towards the Jews. They did it unthinkingly. Now, if they are to help, they must understand the issues. What I heard tonight about Belgium and how it managed to keep the peace does not apply to us. If Europe wants to play a role it must first of all understand the unique nature of the problems we're facing and apply pressure on Israel to stop building settlements.'

The Belgians had not invited us to preach to them. They wanted to know our views on what was going on and what to expect for the future. That's why they didn't react to my challenge.

I could see in the corner of my eye the consul's wife waiting for me to finish speaking so that she could invite everyone in to dinner. As soon as I did, we stood up and moved to the dining table.

On the way we lost our host, who declared that he had a bad flu, which he called 'that Jerusalem flu', and had to go to bed.

Our conversation continued at the dinner table. After we sat down I heard Yehuda asking the Palestinian who, after his many years of service with the Belgians, had come to look French and speak English with a French accent: 'Did I go too far? Am I being too harsh in the way I speak?' The tactful Palestinian said: 'Not at all.'

Next to Yehuda sat the Belgian economist. He had

a deadpan face, which reminded me of the portraits of Flemish men done by seventeenth-century artists. When spoken to, his head turned and the eyes followed without him changing his expression. He was there to listen and take note of what we said, not to give his opinion. He listened without betraying any reaction and was a complete contrast to Yehuda, who continued to be animated as he pronounced more of his dire assessments of the situation.

The food was good. The discussion that went on during the meal only confirmed my growing conviction that the Palestinians whom I knew well and had worked with for many years—all experienced, long-term activists in the struggle during the Intifada—were utterly deluded. I agreed with Yehuda that we were entering a new period as destructive to our country as the Nakba[4] had been. It was both bewildering and sad to observe how the Palestinians were unable to confront the truth of what was taking place. It was also clear that I had scant opportunity to influence the course of events.

During the discussion that continued after dinner I also observed that the Israeli guests were as anxious as I was about the fate of their country and their future role in it. Yet I was more concerned at that point with what was happening to my side, the obvious self-deception of those being groomed for a leadership role in the prospective lame Palestinian Authority.

As though to prove Yehuda right about Rabin's constancy, it was less than two years after that dinner, on 4 September 1995, that the Prime Minister stood on the stage erected in eastern Jerusalem for the celebrations marking the three-thousandth anniversary of the establishment of Jerusalem as the capital of the Kingdom of Israel and declared (in language so untypical of this military man): 'Jerusalem is the celebration of the glory of the Jewish people from the day it was created in the Image of God. She is its heart and the apple of its eye; and our festivities here today are only meant to once again elevate Jerusalem "above our chiefest joy" as was the custom of our fathers and forefathers.'

Now, many years later, when I think back over the course of my life during these past 26 years, how I managed to distance myself from any political involvement, and how the activist that I had been during the Intifada has turned into the observer and writer, I realise that the transformation began after that fateful dinner. It was then that it became clear to me that if these Palestinian friends whom I had admired and worked with for many years were so deluded, I could not partner with them to turn the tide.

The anticipated agreement between Israel and the PLO, I believed, would be tantamount to a surrender document. It would give rise to new political realities impossible to alter through documentation of human rights violations. No amount of critical writing could bring the parties to change it. Now was the time to move beyond the limited audience of readers of human rights documents, and address a larger public through literary writing to help rehabilitate the tarnished image of the Palestinians. To do what politics cannot do.

That dinner led me to decide not to attempt, as I was wont to do, to own the failure but to move on to a more solitary pursuit. And so I did. I shifted my concentration from political activism to literary writing and never turned back, never thought my work was futile, and never regretted the move.

Indeed, in 1993 at the Belgian Consulate in Jerusalem, a dinner changed the course of my life.

The Life and Death of Pakistan's Sabeen Mahmud

Bina Shah

PAKISTAN IS NOT an easy place to have an opinion, and it can sometimes result in your death. At least, that's what people said when Sabeen Mahmud, the 40-year-old human rights activist and founder of The Second Floor, was killed in 2015. The assassination of Sabeen Mahmud resulted in the silencing of a voice, and then, paradoxically, the amplification of many others, raised in protest and anger and fear and sorrow. Yet it also illustrates the deadly struggle in Pakistan for freedom of opinion, thought, and action: precious values in open, democratic societies which are seen by many in this deeply conservative country as threats to national security, and perfidy to the country's core values.

Sabeen's murder rocked the foundations of Pakistan's civil society: its target, its heartlessness, drove citizens into a state of shock and incredulity. Who would want to kill Sabeen? A gentle, tall woman with cropped hair who wore jeans with a Pakistani-style short tunic and Indian Kohlapuri sandals, she loved computers, worshipped Steve Jobs, and was obsessed with the actor Hugh Laurie. Not much of a one for makeup, she indulged herself with the occasional Body Shop fragrance or lipstick. Nobody could imagine this self-described postmodern flower child, whose favourite flower was jasmine, had enemies who hated her enough to take her life.

There is a well-known photograph taken at the scene of the crime: Sabeen's Kohlapuri sandals abandoned in the well of the driver's seat in her car. It speaks louder than the gunshots which entered her body, in her chest, cheek and neck, killing her immediately. A final sigh, a slumping of the head to the left, and silence. A brave voice gone forever—this is Pakistan's curse.

In 2007 Sabeen left a successful career in IT to start a movement for positive social change in Pakistan and opened The Second Floor in Karachi, a unique space where she proffered dialogue, critical thinking, the arts and science along with low-priced cappuccinos and cookies. Over the years the café became a breathing space in a city wracked by years of political violence. People of all generations went there to talk, to dance, to create art, to practise yoga, to listen to lectures on quantum physics, politics and philosophy. Things that seem normal to anyone living in a 'normal' country, but Pakistan is not a normal country.

In Pakistan, 'normal' is a shifting paradigm. What is normal when a country has been born out of a violent earthquake, the cleaving of a nation in two, the transfer of millions and the death of millions? Historian Ayesha Jalal gets to the heart of what happened to Pakistan both before and after Partition, which set it on its path of military rule, itself only one iteration of that abnormality. 'When Pakistan was created, it got a financial structure that was 17.5 per cent of undivided India, and a military that was one-third of undivided India,' she wrote in Scroll.in. In other words, the army's prominence in Pakistan is a structural reality of Partition, as Jalal notes: 'Pakistan is a state that was not supposed to survive. The real history is that it did manage to survive. Military dominance is the price Pakistan has paid for its survival.'

Pakistan occupies a low rung on the scale of personal freedom according to the Universal Human Rights Index and is listed 139th out of 180 countries on the 2017 Press Freedom Index. In this troubled South Asian nation stumbling out from years of military dictatorship towards a flawed parliamentary democracy, plagued by corruption, nepotism and military interference, rulers still view those voices that question their motives and methods as a threat to their authority.

Artistic and intellectual pursuits had been clamped down during years of Islamisation under General Zia ul Haq's dictatorship (1978–1988) and 30 years on people are still shell-shocked from the loss of their civil rights and cultural spaces. From 2007, and then over the course of the next short eight years, Sabeen inspired and encouraged people who were tired of helplessness and inaction just by providing them a space where they could think differently.

Under Sabeen's stewardship The Second Floor was a place like no other in Pakistan: a safe space for those who didn't feel they belonged in this conservative society. It was staffed by mostly Hindu-minority young men (there are 3.6 million Hindus in an overall population of almost 300 million). These young men were hired and trained by Sabeen herself, who wanted to give employment opportunities to a marginalised community. Young men and women met and romance blossomed, trans rights activists gathered to talk about their work and gay artist Asim Butt painted murals depicting scenes of love and affection between men. In Pakistan, where men and women don't show physical affection in public, where obedience to parents and authority figures is valued above individualism, The Second Floor was oxygen for people who were suffocating in the country's cloying conservatism and who badly needed to breathe. Over the years, I participated in T2F's many cultural events, wrote two novels there, and was a supporter of Sabeen's vision for a better Pakistan arrived at through dialogue and critical thinking.

Critical voices, if loud enough, can threaten the flow of money and power of which Pakistani politics is a conduit. Both the Pakistani state and non-state actors—terrorists, the building mafia, religious extremists—use similar tactics of silence and violence to quell the debate, dissent and dialogue so vital to democracy. Working towards a truly progressive society can be a life-threatening undertaking for many of its civil-society activists. In 2017, Pakistan's establishment became locked in the throes of a low-key war with proponents of freedom of speech—driving prominent journalists into exile, jailing and disappearing bloggers, threatening and kidnapping activists.

The night Sabeen died, on 24 April 2015, she moderated a discussion called 'Unsilencing Balochistan' which addressed the topic of missing persons in Pakistan's restive southwestern province. Many in Pakistan believe that this last discussion was what led to her death, but the danger Sabeen faced began years earlier than that. Sabeen was killed by self-radicalised men who found her liberal, secular views anathema—or so they claimed in their confessions to the police. Writing in the *Herald*, investigative journalist

Naziha Syed Ali recounts how the alleged killer, Saad Aziz, spoke quietly and calmly about the extremist gang's plan to murder Sabeen. It was based on his dislike of her social stance, which he'd scoped out while attending previous events at The Second Floor. On the night of her killing, Aziz drove up on a motorcycle to Sabeen's car and shot her through the window then raced off to meet his accomplices far away from the crime. Two weeks later he and his gang allegedly committed the Safoora bus attack, where they opened fire on a bus of Ismaili Muslims in Karachi, killing 46 members of the minority Shi'a Muslim sect.

Sabeen's pro-Valentine's Day campaign in 2013 particularly enraged these educated, upper-middle-class men, their education and status putting paid to the theory that religious extremists in Pakistan are poor and uneducated. Saad Aziz was a member of Karachi's middle class, and a graduate of the Institute of Business Administration, an independent university in Karachi founded in 1955—it is the oldest business school outside North America. This type of educated religious extremism is motivated by the same bid for money and power that motivates politicians and government officials in Pakistan. The extremists cloak their baser designs by proclaiming their end goal as the preservation of Islam and the glorification of God. Some also oppose the Pakistani state and its nation-building project in an attempt to align themselves with global Islamist movements. And there is always the possibility that Saad Aziz wanted fame and notoriety and sought to gain it through murder and terrorism.

Four years later, Sabeen's murder seems arbitrary and ill thought out, even though it was meant to silence and intimidate people like her. That they chose to kill a prominent woman activist is less about eliminating Sabeen the woman, and more about angry young men—intelligent bit players trying to prove their influence over Pakistan's social fabric. Religious objections to a 'secular' space may have only been part of this story. While some accept the police-recorded confessions of Saad Aziz and his cohorts claiming Sabeen's secularism as the reason for her murder, others maintain the state had her killed for hosting the discussion on human rights violations in Balochistan.

Pakistanis have learned over the years never to accept official explanations for major events, especially high-profile assassinations (former prime minister Benazir Bhutto's 2007 murder still remains a mystery), as the state often acts to protect those people complicit in the attacks. Nor do the Pakistani people trust the state to resist the lure of extra-judicial murder when it comes to silencing an opponent. Some in the intelligentsia thought Sabeen was silenced by the state; over the past ten years people have grown suspicious that anyone who promotes Pakistan's nascent civil society and social consciousness does so as a ploy for foreign money, or is a traitor who wants to destabilize the nation. Sabeen's murder was seen by some as retribution for these imagined crimes.

One of democracy's key values is inclusion, and Sabeen worked hard for it, carving out a space for the people who couldn't find a place for themselves anywhere in the traditional strata. Artists, students, philosophers, scientists, ordinary citizens and social activists alike found refuge and relief at The Second Floor and they also found themselves. Once they began to organise and raise their voices for reform, they became brave enough to challenge authority. They demanded accountability and transparency from the city's administration, from the bureaucracy and, perhaps fatally, from the military.

The Pakistani intelligence services were said to send agents, both undercover and as official representatives, to observe the debates and sometimes to disrupt them. Yet everyone respected Sabeen's rules for civil discourse and debate in the café's safe space. Many opponents found themselves won over by her personality and her decency; to them Sabeen was the one of the best disruptors of her generation because she challenged the status quo, but always with politeness, decency and respect. Aziz cited the pro-Valentine's Day campaign, with its slogan *Pyaar Honay Dey* (Let There Be Love), as a major provocation for his attack. The *Herald* magazine recounts this story in its report on Sabeen's death: 'At the groundbreaking Creative Karachi Festival organised by The Second Floor in 2014, the *azaan* (Muslim call to prayer) went unnoticed for a few moments in the hubbub. A young man angrily demanded that the music be stopped instantly. Sabeen went up to the guy, took him aside and spoke to him for a while; a little later, he actually brought flowers for her by way of apology.' We will never know what exactly she said to him, but we can be sure that she said it with love.

In the wake of Sabeen's death, it seemed that everyone needed to react and respond, not just to make sense of the assassination but to also analyse what in Pakistani society had caused the murder of someone so beloved. Sabeen's violent death provoked an urgent examination of how Pakistani society was attempting to transform itself along progressive lines, a critical analysis of the powerful forces that opposed this transformation, and consideration of how far they were willing to go to resist it.

But first the grief and pain had to be expressed. Scores of op-eds and columns appeared in newspapers in Pakistan and around the world, written by everyone whose lives Sabeen had touched. Pakistani writers, many of whom had known and been encouraged by Sabeen, added their words to the obituaries and commendations, and began to weave into their eulogies strong responses to extremism and oppression, providing a historical context and background to the climate in which the assassination took place. Common to all writings was the observation that Sabeen had created a catalyst for turning the tide in favour of a more open society, but that the backlash against that opening destroyed her in the end.

Sabeen was said by many to have started a social revolution, but another movement was under way at the same time: the outsourcing of political violence from an oppressive state to individual actors—vigilantes, extremists and sectarianists—who take up the mantle of maintaining Pakistan's security or ideology or whatever vision inspires them to pick up guns and shoot at innocents.

Writing in *The Guardian* immediately after the assassination, novelist Kamila Shamsie asked why Sabeen, who wielded relatively little political influence, had been murdered. 'She didn't seek political power, she didn't have the sort of reach that major TV personalities command. Perhaps it was enough that, like Malala Yusufzai, she wasn't frightened of those who seek to control through fear.' She continued: 'Sabeen and other members of civil society were contesting the control of the state by raising issues such as minority rights, opposition to religious extremism or freedom of expression.'

Fuelled by optimism and courage, Sabeen planted herself

firmly on the side of civil society, setting a high bar of belief in the truth. Her death does not indicate a turning point, only a marker in the long, tortured evolution of this nation towards a more open society, if not a 'normal' one. For Pakistan was never fated to be a normal country. Normality has been suppressed for decades; it continues to be contested as the civilian and military leadership actively stifles dissent and harnesses the powers of religious orthodoxy within the political system and extremism without to achieve its goal of indefinite power.

These issues and more were discussed in Pakistan's teahouses in the 1960s by writers, poets, artists, students, Communists and Marxists. The Progressive Writers Movement of India in the 1930s had carried over into Pakistan after Partition; writers like Sadaat Hasan Manto and Ismat Chugtai fought societal disapproval and state censorship when they wrote about sexuality and society in their books and stories. Yet repressive dictatorships and regimes over the next 30 years drove freedom of expression underground. In 2007 Sabeen began to open the locks once more—and emboldened others in civil society to do the same.

Mohammed Hanif, another celebrated Pakistani novelist, wrote about military executions in the *New York Times* (2017), focusing on the death sentence handed to Sabeen's killer. Like Kamila Shamsie, he first tried to understand the motivation behind her killing. 'Was Sabeen killed for taking a stand against the Pakistani Taliban and their supporters in the mainstream? For defying the powerful military establishment? Because she insisted on drawing red hearts on walls around the city to mark Valentine's Day?'

But very quickly he turned this into a sharp analysis of Pakistan's penchant for secret military trials of terrorists, insisting that open trials instead offer us the chance to comprehend those who seek to undo us as a nation. 'The gory details are what we need to know if we want to know our enemy...court hearings in the open...might reveal how a theological argument can lead to a massacre, how prejudice can lead to sectarian violence.'

In Pakistan freedom of expression is not considered an inalienable human right. Instead, it is seen as power wielded irresponsibly by traitors and rogue elements who want to cause harm to the nation. Nowhere is this more evident than in the dangers faced by Pakistani journalists. For several years Pakistan has been ranked one of the world's most dangerous countries for journalists, and it is common knowledge that if you report on the conflicts in Waziristan and Balochistan, you will be harassed by Pakistan's secret service, the Inter-Services Intelligence agency. Reporting on corruption or other crimes committed by civilians will lead to threats and danger from non-state actors who want negative stories about themselves suppressed—among many such cases are award-winning journalist Taha Siddiqui (exiled), the famous television anchor Hamid Mir (shot at), and investigative journalist Saleem Shahzad (murdered).

The tension between journalists and the state escalated before the Pakistani elections in July 2018, which saw Imran Khan's Pakistan Tehreek-e-Insaaf (PTI) party come to power. In the run-up to the elections, attacks on journalists and social-media bloggers rose exponentially. Anyone who expressed dissent against the state or the military's apparent backing of PTI experienced harrowing attacks on social media by numerous Twitter accounts. *Dawn*, Pakistan's biggest English-language newspaper, faced immense pressure from the military to stop reporting objectively about former prime minister Nawaz Sharif; in military cantonments the newspaper's distribution was halted and a smear campaign against *Dawn* reporters on social media raged for months. Gul Bukhari, a British-Pakistani journalist known for her scathing opposition to Pakistan's military and her support for Nawaz Sharif, was briefly abducted the month before the election; she has since never spoken publicly about her experience or who may have been behind the kidnapping.

Over the years, Pakistan's civil society has been brutalised by both dictators and demagogues, and the war on freedom of speech, tolerance and secular ideals rages on in Pakistan still. This is a war conducted by so-called patriots and protectors on one side, artists and provocateurs on the other. Maybe it is a perpetual war, one that is never truly meant to end, but to instead be a pendulum, swinging back and forth between one side and the other.

Sabeen's murder was one of many deadly events in Pakistan's short history, but her death spurred a movement. The violence enacted upon her did not result in silence; over time, as the grief wore away, it was replaced by a characteristic Pakistani determination to withstand the forces of oppression and fear. Ordinary people began to speak up, working harder for dialogue, continuing to strive for tolerance and an open society. Artists, computer buffs, writers, all pledged to continue the movement that Sabeen started. Artist Sheba Najmi created 'Code' for Pakistan, a non-profit organisation that builds social impact through civic use of technology; the Digital Rights Foundation (DRF) held a feminist global hackathon in Sabeen's memory; DRF's founder Nighat Dad in 2016 won the Dutch Human Rights Tulip award for her work on protecting women and girls on social media. Civil society has grown bold in the years since

Sabeen's death, as if it were a plant that could only bloom when drenched in blood.

Journalists are a stubborn lot, and so are writers. Sometimes we cannot keep silent even when we know that speaking out might endanger our lives. My most recent novel, *Before She Sleeps* (2018) is a feminist dystopia in which most women have died because of nuclear war and disease, and an authoritarian government uses technology and terror to control its population. Living underground in this society is a band of brave women who resist, led by Lin, a fearless woman with uncompromising integrity. The main character is called Sabine; I named her years before Sabeen's death when I started to write the book in 2012. After Sabeen's assassination, the book carried the weight of my mourning, my need to survive the pain and trauma of losing her, my hope that through writing this novel, I could achieve a kind of redemption for not being as brave as her. I dedicated the book *to her*. It didn't need to be said who *she* was. She lived on every page of the novel. I carry Sabeen in my head and my heart all the time now and, when I face a moment of doubt, I refer to her almost as a mantra, a silent prayer: *what would Sabeen do?* In death, as in life, she provides the courage for us to continue.

The Politics of Writing Popular Fiction: challenging the African literary tradition[1]

Mukoma Wa Ngugi

I

IN 1962 A GROUP of young African writers gathered at Makerere University for a conference titled 'African Writers of English Expression'. This group included Chinua Achebe, Wole Soyinka, Grace Ogot, Rebecca Njau, Lewis Nkosi, Dennis Brutus and my father Ngugi Wa Thiong'o. In short, the writers convened at Makerere would go on to define African literature as we know it today. While they discussed and disagreed on a number of issues, including whether African literature should be in English or in African languages, who could be defined as an African writer, or what could be called an African novel, the one thing they agreed on was that literature should be in the service of decolonisation.

In just a few years most of them would be detained or forced into political exile. In fact, they were so fiercely political that their publisher, Heinemann Educational Publishers through the African Writers Series, which gave us titles like *Things Fall Apart* (1958) and *The River Between* (1965), had a section titled 'Authors in Prison' in their monthly newsletter. Closer to home, my father would in 1977 be detained by the Jomo Kenyatta government for his anti-neocolonial Kenya/Africa political writing. In a lot of ways, the more the African governments jailed and tortured the writers, or killed them as in the case of Ken Saro-Wiwa, the more it showed just how powerful their pens were.

What emerged aesthetically from the Makerere Conference was a consensus that African literature had to be in English, the novel realist and most definitely political. To be sure the consensus was contested—for example on the language question—but those contesting were lone voices. I therefore see myself writing both within and outside of that literary tradition. Within, because I have grown up reading and admiring the literature produced by the Makerere generation and because I too believe that the act of writing is a political act; outside, because I also write detective fiction in addition to poetry and 'literary' fiction. It is my literary tradition. This is because I fell into detective fiction by accident.

Much like a found poem, *Nairobi Heat* (2011) is a found novel—at least the bare bones of the story that my imagination in turn fleshed out. While doing my PhD at the University of Wisconsin at Madison, I lived very close to the football stadium where tailgating started as early as 8.00am. I was not surprised when on getting home after a late night elsewhere (there is a reason UW-Madison tops party school lists) I found a white female student dressed in a cheerleader outfit passed out by the door to my second-floor apartment. I did not know her so I called 911, explained the situation, and shortly afterwards an ambulance accompanied by an African American policeman arrived. She was barely conscious, and as the policeman tried to get her details through her getting sick, it suddenly hit me. Here I was, an African student with an African American policeman, and a barely conscious white woman. In the novel, Ishmael Fofona is an African American working to solve the murder of a white woman in racially polarised Madison, Wisconsin. His suspect is a Rwandan who became a hero during the 1994 genocide by saving thousands of lives. He lived in Nairobi before coming to UW to teach courses on human rights. Of course, much like a poet is predisposed to a see a stop sign as a metaphor of one thing or another where for other drivers it's utilitarian, I was predisposed to finding *Nairobi Heat* in what would otherwise have been an anecdote to narrate at parties. For one, as a scholar and reader, I have found the divide between the literary and the popular to be a false opposition. African writers and literary critics, it seems to me, inherited from the British literary tradition the English language and aesthetic standards through colonial education. But the reality for my generation, which grew up at the height of the neocolonial dictatorships with all their serious punishable ridiculousness (for example, it was illegal to dream and talk about the president's death and you needed a permit to gather more than five people), was that we read the literary alongside the popular—James Hadley Chase, Frederick Forsyth and Robert Ludlum. But we also devoured popular fiction by African writers like David Maillu, Meja Mwangi, Mwangi Ruheni and John Kariamiti.

While their writing is diverse—for example, Kariamiti's *My Life in Crime* (1984) is a semi-autobiographical account of his days as a bank robber, while Maillu specialised in borderline pornography—their books also contained social commentary: joblessness, alcoholism, hopelessness, patriarchy, history of the Mau Mau, and so on. They were entertaining to read but, considering the Kenya of the 1980s, where the literary writers like my father, Ngugi Wa Thiong'o, were in exile or in detention, it was the popular writers who kept us reading and thinking about neocolonial Kenya.

For Kenyan writers of my generation, it is impossible to think of an African literary tradition that does not include the popular fiction writers. And it's why the canonical African literary criticism feels false and pretentious—we want literary criticism that will follow us into the gutter where, alongside William Shakespeare, Mikhail Lermontov, Bhabani Bhattacharya, Achebe and Ngugi, we read the Maillus and Ruhenis.

I was also influenced by Walter Mosley's Easy Rawlins mystery series, especially the novel and movie *Devil in a Blue Dress* (1990). I cannot think of his antihero, Mouse, without smiling. I might as well have been describing him when O, my antihero in *Nairobi Heat*, tells Ishmael: 'we are bad people too... The only difference is that we fight on the side of the good.'[2] In addition to telling an entertaining story, Mosley is able to organically bring out issues of race and class within the entertaining form of the detective novel. Through reading him I realised that setting and plot have everything to do with it if you want the issues to emerge organically.

When Ishmael makes his way to Nairobi, as an African American he has to confront issues of his own identity. I also introduce issues of gender and violence through Muddy, the femme fatale who survived the genocide and joined the Rwandan Patriotic Front. She tries to escape her violent past through the spoken word, but she is also addicted to violence. And the Nairobi urban setting means that issues of class are organically intrinsic to the form.

I was born in Evanston, Illinois, but spent the first nineteen years of my life in Kenya before coming back to the United States for my bachelor's degree. At the time I was writing *Nairobi Heat* I had been in the United States for over half my life and the questions around the tensions between being African American and African had been growing. I was therefore intellectually and imaginatively already predisposed to recognise that the meeting in that puke-stained stairway fumigated with alcohol breath could lead to a story. After the policeman, young woman and paramedics had left, I called a fellow writer friend of mine and told him I had found a story to enter into a competition. When I started writing the story it turned into the novel *Nairobi Heat*, which I dedicated to David Maillu and Meja Mwangi. Because of growing up in Kenya and later living in the United States, I have always been interested in the relationship between Africans and African Americans that is at times one of solidarity and at other times one of tension. Therefore, while the novel went on to reach readers outside my intended global black audience, I cannot say I was writing for everybody. Crime and detective fiction, perhaps more than any other genre, will reach beyond the writer's intended audience—the form, even when used differently, is universally recognisable, with its bad and good guys, femme fatales, violence, and so on. *Nairobi Heat* and the sequel, *Black Star Nairobi* (2013), have been popular with readers who do not necessary read African literary fiction. In Germany, where both novels have been translated into German, the novel has done well with aficionados of crime fiction as opposed to African literature. For these readers, detective fiction might very well work like a gateway drug and start them on other African works of literature.

II

The larger problem for writers like myself working inside and outside the canon is that the African literary tradition as currently constituted rests on a false foundation. But it is not just the cutting away of, say, early Arabic, Amharic, Kiswahili and South African literary roots. It is also a forcing of African literature into European aesthetic standards—a privileging of the African novel in English while banishing popular forms from the African literary tradition. African crime fiction, Hausa women's literature, science fiction, romance fiction—in other words, the reading that makes our daily bread—are left outside the literary canon. And the point, as I said earlier, is that we should not read African popular fiction as a separate category but rather as an integral part of African literature, within an African literary tradition. Then it becomes possible to ask the question: what is African detective fiction doing that is different from the realist novel?

In a 2008 symposium, 'Beyond Murder by Magic', held by the Jahnheinz Jahn Foundation at the Johannes Gutenberg University, one of the questions discussed was 'What makes African crime fiction "African"?' While seeking to avoid falling into the pitfalls of the Makerere discussions around what is African literature, the participants instead worked with the question of 'the interface of African literature and crime fiction'. What they found was that what they have in common 'is their emphasis on the "double" function of literature. Many African authors have a strong sense of responsibility towards society, which, independent of the genre they choose to write in, is reflected in their creative writing. Likewise, crime fiction exerts such a pull on contemporary African writers'.[3] But can't that be said of all writers and all literature? Or, if not of all writers, all literature to the extent that the imagination, even in science fiction or magical realism, ultimately draws many of its stories from society? The question, rather, ought perhaps to be: in what ways does popular African crime fiction differ from the well-known African realist novel, say *Things Fall Apart*, in terms of politics and aesthetics?

If we look at the treatment of the politics of violence primarily in crime fiction and realist fiction, the differences in themes and aesthetics emerge primarily around agency, social change and translatability into political action. For the revolutionary psychiatrist Frantz Fanon, violent resistance to colonial rule was an integral expression of the colonised's agency. He argued that 'decolonisation is always a violent phenomenon' and that '[a]t the level of individuals, violence is a cleansing force. It frees the native from his inferiority complex and from his despair and inaction; it makes him fearless and restores his self-respect'.[4] In the realist African novel, violence is treated within a larger social and political context. In Ngugi Wa Thiong'o's *A Grain of Wheat* (1967) and *Matigari* (1987) the violent resistance to colonialism and a neocolonial dictatorship is political. Or in Achebe's *Things Fall Apart* the violence, no matter how futile and individualised, is within a colonial context. In this sense violence is institutionalised and follows the Manichean colonial world of coloniser and colonised. In *Things Fall Apart*, Okonkwo's individual acts of violence may be said to offer a critique of individual violence, but it is also very clear that this is happening within a growing, encroaching and violent colonialism.

In contrast to *Things Fall Apart*, where the violence speaks to and transforms the whole society, the violence in detective fiction affects individuals with no revolutionary consequences. Kwei Quartey's *Wife of the Gods* (2010) features a marijuana-smoking police inspector by the name of Darko Dawson. Darko is investigating the murder of Gladys Mensah, a medical student, who is helping in the educational campaign against HIV/AIDS. He is also investigating a second case—the disappearance of his mother. *Wife of the Gods* covers the same thematic terrain as African realist novels. His suspect is Fafali Acheampong, a priest in the village of Bedome who practises the Trokosi system—this is where families give up young girls and women to the priest to atone for their sins. On the face of it, *Wife of the Gods* covers similar ground to that of the Makerere generation: there are questions of gender and violence teased out through the Trokosi system, African versus Western culture, the divide of city and country, police violence, corruption and poverty. But the novel is not a meditation on the larger issues; instead, they become the backdrop that makes the plot possible. In *Things Fall Apart*, individual acts of violence transform the whole society. In *Wife of the Gods*, individual actions transform individual lives.

The two murders and suicide happen to individuals, and in the end the cultural, economic and political systems remain—that is, the oppressive structures remain intact. The society has not been transformed for better or worse, but individuals have. In *Nairobi Heat*, while I work with the Rwandan genocide, racial violence in the United States, and historical and criminal violence in Kenya, the trauma is individual. This, I believe, is something demanded by the form itself—it is individuals working within the limitations of their societies. Even in times of great upheaval, the detectives and criminals are working within society, working within the rules even as they break them. In other words, a detective novel cannot show revolutionary violence as an act that transforms society for the better. If, for Fanon, violence expresses the newly found agency of the colonised, violence in crime fiction is a symptom of a sick society and a necessary but evil tool for the detective. Is this a limitation? I do not think so—it just means that the detective and literary African novels do different work. And crime fiction, I think, is so organic to the societies that produce it that it imaginatively links the reader, the novel and the society. In a sense, crime fiction is more of and about the place than the realist novel.

In *Wife of the Gods*, Efia, one of Acheampong's five wives who has had to endure beatings and rape, eventually cuts her husband's penis off—recalling the revenge of Firdaus in Nawal El Saadawi's *Woman at Point Zero* (1975). In this novel, Firdaus, an oppressed woman who seeks agency through high-class prostitution, kills her pimp in an act of vengeance and is sentenced to death. But the novel is also an indictment of patriarchy fuelled by neocolonial economic marginalisation. There is a larger indictment of society and repressive politics. We get to see the intersection of women's oppression via gender, decolonisation, psychology of resistance and religious oppression. In Tayeb Salih's *Season of Migration to the North* (1966), Mustafa engineers the self-destruction and suicide of white women to avenge colonialism. Mustafa's actions are understood within the alienation that came with colonialism. Here, all three novels are clearly indicting women's oppression but do it differently. In Salih and Saadawi, the violence of revenge is stylised. In Quartey's *Wife of the Gods* an individual woman finally finds agency and cuts off the instrument of her oppression, but the whole society, while indicted, is not threatened. But is that not the way it is in real life? In a strange way detective fiction is more realist than the realist novel. The last section of Frantz Fanon's *The Wretched of the Earth* (1967) details clinical cases—giving examples of the psychological toll that violence and torture take on the tortured and the torturer. One French police torturer traumatised by the violence he inflicts on the Algerian nationalists comes to Fanon for treatment—not so that he can stop but so that he can carry on his work. Fanon narrates that the police officer 'could not see his way to stopping torturing people (that made nonsense to him, for in that case he would have to resign) he asked me without beating about the bush to help him to go on torturing Algerian patriots without any prickings of conscience, without any behaviour problems and with complete equanimity'.[5] This is precisely the kind of character one meets in crime novels, an animation of the kinds of societies that produce the torturer and those who resist repression. The crime novel, I think, represents society in shorthand; the realist African novel is society in longhand. They speak to each other—after all, the characters, like the authors, would have all read *Things Fall Apart* as a set book, and probably David Maillu's thin *My Dear Bottle* (1978) as an insert, hidden away from parents and teachers between the covers of the more literary novels.

III

There is one thing that worries me, though, and that is the portrayal of African cities in detective fiction as violent, misogynistic, hard-drinking marijuana hubs. The US cover design of *Nairobi Heat* has Africa shaped like a gun against a green background. It is a very arresting, innovative cover, yet it is one that presents Africa as a violent place. The cover of the German translation is literal—it shows a black man keeping warm by a charcoal burner. The US version of my earlier novel *Black Star Nairobi* shows Kenyatta International Conference Centre with a time bomb on top whereas the German version shows a black man screaming with fists raised and, in the background, black coffins burning. And my response has been—why are we obsessed with how the West sees us? Why are we still judging African literature by how it's received by Western readers? What interests me most as a writer is contradiction. That is, portraying Nairobi as a city of contradictions—where a wall separates rich estates from slums, wealth at the expense of the poor, where the poor kill each other to vote for the richest families, or fight each other for land when the ruling family owns half a million acres.

And at the same time the violence is real. I set *Black Star Nairobi* during the 2007–08 post-electoral violence in Kenya and the 2008 US elections. The photo that is the cover of the German edition was actually taken during a pro-democracy demonstration.

In the end, it is not a question of whether the literary or the popular is better, and therefore deserving of more attention. The task for writers from Africa and their readers, it seems to me, is to normalise the African literary tradition without regard to high or low forms of literature. The crime novel, working from a genre with its own demands, and written by writers who are dedicated to the form, is part of the African literary tradition. And as long as people are fired by reading and talking about these works, we have a duty to study and teach them alongside the other literatures, teasing out their radical politics.

The more borderless we allow African literature to be in

terms of its literary history, languages and genres, the richer the African literary tradition. The literature exists; it just needs critical attention. In the end, though, what lies at the heart of it all is the kind of African literature and tradition we want. And the reason is very simple—it is already borderless. The work of Chimamanda Ngozi Adichie flows directly from that earlier Makerere consensus in that her novels are political and realist. She sets *Americanah* (2013) in the US, Nigeria and Britain and, like most of her other work, it is fiercely political and feminist. NoViolet Bulawayo's *We Need New Names* (2013) is a searing critique of globalisation and is set in Zimbabwe and the US. And then you have books like Nnedi Okarafor's *Who Fears Death* (2010), an African science-fiction novel that is radically political and feminist as well as works by diaspora writers like Yaa Gyasi's *Homegoing* (2016), an intergenerational epic on Africans and African Americans. Where the African novels from the Makerere generation were concerned with decolonisation, contemporary writers contend with the politics of sexuality, globalisation and global blackness to name a few.

Frantz Fanon in *The Wretched of the Earth* concludes by pleading with Africans to not follow Europe through imitation into the abyss of constant wars, conquest and dehumanisation, into the betrayal of humanism. He wrote: 'If we want to turn Africa into a new Europe, and America into a new Europe, then let us leave the destiny of our countries to Europeans. They will know how to do it better than the most gifted among us. But if we want humanity to advance a step farther, if we want to bring it up to a different level than that which Europe has shown it, then we must invent and we must make discoveries.' [6]

We have had and still have the same choice. Why not

follow Fanon's plea and let the form and content of African literatures be many things? Why not listen to Achebe when, in the essay 'Thoughts on the African Novel', he writes, 'What I am saying really boils down to a simple plea for the African novel. *Don't fence me in*.'[7] Writers and the literature they produce is of use, whether in an aesthetic or political sense, when society gives them the freedom to roam free.

When Bodies Speak:
the politics of rewriting Draupadi

Githa Hariharan

A WOMAN CLOTHED. Then stripped, so she is just a woman's body; bare skin on which battles are fought for power in all its guises, from honour to state security. What happens when this woman's body speaks? What is its language? And can such a language live apart from the vocabulary of politics?

Here stands a beautiful, dark-skinned woman, the princess Draupadi. 'I've so much,' she says, 'so much more than other women. I have five husbands, the eldest the prince of justice. But I stand in full public view, like a widow with no one. And look, a man tugs at my sari; other men leer.' In the *Mahabharata*, a story of epic proportions, Draupadi, born of fire and earth, is quick to curse. She nurses her desire for revenge. She is earthy, very different from her pious counterpart, Sita, also born of earth and the heroine of the epic *Ramayana*.

As with all matters in India, we begin with an old story that leaks into our times through parallels and metaphors.

These form a part of that contested territory, *culture*, through the ideals they raise on pedestals and the interpretations they inspire from multiple voices. Inevitably, in a culture that is a composite of cultures, they give rise to challenges through counternarratives.

In the *Mahabharata*, Draupadi has five husbands; they take turns with her a year at a time. Each has one of the qualities that make for a perfect husband. One is handsome; another is a scholar. The third is a skilled warrior; the fourth has the strength of ten bears. And the eldest among them has a fine sense of justice because he knows the rules and how to uphold them. This worthy has just gambled away all their money. Left with nothing, he gambles himself and his brothers into slavery; then he stakes and loses their shared wife, Draupadi.

Draupadi is dragged by her hair to the royal court. She is no meek victim. 'What kind of man,' she asks, 'stakes his wife in a game?' She also tries a legalistic defence. If her husband was a slave, no longer master of himself, could he stake his wife? Her cleverness only makes her unpopular with the audience, including her erring husband, who stares glumly at the ground. Her words fall on deaf ears. Only her body remains.

The man who has tugged at her sari begins to unwrap it. Draupadi is unravelling. She prays to Krishna, the cowherd philosopher-god who has an impressive scorecard with women. A miracle happens. The gift Draupadi receives from a womanising god is, ironically, cloth that will keep her body covered. Her sari grows, every six yards a different colour. Draupadi's tormenter unwraps endless yards then swoons, exhausted. Draupadi's body remains covered, though she has provided humiliating titillation for the male audience.

She makes a couple of promises to herself and the court. She will wash her hair in the molester's blood; and till she does this, she will not tie her hair. She will leave her hair free like an angry river, like a devouring Kali. Then, despite her anger, she manages to get her husbands and their money back. Draupadi, a privileged woman, what we may consider part of the establishment today, is, nevertheless, a rebel—a woman who acts.

This old story still lives in many ways, in the community worship of Draupadi as a village goddess, and in plays, films, art, poetry, novels. The *Mahabharata* is a complex legacy for 'tellings' of every sort. These tellings and retellings are not always set in times of warfare when the woman's body is used to define, defend, lose, or win the battle. Draupadi's story also lives in times of peace; it is the ancestor of a range of contemporary narratives. These challenge sanctioned ideas about 'heritage' or 'Indian Culture' by placing a woman's naked body centre-stage—an Everywoman's body, a favoured site for power struggles.

Perhaps the finest example of Draupadi's body as a victim resisting victimhood is a story by the great Bengali writer and activist Mahasweta Devi. 'Draupadi' appeared in 1978, soon after Indira Gandhi's infamous State of Emergency was lifted.[1] Why is this story so important in the larger narrative of cultural politics? Mahasweta's Draupadi is real, not a princess but a 'tribal'—an *Adivasi*. She does not have five husbands who define her purpose in life. She has one, a comrade in the fight for the rights of indigenous tribes. Possibly this Draupadi cannot even say her Sanskritised name; but it makes sense for a guerrilla Draupadi to be vernacularised to Dopdi. Her husband, like so many Adivasis, is killed in an 'operation' by the special security forces in charge of 'encountering leftist extremists'. So prolific is this state-sanctioned killing that the noun 'encounter' becomes the verb 'counter,' then Indianised to *Kounter*.

This is 1971. In an 'operation against militant tribals', three villages are cordoned off because a landlord has been murdered, and tribals have occupied upper-caste wells during a drought. In the wry tone she uses throughout the story, Mahasweta writes, emphasising the words imported from English into Bengali: 'In the forest *belt* of Jharkhani, the *Operation* continues—will continue. It is a carbuncle on the government's backside… Catch Dopdi Mejhen. She will lead us to the others.'

Draupadi moves carefully in the forest, cold rice knotted into a cloth that hangs at her waist. Her head itches; she longs to rub her scalp with kerosene and kill the lice, but she is afraid the smell of kerosene will give her away. Despite her precaution, she is 'apprehended' and taken to the police camp. Before he goes to dinner, the encounter specialist in charge, Senanayak, tells his subordinates: 'Make her. *Do the needful…*'

It is night. Her arms and legs are tied. She is raped by more people than she can remember. Over her still body, 'Active *pistons* of flesh rise and fall, rise and fall… Her breasts are bitten raw, the nipples torn.' In the morning, the big boss, Senanayak, orders that she be brought to him. But there is a problem. Draupadi refuses to wash herself or wear her clothes. Senanayak sees Draupadi 'naked, walking towards him in the bright sunlight with her head high. The nervous guards trail behind.'

'Draupadi stands before him, naked. Thighs and pubic hair matted with dry blood. Two breasts, two wounds.' Draupadi's black body goes closer to him, her lips bleeding as she laughs. She wipes the blood on her palm and asks Senanayak in a terrifying voice: 'You can strip me, but how can you clothe me again? Are you a man?'

She spits a bloody gob on Senanayak's immaculate white shirt and demands: 'Come on, *kounter* me—come on, *kounter* me?' She pushes him with her two mangled breasts. For the first time in his illustrious career, Senanayak is afraid of 'an unarmed *target*, terribly afraid.'

What happens when a woman's naked body speaks? Draupadi does not suddenly turn into a leader. But she becomes a source of power insofar as she turns her wounded body into a weapon. In that brief lightning flash, her ravaged woman's body, the 'unarmed target', terrorises her plunderers. It threatens Senanayak's manhood, the source of his power.

When a woman's naked body speaks, its language can turn the victimised body into a speaking, fighting one. Her body is no longer only for the powerful male to inscribe upon; her body turns her into an inscriber. Surely we have heard this language before, in homes or on the streets? It should be familiar, but something, its challenge to acceptable language, perhaps, makes it bold, even shocking.

Draupadi's story travelled from Bengal in the East to Manipur in the Northeast. The Northeast, like Kashmir, has long suffered the brutalities unleashed by a combination of 'security forces'. Their misuse of power, whether by 'encountering' people, 'preventive detention', or the rape of women, is exacerbated by laws that provide the armed forces with immunity. For instance, the much-hated Armed Forces Special Powers Act, popularly referred to as AFSPA, gives the armed forces special powers in what are categorised as 'disturbed areas'. From the 1950s onward, the Northeastern states have reeled under these special powers manifested in some form or another. As in Kashmir, the security forces have ensured that state security, or the war against insurgency or terror, always, and anywhere, means brutalising civilian lives. It means people living with permanent collateral damage, or dying from it. And, as always, a good number of these people are women; women with bodies that can be assaulted, tortured, raped or killed.

Draupadi's story found its way to the theatre director Heisnam Kanhailal in Imphal, Manipur. Kanhailal, known for his politically potent theatrical productions, had already worked with a constituency important for both culture and resistance in Manipur: the Nupi Keithel or the women's market in Imphal, the capital of Manipur. Kanhailal was also the force behind the Kalakshetra Manipur, a group aspiring to a sharper cultural creativity that would combine the power of austerity, silence and the body. 'What we need is the creation of a new body culture,' Kanhailal once said. He showed what he meant with his production of the Draupadi story. In the last scene, Kanhailal's actress-wife Sabitri, playing Draupadi, discarded her clothes one by one. Her protest against her rapists must have meant something powerfully real to the audience in Manipur, given that they knew what the AFSPA-supported army personnel were capable of doing, and what they actually did.[2]

The play was staged in the year 2000, twice in Imphal, and many times in the rest of India. It stunned audiences everywhere. Was it possible for theatre to take such a bold political stand? In Manipur, the play spoke to some; it enraged others and was nearly banned. After two performances, wrote Kanhailal, the theatre group decided not to perform the play in Imphal rather than give in to demands to drop the nude scene.

And four years later the play was called prophetic; Kanhailal was hailed as a seer by local newspapers. In 2004 real life brought together a tale from a literary epic, short fiction and theatrical defiance. Draupadi's story came full circle with ordinary women living their anger on the streets, their only armour their own bodies. Twelve middle-aged women stripped naked in broad daylight to protest against the brutality of the Assam Rifles army contingent.

This is how fiction met real life. First Draupadi's story morphed into another woman's story. On 10 July 2004, a 34-year-old woman called Thangjam Manorama was identified by the Assam Rifles as Corporal Manorama Devi, alias Henthoi, a militant who was an expert in 'IEDs or improvised explosive devices'. In the 'night operation' that followed, the Assam Rifles personnel barged into her house, gagged her, and dragged her out of the house to the courtyard. Her mother and brothers were beaten up and told to stay in the house. But they could see Manorama through the windows; she was slapped, pulled by the hair, and thrown to the ground. Manorama struggled. A man (not in uniform) inserted a knife under her phanek, a sarong-like skirt. Her phanek was pulled down from her waist to her knees; her long blouse was pulled up, unbuttoned. At the same time, she was questioned about arms – whether she knew where they were stored. They took her away around 3.30am, telling the family she was being taken into custody. She was still alive. Two hours later, her bullet-ridden body was found four kilometres from the house. There were scratch marks and semen on her body; there was a deep gash on her left thigh. There were bullet wounds on her genitals, as many as sixteen. People were traumatised; there was great pain among the public; there were tears. Then followed the public protests, marches and demands for the repeal of AFSPA.[3]

The rage simmered. It had to boil over. On 15 July 2004 a few women reached the office of the Nupi Samaj as early as 7am. They removed their underclothes and dressed again in their phaneks and white blouses. They took a banner and made their way to Kangla Fort where the Assam Rifles were stationed. Other women met them at the Western Gate of Kangla. By 10am there was an air of waiting—and of suspicion among the officers on duty. Why were so many women at the gate? What were they going to do next? Suddenly, without warning, twelve of the gathered women took off their clothes. Their hair was untied—a traditional sign of mourning. They held up a banner that said, 'Indian Army: Rape Us'. And they called out, at first hesitant, then stronger, so that the air rang with defiant women's voices: 'Rape us, kill us! Rape us, kill us! Indian Army, rape us, kill us!' One woman shouted: 'We are all Manorama's mothers. Come, rape us, you bastards!'

Hair untied like the *Mahabharata*'s Draupadi, naked like Mahasweta's and Kanhailal's Dopdi, shouting out a challenge with body and speech, from epic to story to theatre to real life on an Indian street in broad daylight: Draupadi had come full circle in the naked bodies of the *Imas*—the mothers of Manipur.

A continuing chain of stories, twists, and reimaginings—metaphorical and real-life Draupadis exist for the people, for the times, and for different instances of injustice. It would seem clear at this point that, like epics, stories, and the history of real events, the Draupadi legacy belongs to all. But the depiction of Draupadi triggers controversy in new ways. There is no end to the fight, it seems. The Draupadi story still has to resist those who distort her challenge and empty it of meaning.

In 2010 one of the most highly acclaimed Indian painters, MF Husain, was hounded into leaving India at the age of 94. He gave up his Indian citizenship and became a Qatari. As a Muslim, his paintings of Hindu deities and icons were attacked by the self-appointed custodians of Indian culture as 'insulting' women. These groups, as right-wing as they come, threatened the artist and filed legal cases against him. They vandalised galleries exhibiting his works. Perhaps the most controversial of Husain's paintings was his portrayal of 'Mother India' (Bharat Mata) as a woman being raped. Husain also got into trouble for two paintings of Draupadi. *Draupadi* (1971) is a large female nude, surrounded by miniature male figures, the men in her life controlling her. *Draupadi on Dice* (1971) has the heroine of the Mahabharata midfall, midscream, surrounded by dice.

Around the same time, the National Academy of Letters (Sahitya Akademi) announced an award to the Telugu writer Yarlagadda Lakshmi Prasad's novel *Draupadi*. A group of Hindu 'activists' claimed the novel made Draupadi 'indecent' and threw shoes at the author when he was onstage. Again, in 1984, the Oriya writer Pratibha Ray published a novel called *Yajnaseni*. The title ('born of the sacrificial fire') refers to one of several names for Draupadi. The award-winning novel imagines the *Mahabharata* story from Draupadi's point of view. It traces the life of a woman who grew up 'like a son', wrote poetry, and asked questions, only to be married to five husbands and make her life subservient to their duties and destinies—their *dharma*.

Decades later, in 2013, the right wing, slow readers all, objected to Ray's all-too-human Draupadi, a survivor who fights and rages. In March 2013, a local edition of the newspaper *The Pioneer* carried one example of these shrill reactions:

> *Yajnaseni* has dishonoured Draupadi... The modern feminist Draupadi...is aflame with anger and is upset beyond limit at the proposal of marrying all the brothers... Draupadi's character is an established one and hence a writer has no freedom to redesign it or play with the same... As an ideal Indian woman, she is committed to her husbands in her mind, body and speech. Draupadi is like a jewel that adorns the crown of Indian womanhood. In a faithful wife's heart, her husband occupies a place higher than that of God.[4]

Draupadi has now been turned into an untouchable idol by a different kind of police in India, the thought police. For these new cultural experts, cohorts of the right wing led by the Rashtriya Swayamsevak Sangh (RSS), who want a Hindu nation ('Hindu Rashtra'), the rebellious spirit of Draupadi must be crushed. Maybe they are afraid of what it is capable of inspiring. Certainly, they are allergic to multiple tellings of the same story, an inescapable cultural transaction in a diverse country like India. The right wing wants to tie a chastity belt on all the stories—in fiction or real life—that may question a woman's place in society, or challenge the woman's body as a site for the exertion of power. Most of all, they object to us making a story our own, mining it for meaning in our lives today. It's not surprising that the thought police would want literary chastity in a story in which a woman has to marry five husbands and is stripped in public. How do they censor the multiple readings of such a story? By making the woman a chaste goddess. Allowing her to be human, a real woman, even in a novel or a poem or a painting, may mean questioning the continued belief in the husband as the god of the ideal Hindu woman—whether in art or in real life.

The mocking of Draupadi—and her descendant Dopdi—continues. In September 2016, the current Indian government paid fulsome tributes to Mahasweta Devi on her death. Soon after, it was business as usual for the new guardians of culture. Students and teachers in the University of Haryana staged a play based on Mahasweta's story 'Draupadi'. But the right wing, from official to garden-variety thug, has made itself the arbiter of what is 'nationalistic' behaviour and what is 'anti-nationalist'. Eating beef is anti-national; expressing solidarity with those resisting the army atrocities in Kashmir or the Northeast is anti-national; not hating Pakistan is anti-national; women refusing to be subservient is, of course, anti-national.

In the case of the Haryana University adaptation of Mahasweta's story, the right-wing student group Akhil Bharatiya Vidyarthi Parishad (ABVP) attacked the play—and the students and teachers involved—claiming that the story dishonoured the army. It is doubtful that these protesters had even read the story, let alone read it for what it is. But they succeeded in changing the story so it was no longer about Draupadi or Dopdi. It was about the soldiers—'brave hearts', 'martyrs'—who must be valorised at all costs by 'nationalists'. Draupadi, women, the woman's body are merely unmentionable collateral damage.

The combination of attacks on free speech is a poisonous mixture of hate-mongering, distortions and idiocy. Recently, Facebook took down posts of the naked mothers of Manipur protesting against the Indian army. As in the case of the famous My Lai photograph from the Vietnam War, Facebook found the protesting Manipuri women obscene because of their 'nudity'. In an angry response, a college teacher posted: 'Powerful women in Manipur shamed the Indian armed forces through this protest and today, Indian "patriots" find the image offensive while being complicit with "their" boys. What does Facebook do? It sides with the patriots rather than realising this image is iconic.'

In Pratibha Ray's novel, Draupadi says: 'All the rituals and rules...built around the distinction between rich-poor, high-low, Brahmin-Chandal, male-female...the profound inequalities...based upon considerations of virtue and sin—against all these a lifelong war would have to be waged.' This means a lifelong war against intolerance of free speech, debate and imagination. It means cultivating a lifelong habit of asking questions. How do we let the myriad challenging narratives of an inclusive culture flourish? Draupadi lives in India today with her tongue almost tied. Can that clothe her naked body?

The Myth of Integration: continuing racisms and inequalities in the Global North

Hsiao-Hung Pai

THE POSITION OF A WRITER and journalist in the world today must be one of making a stand against inequality, against the borders created by the state and the market—and the borders of the mind. For us, it is a constant battle with the powers that impose these borders on us. When we write and report, we may contribute a little towards enabling others to open their eyes and know where they stand in front of injustices. In the 1920s, the Chinese writer Lu Xun said: 'It is high time that our writers take off their masks, look honestly, keenly and boldly at life, and write about real flesh and blood... It is high time that some brave fighters charge headlong into battle.'[1] His words remain prescient and speak to me almost a century later: to write today is to interpret and change the world.

In Europe right now, we are witnessing a resurgence of a politics of regression pushing societies back to battles that were fought decades before. We have far-right forces coming on to the central stage across European states, winning votes on pledges to restrict or end the movement of people from outside the fortress of Europe and making lives much harder for those already here.

My enquiry begins here—I've been on this journey for many years, witnessing and documenting the impact of such borders on people from the Global South. I chose to look at what has been going on in Italy in this piece as the country voted in a far-right government in March 2018. I've been living in the southern regions—Sicily, Calabria and Puglia—to look at how anti-migrant policies have impacted people's lives and how such internal borders continue to marginalise and segregate a large number of people from society.[2] There is a long story to be told and, in the end, it will not be pleasing to everyone. But a writer doesn't write to please.

Integration, integration, integration. In Britain, this word has always been part of the discourse that frames immigration and the presence of immigrants as the problem and their 'integration' into 'Britishness' and 'British values' as the solution. It is part of setting the imperial centre and the colonised in their place. Embedded in colonialism, 'integration' presumes your belonging and determines your right to citizenship on the basis of how much you 'fit in'. The word 'integration' asks those targeted to be invisible, according to Pierre Tevanian, the French essayist, and Saïd Bouamama, the Algerian sociologist, as inequality and domination always require the social invisibility of dominated groups. This 'invisibilisation' has been reproduced in the sphere of immigration where the immigrant is reduced to an indebted position (*position d'obligés*) vis-à-vis the host society.

'Integration' is also a word that I have heard repeatedly

since I lived in Italy in 2016 and continue to hear, particularly in liberal circles. It has been a dominant ideological component in the asylum reception system where tens of thousands of displaced people from Africa, Asia and the Middle East have found themselves when entering their first European country. 'Integration' has been part of the 'common-sense', fund-securing phraseology that has operated in the profit-making business of welcoming new arrivals for at least a decade. However, since the Far Right came into government in Italy in the summer of 2018, with Matteo Salvini as its figurehead, the rhetoric of 'integration' at times has acted as the rallying point for many in liberal circles who were opposing the government's anti-migrant policies.

Rather than offering any solution, the integration discourse is, in fact, part of the problem. In Italy, following the first stage of emergency reception when people are rescued at sea and arrive in ports, asylum seekers are often transferred to a secondary reception centre known as SPRAR (Protection System for Asylum Seekers and Refugees), the stated aim of which has been to help 'integrate' people by equipping them with language skills, and vocational training and guidance. It is a well-known fact that very few SPRARs have actually achieved their stated aims. Instead, the reality has been that there are few qualified teachers available and no proper curriculum for learning Italian. Language teaching is dealt with as a gap-filler, not aiming to equip people for life as equals in Italy, but to supply them with the basic conversational skills so that they can go out to do the menial jobs required of them. Many under-age asylum seekers who are experiencing such inferior education understand this. 'With their language teaching, I'm never going to become a minister in Italy!' one joked bitterly. These children's journeys to reach Europe have already delayed their starting point of education, and now their schooling, if any, places them permanently behind Italian citizens.

Also, in most SPRARs, there is little introduction to the job market and the outside world. At best, people are left to their own devices. In the worst-case scenarios, certain SPRARs have arranged for asylum seekers to get work and have taken a percentage of their wages. This is why the young people in SPRARs often feel they have no future in this country. Behind the disguise of 'integration', the reality for people trapped in reception shelters and camps has been that of exclusion, which reflects their marginalisation in Italian society.

In recent years, liberal advocates have often talked of migrants resettling in dying old villages in Italy and reviving them as models of 'integration'. This is celebrated as a positive example of migrant contribution and highlighted as a 'win-win situation' where Italy receives migrants and migrants 'pay back' the country's hospitality by repopulating Italian villages whose decline was the result of decades of lack of investment and youth emigration. 'Integration', in other words, refers to a process of assimilation: we receive you, you fit in, adopt our ways and values, and make the necessary economic contribution.

Let us turn the perspective around and not talk about asking new arrivals to prove themselves worthy of acceptance by contributing economically, and instead look at it from where they stand and ask this question: are 'integration' programmes and projects benefiting *both* local communities and migrants?

Riace and Camini are two Calabrian villages that followed the path of regenerating themselves with 'integration' projects. Two decades ago, Riace was threatened with depopulation. In the summer of 1998, a boat left Greece in poor weather and landed at Soverato, 40 kilometres north of Riace. On board were 218 people; these men, women and children were all Kurdish, most of them from northern Iraq. Domenico Lucano, locally known as 'Mimmo', who later became the mayor of Riace, proposed that the Kurdish people should stay in the village. He soon came up with the idea of rejuvenating Riace and housed the new arrivals in properties that had been left vacant by former villagers who had migrated to northern Italian cities, like Milan and Turin, or abroad. Lucano and his colleagues set up several projects, the most prominent known as Città Futura (City of the Future), with a stated focus on 'integration'. The funds that came with the projects started changing the face of the village. Jobs were created for villagers and there was turnover in the shops. Within two decades, Riace's population had grown from 900 to more than 2,300. The village's economy was, indeed, saved by the migrants' arrival.

Camini, a tiny village situated a couple of miles from Riace, followed in its footsteps. It had survived on agriculture based on small landholdings producing citrus fruit, oil and wines. As in Riace, the young people of the village had deserted Camini two decades ago, seeking employment in northern Italy or in Germany. The village's mayor today, Giuseppe Alfarano, was once part of that exodus. When he was eighteen, he went to study at the University of Florence. Wherever the young went, they would eventually settle there. Almost no one would return to Camini to live. As a result, the village suffered the fate of steady depopulation, with only 250 people remaining in the late 1990s. Alfarano recalled Camini as a 'dying place' before the SPRAR project came about. As young people moved away, there were few births: between 1998 and 2001, the total number of children in Camini was eight or nine. The school closed.

Giuseppe Alfarano had returned to Camini to live. He and Rosario Zurzolo of the social co-operative Eurocoop believed that the way to bring life back into the village's economy would be to loyally follow the Riace model. They consulted Lucano regularly. They sought state funding in 2010 and a SPRAR project was initiated by Eurocoop Servizi, managed by Jungi Mundu (the World Together) Association. Initially, there were only thirteen refugees on the project. The number later increased to 30, and eventually to 113. With the funds that came with the placements, the project aimed to revive the village. Abandoned houses were refurbished, the school was reopened, and jobs were created for the villagers. The project manager's office on the second floor of the Jungi Mundu building was staffed by numerous people—all of them Italians—including administrators and a cultural mediator who showed guests around the various workshops where 'migrants are taught by locals to make wood and ceramic artworks and pottery'. Overall, around 30 Italians are employed on the SPRAR project. Local residents have also been employed in construction and other work created since the project started.

The project has also brought in a lot of interest from the outside world, in the shape of the media, researchers and volunteers, which boosted consumption in the village. Looked at more cynically, with the model of 'integration' widely advertised, refugees found themselves becoming a tourist attraction. 'Refugee tourism' flourished. Italian tourists would travel to Camini to 'take a look at the brown and black people' while relaxing in these mountains.

Under the SPRAR project, more people from Syria, Eritrea, Nigeria, Gambia, Pakistan and other countries, have been transferred to Camini since 2016. Between 2017 and 2018, twenty children were born in Camini, to both local and refugee families, compared with just one child a year before the project. As the number of children grew, the school was re-evaluated and relocated to a newly refurbished building. Clearly, the SPRAR project had positively impacted the local economy and revived the village. It brought the population to an estimated 820 people. When Alfarano ran as a mayoral candidate in 2016 (for a five-year term), he included the SPRAR project as part of his manifesto. He did not need to convince the villagers. He won the election. 'People in the village could see the benefit of the project,' Alfarano said. 'It is transforming Camini into a place like Taormina.'

At the same time, how have the projects worked for the new arrivals in Camini and Riace? Did they see the villages as presenting them with any real future?

The reality is that the migrants who were sent to Riace and Camini were surprised by their isolated location and dismayed at their socio-economic prospects. It was not their choice to live in a remote rural area. If given the choice, they would have always wanted to live in a town or city, to have access to employment and to be near existing migrant communities (which are only in urban areas). But would the new arrivals be given the same welcome if they chose to go to an industrial city or town where the jobs are? Would they then be called 'foreigners coming here to take our jobs' instead of 'migrants rejuvenating our economy'?

Moussa, from West Africa—his real name and country of origin cannot be revealed for his own safety—was one of those transferred to Riace on a SPRAR project in 2016. He was a soldier who fled persecution and ended up in Libya. He never expected to come to Europe but the hell of Libya pushed him onto a boat. On arrival in Italy, he wanted to rebuild his life and support his family. He was shocked at being sent to the village and resented it very much. 'I didn't come here to retire,' he said. The SPRAR project in Riace was said to have created jobs for the new arrivals. However, what was actually created were artisan 'laboratories' (workshops) for woodwork, glassware, ceramics and embroidery—none of the skills were useful to migrants for future employment. Moussa, placed under the auspices of Project Welcome, one of Lucano's projects, is one of the many Africans who have never received employment advice, vocational training or work placements from the SPRAR project, let alone any paid work, in the three years they have been in Riace. 'There was no real work for migrants,' Moussa said. Media reports had portrayed migrant women working in traditional handicrafts shops in 'Global Village', an area in which stalls and shops were set up where they were taught to make things to sell. In reality, there was no daily wage for the migrants. The profits from the sales of products did not go to them either.

For those who managed to find some casual work in the village, non-payment was common. On the rare occasion when Moussa obtained work as a security guard for Lucano's brother, who was running a reception centre for minors, he did not get paid for five long months. The employer's justification for non-payment was always: 'We haven't received cash from the authorities.' Apparently the provincial authorities of Reggio Calabria, where Riace is located, had not been paying the funds due since June 2016. With payments falling behind, a huge debt of two million euros was accumulated. Wages were not paid and asylum seekers feared being made homeless. (Later, Lucano's brother tried to pay back the wages owed to Moussa by letting him stay in his friend's apartment, rent-free.)

So much for the SPRAR project's aim to help people become independent and integrate with society. Most migrants in Riace actually ended up impoverished and desperate. Although Moussa wanted to be independent, he could only live on the state allowance of 75 euros per month until his time on the project ended. Even after this, Moussa and others had to live by occasional farm work for a maximum pay of 30 euros a day. Mayor Lucano's arrest for fraud and 'aiding illegal immigration' in October 2018 under the directive of Salvini, who didn't want to see migrants 'living in the community', sealed the fate of the Riace projects. While Lucano was being investigated, there was barely any work for migrants in the winter and by the end of February 2019 most of Moussa's friends had left Riace. Only fifteen migrants remained.

Daraja, a Nigerian woman in her twenties, was one of them. She was transferred to Riace in 2016 and spent a long time searching for work in the village. She eventually found a job in a nursery doing cooking and childcare, but had not been paid a penny—and nor had her four colleagues at the nursery. Yet they were trapped in Riace because they were still waiting for their humanitarian protection documents. Under the Salvini decree that had come into effect in November 2018, it was looking increasingly unlikely that they would be granted these.

In Camini, while the village may have been a sanctuary for recovery for Syrian families, isolation was clearly not a long-term option. One of the 35 Syrian families on the project had been housed in a farmer's empty property on the edge of the village and had been living there for two years. The mother had been hospitalised after a breakdown. She had suffered tremendous emotional turmoil on the journey, knowing her disabled baby son's condition could have been worsened by the hardship before and during their escape. The family was barely coping with her absence. The father was looking after six children on his own, with help from a carer, who came in several days a week. For the time being, with all his childcare responsibilities, he could not consider looking for work. The exhaustion was written on his face.

His disabled son was three and, despite being paralysed from the waist down, he was an active child, enjoying talking with all the adults around him, in Italian. For a few days a week, a volunteer would come to their house and pick him up to go to 'baby parking' (a crèche), consisting of two well-maintained playrooms in a building renovated by the project in the village centre. It was a well-staffed place, open to villagers and migrants alike. Unable to move, the boy would sit on the mattress in the playroom, playing with the toys around him and interacting with other children. This was a much-needed facility that families like his could not do without.

If anyone asked this family about their home country, the father would play a video of bombing and destruction on the streets of Damascus. Right now, all they could do was try to recover, although it looked like they had a long way to go. They were trapped by illness, the child's disability and the hardship of trying to rebuild their lives in the middle of an isolated village. All that they could think of was the here and now. They had no means to think of the future.

Others felt trapped by the lack of opportunities. Charlotte's family was one of those attached to the project.

She had come from Nigeria with two girls and two boys, and they had been placed in a shelter in Milan when they arrived. She and her family had then been transferred hundreds of kilometres south, to Camini. She was shocked to find it a small village, and felt angry about the authorities' decision. 'Why were we sent to a place in the middle of nowhere?' she asked. Charlotte looked around and saw no business or trade in the village and many locals were unemployed or had moved away for work. From the start, she feared that she would not be able to find ways to support her children.

Having been given no possibility to move away, Charlotte tried to come to terms with the situation. She tried to get used to village life. She made friends. She tried to feel settled. Then, a while later, she was offered the rented space of a design workshop by the project for her to practise her handicraft and dress-making skills—she had studied fashion for two years in Nigeria—and to display her products for sale. Colourful women's dresses, handbags, purses and items of jewellery were all laid out and hung on walls inside her workshop. Over two years, Charlotte invested a lot of hope in the workshop and tried to reach out to villagers so as to earn a living from her products. Eventually, though, she saw that the workshop was more of a display window for visitors. She was not going to make a real living out of this—villagers could hardly afford these handicrafts.

She and her family were offered a basic apartment for which rent was paid by the project. The allowances she received were given in vouchers, which could be used in the only three shops in the village. The voucher system, as always, was stigmatising. It singled out the 'outsider' status of the migrants and limited their ability to purchase the things they needed. It certainly did not foster a sense of belonging. Apart from these day-to-day difficulties, Charlotte had not been able to earn enough to support her children. Then Charlotte met a Nigerian man in Camini and they decided to get married. Her wedding ceremony was a glamorous event in the village. To this date, she cherishes the professional photographs taken of her wedding that were compiled as part of 'Un Mondo Nuovo' (A New World), the photo album of the SPRAR project.

Meanwhile, Charlotte knew that the reality of employment and opportunities for migrants were less pleasing to the eye than the 'diversity' signposts and flagship workshops, which generated no income for them.

In 2017, Charlotte's time in the SPRAR project ended, thus ending the allowances and the accommodation. She was finding it harder and harder to cope. She tried to bring in an income by taking up hairdressing and braiding—but customers were limited to Africans. Her husband remained unemployed. Throughout 2017, many of the original arrivals were gradually moving away, one by one, because there was little prospect of employment. New transfers continued. By February 2019, the overall number of 118 people on the project had decreased to 89.

The lack of work continued through the winter for Charlotte. Having waited for her documents for a long time and not been granted them, Charlotte decided enough was enough and that she had to do something to support herself and her children. One early morning in late February, Charlotte and her family left Camini. They took a bus all the way to Naples, where they planned to stay for a while. In the longer term, Charlotte thought about going to Germany, to seek better opportunities there. Ironically, that was where many young villagers from Camini had gone two decades ago. If Charlotte did eventually go to Germany, she would need to apply for asylum from scratch and to relive the limbo of the past few years in Italy.

The one family man who had regular work in Camini while I was there was Jemal, from Eritrea. He had been given the job of running orchards at the bottom of the village. He was growing fennel and other vegetables and was in the process of building a greenhouse. His monthly earnings were around 900 euros, some of which had to go towards paying the rent as he was no longer on the project. He shared the income from the orchards 50-50 with Jungi Mundu.

By February 2019, only around ten people were in employment, mostly part-time or low-paid casual work, out of the entire migrant population in Camini. The lone adolescents and young adults who were transferred there fared the worst. There were three building sites in the village. The Gambian boys on the project who had been employed as labourers on these were being paid 2.50 euros per hour.

Nineteen-year-old Drissa, from Mali, was one of the two African youths who worked as casual street sweepers for the project and the local authority. He had been transferred to the village eleven months before. In December 2018, he started working as a street sweeper for only three hours a week. He worked for a month and did not receive a penny for it. Nor did his co-worker, another transferred teenager. When the job started, Drissa was told that he would only know how much he was to be paid when the month was up. Drissa did not feel in a position to talk about wages; he felt he was a visitor, a stranger, and somehow whatever was given to him was seen by society as some kind of a 'favour'. Besides, he was still waiting for his documents and had a stake in the project. Therefore he did not want to 'rock the boat'. Drissa was paid eventually, although delayed payments remained common.

The same approach to migrant labour has been behind dozens of volunteer projects in the name of 'integration' set up by municipalities in northern and central Italy since 2011. These projects openly organise asylum seekers to do unpaid work. With help from the media, it has been presented as a way to 'integrate' migrants into the local community and for them 'to give something back to Italy' for receiving them. The popular media are good at circulating these ideas, which are easy to sell, because much of the general public has already bought into the belief that asylum seekers are like 'parasites'. Getting them to do free work is seen as a good thing: street cleaning, gardening in public areas, or even harvesting fruit for church charities. Two years ago in Ciminna, a Sicilian town 40 minutes outside of Palermo, a priest, Sergio Mattaliano from the Catholic charity Caritas, started running a programme that aimed 'to offer agricultural job skills to migrants and refugees...providing a model for long-term integration'. African boys were required to harvest crops and produce olive oil, and tend to chickens, rabbits and sheep. In the name of integration, they were not paid a penny while their produce was actually for export.

These voluntary integration projects are growing in number from small towns to cities like Milan and Rome. While the local authorities have championed these 'free workfare' schemes under the banner of 'integration', the voices that have not often been heard are the ones that demand a wage. People, understandably, want to get paid. Several protests against these unpaid work initiatives have been organised by migrants.

However, state integration schemes were further developed under the previous Italian government when it announced its plan on immigration and asylum in September 2017. The plan specifically listed 'voluntary work for asylum seekers' as one of the top items, along with the speeding up of forced returns and extension of the detention system. The interior minister at the time, Marco Minniti, said that during the 'empty wait' (referring to the state of limbo endured by asylum seekers as they waited for decisions), they could carry out 'public utility works'.

The idea that Africans and other migrants can be put to work for free comes from the deep-seated racism that permeates Italian society. It is precisely because they are seen as inferior and less human than Europeans that they are categorised as 'deserving' and 'undeserving' migrants. The idea is that Africans and other migrants must contribute economically and sell their labour cheap—or work for free in these programmes—to become 'deserving'. This racism impacts deeply on every migrant's life here, in all kinds of aspects, from employment to housing, to everyday social interactions.

Currently, this racism is being amplified under the new far-right government as Matteo Salvini is working fast to put Africans out of sight by differentiating the 'deserving' from the 'undeserving'. On 6 March 2019, as ordered by the local mayor and directed by Rome, the *tendopoli* (shanty town) of San Ferdinando in Calabria was dismantled, with over 600 heavily armed police officers enforcing the eviction of more than 1,000 African migrant workers who had been living there as the result of the unwillingness of local authorities to provide adequate housing. Most of the migrant workers disappeared into other agricultural regions, while others were processed at an immigration checkpoint and were sent to a variety of centres far away from their work. Five of them were transferred to Camini, not knowing what awaited them or how long they would be placed there. This is not 'integration'; this is human beings being treated like cargo and dumped in remote areas.

In Italy, as in other European societies, rather than acting as an alternative to segregation and racism, 'integration' is used as an instrument for the legitimisation of racism. 'If racism is the denial of equality, then integration is the credo that evacuates the issue of egalitarianism,' said Pierre Tevanian and Saïd Bouamama.[3] As they suggest, the vocabulary of 'integration' was used in much the same way in the colonial period as it is in today's supposedly postcolonial era: it works as a way of pushing back against demands for equality.

Thus, in Camini, while there are migrants 'living in the community' (rather than in segregated settlements, as in many Italian towns), Muslim migrants can only practise their religion at home, and the request for the local authorities to provide a prayer room in a public space has not been accepted. Taking into account different religious practices is a basic necessity if people from a variety of backgrounds are to co-exist. How could people even begin to feel part of society when their religious practices must remain hidden?

If liberals are truly interested in enabling people to become part of society and fully immersed in the cultural and public life of a country, then they need to start thinking about racism, which is structural and institutional, and they must challenge it on every level. The existing ethnic-minority communities, as well as the new migrant-worker communities, are yet to see any real sign of inclusion, let alone genuine acceptance and solidarity from mainstream

Italian society. It is time to stop covering up the ugly truth of racism in so many present-day European nations with the figleaf of 'integration'.

Given ongoing inequalities and the racism of present-day realities in Italy and elsewhere, the words of Lu Xun, who prophetically encouraged us all to take up our pens and write to change the world, continue to reverberate.

Art and the Lower Orders

James Kelman

REGARDLESS OF CLASS, people are surrounded by injustice. Individuals deal with this in their own way but most learn to live with it. Nobody is exempt from the experience. Not even artists: here applied in its general sense to painters, writers, sculptors, actors, poets, dramatists, dancers and anyone else trying to exist through their own creative output. If directly assaulted, do we defend? If the injustice happens to someone else, do we lend support? What do we mean by support? Do we form a solidarity campaign? Or do we drop money into a cup? The establishment pushes the notion of 'the cup'. They call it 'charity', or 'benevolence', and it operates at the expense of solidarity.

In the act of bestowing charity we overcome those feelings associated with empathy. We suppress our emotional response and give support in a more meaningful manner. 'Meaningful' here refers to the 'economic reality'. There is no point crying over spilt milk, better refill the bottle. We learn not to stop 'doing good' but to do it practically, in regard to personal capacity. Don't waste time agonising or commiserating, it won't get the job done. The military learn this. So too the police. Cynicism is not only practical but 'cool'. Heroic cops and coroners proceed ironically, discussing lunch over a dismembered body. Human beings are 'popped', not killed in cold blood. Mass murderers are 'serial killers' engaged in a deadly game, instead of what they are: mass murderers.

The ruling elite and leisured classes learn not only to live with injustice but to value it as the cost of their own survival, which is contingent upon survival of the State. Injustice affects the lower orders in a different way. 'Lower orders' here refers to working-class people, immigrant groups and diverse minority communities (racial, ethnic, linguistic, religious); and to groups such as single parents, people with health issues, those with learning disabilities. The question of 'choice' remains but the context shifts. Injustice is no longer indirect, but thrust upon us. Allowances aren't made for 'artists'. An artist of the lower orders is a lower-order person. Each day is a minefield of exploitation and humiliation, not only for ourselves but for our families and friends.

When injustice assaults close friends and family members we are scarred, perhaps deeply. How can we stand by when our partners, children and grandparents are humiliated by State authorities? People are driven mad through outrage and despair and become capable of the most desperate actions. What do we do? Should we act or should we endure? We can offer solidarity but should we translate this into action?

A classical dilemma arises in regard to art and political engagement. Is it enough to create art or should I involve myself in something away from my own workspace, something 'political'? Surely art offers a challenge to conventional social value which is an act of political engagement? The outcome of artists doing their best is challenging work. Therefore it is enough to create art as best I can; this in itself is 'political'.

Any artwork is 'challenging' that focuses on an aspect of society deemed negative by the powers-that-be. This includes human beings suffering forms of torment through no fault of their own. Public attention is drawn to the plight of these people. This raises such questions as 'can something be done?' which is construed as a political act, not by the artist necessarily but by the State authorities.

Some artists don't intend challenging anybody at all, they just take photographs of somebody on the street, or make a song about an old guy lying in a gutter, a one-legged girl begging outside a fast-food doorway.

Raising such a matter publicly suggests something significant about these particular individuals. Otherwise why would the artist devote time to 'capturing' their existence? More often than not the significance lies in a particular attribute, e.g. stress, despair, rage, heroism, innocence, or even indifference to their own suffering.

If the artist argues that there is nothing unique about this particular character then this may be even more damaging in the eyes of authority. What do you mean?! Are you trying to suggest that this society is full of beggars?! How dare you! Ours is a better society than that! After all, we put the Great in Britain! Why don't you paint a picture of the Royal Opera House in London. The Lord Mayor could stand outside wearing his or her Golden Chains of Office.

Fictional accounts of historical subjects are most welcome, especially those dealing in the machinations of the upper echelons of society. If we must have the 'lower orders', restrain your sensibility, try an adaptation of a classical text. People find it less upsetting, less of an irritant. Consider composing a song about happy street urchins from long ago; cute little lasses and sturdy lads playing leapfrog in a bombed-out site. Nostalgia is acceptable. It assumes we have dealt with the 'get over it' question and can look back with a wry smile of amusement at how 'we were'.

An artist who persists in creating work whose subject-matter is that vast sections of the lower orders enduring hardship through no fault of their own will be viewed with suspicion by the authorities. Sooner or later the artist who persists with such subject-matter becomes 'perverse'. The cry goes up: Okay you've made your point! Other sections of society deserve attention! There is good as well as bad! Surely balance is important! Every outcome is the effect of free choice! The most crucial attribute of these suffering individuals is that they choose to suffer rather than not suffer! Why don't they help themselves?! If concerned people do want to help them along the way, why don't they contribute to an appropriate charity?!

This is the establishment's position. If there is any perversity here it is psychological. Out trot celebrity specialists, asking gravely: Why do people beg? Why do people choose not to eat?

The State finances populist documentaries based on such topics. Especially those that confirm this is indeed a psychological issue, found not only in the United Kingdom but throughout the world. And if we glance back through the annals of history, lo and behold, the celebrity specialists shall discover that ancient peoples also 'made bad choices' in regard to health and wellbeing. Some individuals will choose poverty, unemployment, homelessness, every time, ensuring that their children suffer the same. How things are is how things always have been. Isn't 'human nature' a wondrous matter in its diversity?! Always human, always natural.

This ends in banality: at heart humanity comprises people. This is reflected in an art which has at its very foundation the concerns of humanity in its absolute generality. It soon moves from there to an art devoid of any political context; an art concerned solely with the expression of what it is to be human. 'Pure art': stripped of everything to do with the world as it exists.

What do we have left? Flesh, bones, brains and blood; sets of organs, muscles and bodily systems. All these mixed together within their own specific relationships and systems produce an entity bound by a certain physical configuration, characterised by properties, qualities and attributes, some of which are mental. A further element may enter the human-complex. It may or may not exist. This element is immaterial but an entity in its own right, typically termed 'soul'. It is defined in an indefinite variety of interesting and exciting ways that touch upon essential philosophical and theological concepts.

The whole entity—a human being—will perceive, judge, create and cope in a manner that distinguishes the species from others. All such properties, qualities and attributes are characteristic. The majority of 'establishment art' begins and ends there. We may create an art freed from smelly old politics.

Such a concept is absurd but how deeply rooted it is within the mainstream, and how rarely challenged. The ideal form is an art beyond reality: 'uncontaminated' by the natural world.

It so happens that within such a 'natural world' some are more equal than others, and can cash in on that at any cost. But we humans are imperfect beings! We endure in a tough reality! This is our destiny. How marvellous it would be if things were different! But they aren't. This is how it is; how it has been: how it must be. It is always providential and has nothing to do with tyranny and authoritarianism. It is the way of things. We should accept reality. Wealth and privilege are a birthright. And always remember that responsibility accompanies privilege. There may well be another world where justice exists. (Check it out with your Elected Whitehall Representative.) One day humankind may discover such a place. Until then we survive, together in diversity, taking what we can, sharing what we can. It is the natural order. Away and buy yourself a cup.

A short step from here may be religion, i.e. a supra-natural order, a spiritual world, a world of forms; a universe of galaxies of worlds of pure form, a galaxy of universes of galaxies, a veritable world of veritable galaxies of...of... veritability! Phew.

Nevertheless, every point can be divided. How many infinities exist? Zeno, where are ye?!

Such far-out worldviews are encouraged by ruling authority. They need not be purely formal. Any old thing will work: as long as it remains 'far out', literally as well as metaphorically, and better off in the future, or leastways 'side by side' with reality. Things can go bump in the night. Ghostly spheres may be sensed all around us. Fortunately for the Upper Orders, none of it impinges on the real world. Landed wealth and privilege are indelible markers in any and all possible worlds where similar moral codes appear to obtain. Stealing is wrong. Envying our neighbour is wrong. Lustful thoughts. Killing people. Coveting their ox. Acts of impropriety. Being smug. Pride. Greed and gluttony. Stealing their dough. Laziness, selfishness. Challenging the basis of a fellow's property holding.

All layers of mainstream society, whether the education or legal systems, advise us that humanity shares experience at the most basic level. We smile at the antics of babies, appreciate the glory of flowers, the pathos of the elderly. We enjoy a song, a poem, a painting. It makes no difference who created the artwork: a monarch, a Tibetan shepherd or an Eskimo hunter. Cut us and we bleed, chop off our heads and we are headless. Even something as sophisticated as irony may be shared. We all experience the vagaries of personal relationships.

Such forms of 'inner sharing' are beloved by the establishment. Human experience is lifted aloft from everyday mundanity into something unstained and spiritual. Another core of populist documentary film-making is structured upon it. Let's put a white celebrity male from Essex into the Amazon jungle and see him bond with all these indigenous jungle-dwellers, sharing their wild life experience. How about a celebrity actor masquerading as a down-and-out in Kensington Park, or a sex worker in Soho. Anyone who founds a charity to support the victims of envious neighbours will expect support from every segment of UK society. Homeless beggars will empty their polystyrene cups to support the Princess Royal-sponsored Foundation for Hungry Horses. Such feelings, values and opinions are shared from top to bottom in society and are 'safe'. Art derived from here may attain the universal. Beyond mere reality, he said, holding onto his cravat while reaching for his 1922 Moat Chanders and a cracker topped with Bahookie caviar.

It is a matter of fact that many great artists cannot distinguish their own finer work from the lesser. The art may derive from inner states of being but so too does its contemplation. It might be said that the value of great Art lies not in its creation but its contemplation, and the acquisition of the creation allows this. One way or another, art at its most sublime is assumed to be the property of the Upper Orders. This is a hangover from ancient Greece. Only those with the leisure to pursue its contemplation are equipped to behold it in the first place.

What about art created by the Lower Orders?

What about it?

The difficulty with 'inner states of being' is the concept of 'universality'. How may we speak of 'inner states' in reference to the Lower Orders? If such a thing exists it is at a lower level of development such that, strictly speaking, it is not entirely relevant. Working-class people are certainly human. Or, to put it another way, and as a lecturer in English Literature once advised his students: 'We may stretch to conceive of the central character in the novel[1] hearing a Bach composition but making sense of the experience is another matter. Might it not represent something of a contradiction in terms of "working-classness". Surely, one must be attuned to a certain level of aesthetic sensibility in order to grasp the core of such an experience?'

Expressions of spirituality and such concepts as inner states of being are best left to those in a position to afford them. Art created by the Lower Orders is lower-order art. Where lesser forms are concerned, art is decoration in the first place. Traditionally many on the Left have colluded in the theft and allowed the nonsense to pass. Never mind those who struggle through the crap and take a battering in the process. Art is consigned to the world of the bourgeoisie and ruling elite. All art is decoration and all artists bourgeois bastards.

Who cares anyway?—it is an effete pursuit. The configuration of the stars, the size of a whale's belly, the texture of a fly's wings, the snore of a large male after a night on the booze. The real world is a place of materials and matter; living breathing humanity; reality, the world 'out there'.

Artists of the Lower Orders contend with the suffocating myth that the only valid art is an art that serves a purpose that furthers 'the cause'. Generally 'the cause' is the class struggle. But how is that defined? It may equate to the war against injustice. But maybe not. And who evaluates the art? Who adjudicates on validity? What credentials are required?

So many artists fight not only to survive as artists but to engage in art at all. They seek the freedom to create as best they can, at whatever level they choose, unrestrained by external authority whether right-wing, left-wing or from within their own communities.

The notion of representation is a massive constraint. Artists of the Lower Orders are obliged to create an art 'representative' of 'their' community. They are expected to champion the cause. If their subject-matter exhibits attributes regarded as negative, their work may be condemned. This is a crazy notion but unfortunately is taken seriously. No matter the communities an artist belongs to—race, creed, gender/sexuality, family background—their work should 'represent' the community interests.

Immediate problems arise for those who belong to several communities. My parents were mixed-race immigrants. I am a first-generation cross-gender vegan Gnostic. I refuse to wear man-made fibres, nor do I ride any mode of vehicular transport bar the tandem bicycle. Which community should I represent? Which characters must I write about?

Should artists be handed a set of guidelines on what constitutes 'furthering the cause'? They could then appeal to the guidelines and produce a work of art that conforms to them. That reminds me of certain university Creative Writing courses, and those sometimes advertised in *The Guardian* newspaper.

From authorities beyond their own communities the pressures on Lower Order artists are more severe. We are consigned to the ghetto. No matter the work we create, we are never other than community representatives. Our work is evaluated as a function of how closely it reflects 'the reality of our community'. And 'reality' is defined by external authority. As Lower Order literary artists, any characters we create should be bound by these limitations. They should exhibit no tell-tale signs of inner states of being. Existential crises are barred.

Forget all this about 'representation'. We cannot help but work from within our several communities. There is nothing we need do about this except get on with our work in as free and unfettered a fashion as possible. Perhaps the most powerful form of 'representing' my several communities is engaging in art as a free individual, and doing the best I can.

But which authority will advise a young artist on the success or failure of a finished artwork, be it a painting, a story, a play, or a musical composition?

My earliest stories provoked outrage from members of a writers' group I attended. A couple of years later a printer in York refused to print a story of mine and would not print the magazine unless the story was withdrawn. These and other negative reactions to my stories helped me become keenly aware of the political value of art, the hypocritical humbug that masquerades as 'art appreciation', and the 'place' of my culture within the British establishment.

From the 1970s through the 1980s I earned very little and most of the time was registered unemployed. Two individuals came to my support; one was a full-time employee at the Scottish Arts Council and the other a producer at BBC Radio.[2] In 1974 I was awarded an Arts Council bursary of £500 which allowed myself and partner to put down a deposit on a flat. Later I was given a commission by BBC Radio Scotland to write a play. I wrote one set in 1820, tracing the last days of two weavers executed by the British State for their part in the Scottish Insurrection. The play was broadcast on BBC Radio Scotland in 1978.[3] Following the broadcast I hoped other work in drama might be offered but nothing was.

In 1979 I managed to land a part-time job for one year as a writer-in-residence.[4] By the early 1980s I had published three small collections of short stories and one larger collection for which I received an advance on royalties of £200. This was the biggest sum I had ever earned apart from the radio play. My source of survival was my partner. We had two children. She worked full-time where possible. I was back on the unemployed register. Around 1983 the Scottish Arts Council awarded me a £2,000 bursary. This was a tremendous event for us.

I had been under the impression that Arts Council awards and bursaries were non-taxable sums to be treated as a kind of prize. Perhaps this would have applied had I been in a stronger economic position, and not in actual need.

But because we were in need, it did not apply. In those days I was registered unemployed. The British State endeavoured to force me off the unemployed register. Someone at the Department of Social Security heard about the bursary. They weren't interested in taxing the sum. They wanted to use the bursary as a means to withdraw my unemployment benefit. I was to make use of the £2,000 and draw from it on a weekly basis.

I fought against this. I argued that the bursary granted to artists was there to be used howsoever they wished. If not, then the only artists who were to gain by such bursaries were those who had no fundamental need of the money in the first place. 'Pin-money' for Higher Order artists.

I was not opposed to that, I was demanding the same right. I wanted to use the money in whichever way I thought best. If I wanted to buy a car, a boat, a greyhound, then fair enough. Or a new washing machine or a fridge, or a couple of carpets; some new clothes. It was up to myself and my wife how we spent the dough. But it was a difficult fight and took much time and energy. I tried to impress upon the Arts Council how crucial this fight was for artists. If the Department of Lower Order Control (Social Security) was allowed to set the precedent here then yet another obstacle was set firmly in place.

Most public bodies capitulate as a matter of course when confronted by the Department of Lower Order Control. The Arts Council was no different. Its officials were unable to offer support. The reality of Lower Order life in the United Kingdom was beyond their ken. In short, they were out of their depth.

From the earliest period I thought of myself as a writer but was early defined by mainstream critics and reviewers as a working-class writer. Presumably because the greater portion of both form and substance of my work resonated in Lower Order culture and the lives of working-class people. Form and content were not separate entities, but the result of the techniques I had developed over a period of years. That early critical response to my work tends to remain the case generally. It consolidated the potential of art as a political weapon. I didn't begin from that perspective.

My first published novel[5] appeared in 1984. I received an advance of £500. The novel was condemned by the chairperson of that year's Booker panel then attacked in the House of Commons by a Tory MP.[6] This notoriety did not 'further my career', as mainstream critics prefer to believe. The novel was withdrawn from bookshops in Edinburgh and elsewhere. The MP further condemned the Arts Council for providing financial assistance to my publishers (in those days a branch of Edinburgh University Students' Union). Following this, the Arts Council withdrew its publishers' support grant from my second novel. Nevertheless the Edinburgh students went ahead with publication and managed to find the sum of £500 as an advance for myself.

A few years on came my novel about a man who goes blind after receiving a battering from police officers. This too was narrated in the 'voice' of a working-class Glasgow man. I was used to hostile reactions to my work but ill-prepared for the level it reached when awarded the 1994 Booker Prize. Any pretence at literary evaluation was quickly discarded for an elitism so blatant it was racist. Sound is physical. Anyone who speaks in a certain voice is, *a priori*, less of a human being. In my own country—Scotland—the mainstream authorities were less elitist but also hostile. There was the sense that I had shamed us all. Characters such as this should be seen and not heard, preferably not seen either.

Further marginalisation of my work ensued. The managing director of Dillons, a major bookshop chain of the period, withdrew the novel from all its branches. Other bookshops followed suit. Many novels and story collections later, I find that in England nowadays my two Booker Prize-associated novels (1989 and 1994) are my only two left in print, apart from one small collection of my stories published recently by a small independent press.[7]

Over the years I have got myself involved in political stuff. Maybe this has to do with personality and personal experience. From the age of fifteen to thirty I worked at various jobs and became used to work-floor struggles. In 1973, the same year as my first collection of stories was published in the US, I was driving buses in Glasgow and involved centrally in an unofficial strike.

I managed to win my early 1980s campaign against the Department of Lower Order control. I advised the Arts Council that this was a useful precedent and my documentation was available for use by other artists who might find themselves in a similar plight. That is the last I heard. I don't know whether others have been attacked by the State Department of Lower Order Control in the same manner. The majority of artists find themselves in a similar economic position to working-class people. Those who do not come from such a background will find life very difficult indeed. The rest of us are used to it.

Without going further into the matter, it should be clear that any challenge to mainstream or conventional values is a political act or may be construed as such. This is basic. I find it very difficult dealing with people on the Left who either cannot grasp this, or who can but seek to deny it in spite of the evidence. No artist who concentrates exclusively on his or her own work will ever be criticised by me for any lack of engagement.

At the same time, campaigns are full of chores. Writers and other artists have useful skills and some of these can be employed practically. We can write letters, create posters, press releases, explanatory essays and articles and, crucially, record moments of struggle. Beyond that, who knows? I tend to trust the artist.

All the Feels: vulnerability as political vision

Olumide Popoola

Our feelings are our most genuine paths to knowledge.
— Audre Lorde[1]

I WANT TO PROPOSE a commitment to a different way of engaging with politics. At a time where so much of our culture is steeped in complaining and saying 'no' without offering alternatives, we need to perhaps think about the strength and fierceness of vulnerability.

What would it mean for political change if we exposed ourselves, if we outlined what we wanted and more importantly needed, if we showed our vision, instead of shouting 'not like that' *without* a follow-on? What do we desire, once all we are against is eradicated? What would a better state of things look like?

Our online culture can make me distraught. Not just because of the trolls, the anonymous commentators who bring vile messages they would not dare to voice to us in person. We—and people we side with politically and socially—can also be culpable of climbing on too high a pedestal, from which we quickly push away and put down those who we feel are behind on current debates. Often this involves a smug educating and silencing, rather than an engaging with. It is depreciating commentary, which often comes with self-righteous 'schooling' of others who have not 'got it yet' that can feel jarring. It is not the content, it is the lack of generosity we have for each other expressed in such encounters, when we are playing for the same team.

I have muted people whose political opinion and critical views I highly value because it can feel like a one-sided onslaught—sometimes it appears as if they do not want to be anything other than against. I understand the value of letting off steam, of complaining to let go of something that is sitting awry, of naming ills, of fighting back. But I long also to know what we feel enthusiastic about.

The world of now is saturated with one-sided presentations and fast fixes, and social media is where a lot of this plays out. Most of us will have seen articles or statements reposted, with people getting upset only to find out that the posted item is years old, or sometimes has been refuted quite thoroughly and is widely known to have been. It is perhaps in our nature to want easy, clickable, shareable news items, opinions and truths—things we don't have to engage with deeply because we don't have the time, the capacity or the means. Sometimes logic goes out of the window.

I am grateful for the conversations and important discussions that we can have these days across geographical boundaries. It is essential to name perpetrators. Too often we take a vow of silence and supposed decency, sometimes not knowing that we do, because subtle forces are at play which tie us into a structural grip that keeps us and our voices in a certain place. We suppress the information we have, which keeps the larger makeup alive—the white supremacist patriarchal structures, and who gets away with what. Social media can be a place where marginalised people can speak up and out, and find their siblings in struggle.

Especially as women we have been trained to be nice and polite and not make anything or anyone uncomfortable. Often it is to the detriment of ourselves or the victim, online or in real life. Calling out and saying clearly how things are is crucial. On social media this can find a collective momentum, where we don't have to be the single voice naming perpetrators or abusive incidents.

The political importance of naming ills and perpetrators gets muddled in a culture of quick name calling and putting down, of speaking and commenting in a way that ridicules, when it is not in fact the perpetrator we are trying to expose but someone's half-finished views. It is not the lack of politeness that catches my attention but the absence of showing a political vision.

Gaylene Gould, Head of Cinema at the British Film Institute and Cultural Ambassador for London, two among many hats she wears, posed an intriguing question around what the psychology of saying 'no' is on Facebook.[2] She brought attention to the seeming preference for the negative over the affirmative.[3] Gould made her observations in relation to Britain's failure to come to a workable Brexit solution. Members of Parliament were continually saying 'no' to a number of options, and had done so for weeks, which meant no decision was taken, and without any indication of how a decision would be made (at the time of writing). Gould gave another example from the judging of an arts prize. At first, the whittling down of submissions by the jury was done by continually saying 'no' until they came to a smaller number of works. However, one of the judges suggested that, rather than simply continuing to dismiss entries, they should highlight pieces they thought were excellent instead. In her post Gould describes how she initially felt uncomfortable to name what she liked and why. But the discomfort quickly changed to feeling thrilled about choosing something she loved. Saying 'yes' not only made her/them feel better but also took less time. In the discussion that followed on Gould's Facebook post, different commentators highlighted that expressly saying what we want might seem like a commitment and therefore feel like an exposure. In this way, I would argue, the explicit expression of what we want relates closely to the idea of vulnerability, something that we also often try to avoid.

Perhaps this exposure, this making ourselves vulnerable by a public commitment of our views, is harder because we know there is a possibility that it might change our minds. Perhaps we are not ready to commit to any position, and certainly not that openly.

As a fiction writer, when I teach creative-writing courses on character, I always point out that it is flaws and contradictions that make a character believable, and 'round'. Readers relate to the struggles of characters who are trying to juggle contradictions but also keep to their principles. A coherent but flawless character who never wavers from a linear trajectory, whether in feeling or action, seems unreal. Our uniqueness, as individuals, comes from our traits and personalities, but to some extent from how we bridge and resolve our own contradictions. It is hard to find anyone who can entirely live up to their own expectations or ideals. We get to know a person quite intimately when we learn how they deal with that discrepancy.

Gaylene Gould concluded the discussion by saying that the use of 'no' more often than affirming what we want might clarify our positions, may it be politically or culturally (as in the case of her example about the arts prize); but it might also be rebellious and a response to fear. When we sense discomfort, for instance about political changes or questions, rejecting at first instance what is offered might even be deeply rooted as a survival mechanism.[4]

We might in other words be hard wired to fear exposure and therefore vulnerability.

Before I can get to the significance of vulnerability, I need to address anger. It is imperative to call out patriarchy, white supremacy, destructive and exclusionary politics, injustices. Feminists have long talked about the need for rage. As early as 1981, Audre Lorde penned a now-famous essay that specifically talks about 'The Uses of Anger'.[5] More recently, Mona Eltahawy posed a poignant call to teach girls to rage because 'angry women' become 'free women'.[6] Eltahawy argues, like many others, that girls are taught to be polite and submissive, vulnerable and weak, to keep the patriarchy alive. She draws on Ursula Le Guin's commencement speech at Bryn Mawr College in 1986. In her address Le Guin made a powerful call to the graduating students, who were all women, to erupt like volcanoes. The image of the volcano conjures up a force that can destroy and take up space. Eltahawy argues that girls are taught to be pleasant and quiet, to take a backseat when it comes to their needs. Girls are conditioned to support others' needs and dreams, and to be content with that nurturing role without turning the gaze on to themselves. Volcanoes are not polite, they erupt when the hot magma rises to the surface. They 'go' where they need to go, they pave the way for what needs to be released. To erupt like volcanoes means to express themselves and be confident to take up spaces that they might have learned are not for them (but are rather men's domains). With their force they would destroy what stands in the way of free choice and equality.

In another essay, Eltahawy speaks of the language (and perhaps also tone) that is required of girls and women, which demands compliance with oppressive notions of politeness and niceness. Her lectures and talks are prefaced with what she calls her 'declaration of faith: fuck the patriarchy'.[7] She opens with that rallying call irrespective of where she speaks in the world. It proclaims that she will not obey the rules of good behaviour over her freedom, and that of others oppressed by patriarchy. She explains: 'I could say "dismantle the patriarchy" but I don't because I am a woman; a woman of colour; a Muslim woman. And I'm not supposed to say fuck.'

In our current political climate, faced with the global upsurge of the Far Right, anger is not merely a reflexive response, it propels us to action. It carries our voices when we shout: 'No, I am not giving consent, not in my name.'

In 'The Uses of Anger' Audre Lorde asserts:

> Every woman has a well-stocked arsenal of anger potentially useful against those oppressions, personal and institutional, which brought that anger into being. Focused with precision it can become a powerful source of energy serving progress and change.[8]

In speaking for vulnerability as a force for changing how we engage politically, I do not mean that we should silence or even temper our anger. The micro-aggressions we experience every day would destroy (parts of) us if we did not say 'STOP!' loudly and fiercely. Black women in particular are pathologised for being angry, when we are saying what is, when we call out, when we object to discrimination. The stereotype of the angry black woman is a sophisticated tool of oppression, for silencing Black women's experiences and their/our voices.[9]

What I am calling for is an embracing of vulnerability, a reconciling that acknowledges a range of reactions. Keeping the rage alive while also bringing into the mix how revealing what our political desires are (not just what we are against but our ideal vision of the world) can feel exposing and therefore make us fearful.

The notion of the strong Black woman, for instance, which is a widespread trope and a stereotype, can be incredibly harmful. We cannot do it all or bear it all. We cannot fight endlessly and not be affected. We cannot exist in one mode without other parts of us being present. Not if we want a wholehearted experience of life and politics.

What if showing how we are vulnerable did not make us weak or attackable, but rather fierce and fearless? When we have shown all that we are made of, we simply don't need to panic about being exposed. We are entering the political arena, the discussion or the decision-making process fully aware, fully present. If vulnerable means being our true selves, not guarding or disguising parts of us, it also means that our true vision might lie there. Politically, vulnerability is an opportunity to show our political vision, therefore to be seen. That seeing and being seen enshrines the very possibility of leading us forward.

There is growing awareness of the need for self-care, not as indulgent pampering but as an essential element in our mental, emotional and physical health. It has become more widely acceptable, in society generally, to take mental and emotional health into account, even if we are only at the beginning of this understanding. It can sound like self-care is easy, and that it can solve all sorts of things that in reality it cannot address. Rest, recuperation, getting help, healthy boundaries, saying no to things, and the many other actions that can be named under self-care, are important and political, *and* we need them to be included in a wider political analysis. A rigorous approach requires us to acknowledge the notion of community care. Sometimes it is not enough to care for oneself. Certain conditions, certain needs are only met through the care of the/a community. Sometimes the lack of community structures is what is missing altogether. Community care recognises that people are not solely responsible for making better the conditions they find themselves in. Otherwise those conditions get served back to us. This is where the gap lies. Self-care does not eradicate causes, it can only alleviate effects. It does not always respond to the roots of the problem(s). We can't always care for ourselves until we are well (which often simply means functioning) because there are many things in the way, a lack of fairly priced housing, poor wages and unaffordable childcare, to name but a few. There is structural racism, ableism, sexism, homophobia, transphobia and the like. Having a more comprehensive notion of the personal, the community, the public and the political allows us to intersect individual concerns with the larger structures and layers of oppression and disadvantage. Being there for each other is a political tool.

Writers and teachers of fiction often use empathy to give weight to the importance of literature. When the reader walks in someone else's shoes, they know them more intimately. They understand them (the characters) in an inside sort of way. The distance between them shrinks. They feel our shared humanity. This makes for a better world, and creates a climate of understanding. The idea of empathy can also transpire in a different manner, however, leading to little other than a moment of absorption. If reader and text meet for a brief encounter of synchronicity, the fictional world becomes alive and the reader steps in. Does this meeting of another world and its condition, a character's reality and challenges, sink to a deeper engagement, or end at the moment of consumption? Does this 'feeling another' alter how the reader interacts henceforth? If so, what does the reader do with it? Does it stoke political action?[10] As a writer I have heard many times how readers identified with characters they had little in common with, how moved they were, how much they learned. Some used this new awareness to navigate the real world.

When I was a young spoken-word artist one of my signature poems spoke about a series of racist encounters and experiences of racial profiling, like driving across the German border and being flagged down by police who were racing after us with their lights on because we looked Albanian. We were a car full of people of African descent, and Albanians were the 'suspicious people' of that time. Or another moment when I was stopped in the tube station Bahnhof Zoo in Berlin, in the middle of the day, and asked for my passport. When I enquired whether everyone had to identify themselves in this way the police answered truthfully, not hiding: they thought I might be a drug dealer without the official papers needed to reside in Germany. They had no reason to think this. I was simply changing trains with a valid ticket. The poem was full of those incidents, framed by a chorus that paid homage to my Afro-German sisters and brothers.

After one of my performances a white woman (in her thirties or forties) came up to me to tell me, excitedly, how much my words spoke not just to but *of* her. She could see herself in the poem. It was telling, this claiming of an experience that I knew she could not have had because the dominant culture fully embraced her. She did not empathise with me but rather was attempting to deny me my voice by claiming it. It was my first real understanding as a writer that a text I had written did not belong to me but to the reader. She could do whatever she wanted with it if that fitted her worldview. Perhaps she needed to protect herself by making the many incidents I had named untrue. Maybe it was a form of distancing so as not to feel she ought to do something to help change the society that allowed it. Instead of acknowledging the difference between her reality and mine, and the feelings it aroused in her, it seemed necessary for her to make us equal at all costs, as if we both had to deal with racism in our daily lives.

I believe in the power of fiction, and of literature. I see imagination as one of our most powerful tools for change and political vision. If I cannot see anything different, if I cannot cast a glimpse beyond the current situation, how will I arrive somewhere else, and, more importantly, what will carry me through the arduous task of un-doing and building anew? How else will I change deep-rooted habits, break patterns and structures that only reaffirm and uphold what is now but not express where we need to be going in the future?

Imagination is the space where change becomes tangible, where it grows into a picture, something I can face. It is something we can hold, in our minds and hearts. This holding is crucial because it relates to materialising change.

How to address the current political climate with honesty and horror, with empathy and vision? How do we feel when encounters lodge within our bodies, enter our physical self and make their own way? How to relate when thoughts and sensations rage?

A feeling or an emotion gets its meaning through what we have learned and what we believe. Meaning is constructed. It is not bias free. It is not necessarily a logical conclusion. In other words, what we feel is not entirely neutral and does not belong to ourselves alone. It depends, as scholars who engage with affect theory discuss, on learned thought patterns and structures, on culture and tradition. Things that make us, to some extent, feel a certain way. We frame our feelings in the context of what we know, and of what we can therefore allow. As Sara Ahmed argues,

> whether I perceive something as beneficial or harmful clearly depends upon how I am affected by something. This dependence opens a gap in the determination of feeling: whether something is beneficial or harmful involves thought and evaluation at the same time it is 'felt' by the body.[11]

Affects are bodily sensations, impressions on and in the body, encounters with the moment. They denote a being in the moment that is actively defined by what the body experiences. They are registered 'to the side of conscious thought rather than within it, but, as sensory intensity'.[12] We are not entirely aware (conscious) of them, or more precisely, not able to name them in that instant. They are received on a sensory level and we draw on all that is available to us to give them meaning and thereby place them accordingly. It is a sensing before the cognitive, a happening, perhaps unnoticed, perhaps uncategorised, perhaps unspoken.

I am interested in how states of discomfort, which are affects, can function as sites of meeting another, or ourselves. Perhaps they are opportunities for change. What would happen if we let those instances be for a moment, without glossing over them, without 'making us equal' (as in pretending sameness as of course I want equal rights) but with acknowledging the sensation they produce? We usually feel vulnerable then, discomfort uncovers something of/in us: fear of being left behind and deemed not worthy of the discussion or journey; fear of not getting it right. Discomfort could mean we are alarmed that we might get hurt (again), it can reveal that we lack thorough knowledge of something yet feel strongly enough to speak and/or act on it. We could be called out about our lack of insight. We could be exposed as 'frauds'. When we are vulnerable our bodies are implicated too—we cannot hide behind our opinions. What generative moment lies there? Vulnerability can be used to propose that we fully involve ourselves with the complications and contradictions that come with being human even when we have ideals, clear political ideas and visions. In *Radical Dharma* (co-authored with Rev angel Kyodo williams and Lama Rod Owens), Jasmine Syedullah reflects on meditation and social-justice activism, both elements she intersects with in her practice.

> What if freedom is not a means to an end full of more comforts than this moment, right now? We may yet be further inconvenienced along the way.[13]

What if freedom lies in getting used to this inconvenience? As we are not talking about personal freedom but political freedom, other people will have a stake too. In meeting others, encountering and exchanging, it will get more inconvenient. There is an opening in moments of discomfort, and often they are tied to choice: we can try to invite the encounter, the moment, the sensation or we can try to leave it, to bury or block it, as quickly as possible. Moments of discomfort happen all the time. As a writer, I know that I only ever find something new (be it a voice, a topic, an angle on a topic) when I feel uncomfortable, when I am not entirely sure if it is leading me somewhere. I feel exposed following a thread because I am already committing to my idea of it. If I want to find something new I have to go beyond what is habitual to me, and what at first is uncomfortable. Perhaps we need to start embracing the reality that we are different at different times, not only that we are different from each other. Perhaps vulnerability is a practice, the showing and showing up, again and again to discuss and clarify, to grow and refine.

Deborah Gould states that affect is

> a body's registered sensation of a moment of existing relationally, interactively, in the world, affect is an effect of being affected and an effect is itself a preparation to act in response, but in no pre-set or determined way.[14]

She goes on to say that

> Affect is also a key force in social change. Ideas about

the need for change and movement toward bringing it about often begin with an inarticulate and inarticulable sensation that something is awry, that things could be and perhaps should be different, affective states can inspire challenges to the social order.[15]

When thinking about affect, multidisciplinary artist Phoebe Boswell's work came to my mind. I recently visited her show *The Space Between Things* at the Autograph gallery in London (2018/19). Boswell's work draws on the body, to show it functioning 'relationally' and 'interactively' in the world, and layering it within the different contexts she explores. I deeply admire Boswell's work for its honesty and weaving in of African, diasporic, personal and political notions. It is a confronting and stunning exploration of grief and trauma— vulnerable, beautiful and courageous. In it, Boswell uses self-portraits and drawings, and film that shows in close-up surgeries on her eye and heart. Boswell tweeted at the end of its run:

I spent three weeks drawing myself onto the gallery wall in unfixed charcoal; a cathartic act of vulnerability and defiance to remind me that while my body is fallible, I still exist.[16]

In a *Frieze* magazine review of the exhibition, Rianna Jade Parker tellingly writes: 'we heal ourselves, and each other, by living and by speaking our truths out loud. It is only in this way that we can thrive, rather than merely survive.'[17] Vulnerability, and in this case the making known of those parts of us that are difficult to bear, gives permission to others to show our entirety. There our whole selves are brought to participate in the conversation.

This is where it lies, the fierceness required to show what is, in its entirety. Boswell's exhibition, which explores the grief following her trauma, does not only show her own healing process, but also reveals that we have to leave it be and witness it while that healing is taking place. It uncovers a state of discomfort, not a fleeting one but a sustained condition. Allowing this ongoing process of grief, healing and transformation, without glossing over it, without a tidy end, is perhaps what makes it so truthful and in some ways a form of 'thriving'. It is more than surviving. It embraces what it takes to overcome it and stay in the moment of this. This kind of fierceness is about the ability to accept fear and be uncomfortable, whether it relates to oneself, a position, or a need. This ability to expose is an indication of great strength. To claim space for one's own vulnerability is to resist the notion that survival is good enough, that healing is personal and must therefore be hidden. That personal pain, trauma and grief are not part of our collective reckoning.

For myself these reflections begin in my childhood, which was marked by upheaval and uncertainty, and some years spent in foster care and a girl's home. In a sense, the luxury of vulnerability has always been what kids like me could not afford. To expose ourselves further would have been futile. And who has the time when you are trying to survive? Being vulnerable is something I claimed as a right for myself. It was something that grew out of a fierceness that did not let survival be the measure of living because survival only embraces the bare minimum. Vulnerability is a defiant reckoning. It demands that I, and we, do not have to arrive or continue fragmented.

Deborah Gould's essay talks about 'Lauren Berlant, who places nonrationality at the heart of the political'.[18] Nonrationality speaks to affect. We act because we sense the wrongness of something. Paying attention to these irrational cues, these bodily sensations, can perhaps sharpen what we actually want, politically, but also help to strengthen our solidarity with those we ally with.[19] I propose a return to an old-school type of sitting and discussing with each other. A carving out of positions that has listening as its crucial underpinning, and that embraces the friction that comes from difference and growing alongside each other. A talking things through, a learning by sharing and holding space. Holding space means letting be, it acknowledges the other without aiming to pull another over to one's own side, at least not straight away. It perceives first, then examines. We need self and community care centrally placed as essential components of change. To be brave is to show oneself and still do all that you think and feel is (politically) right. To dare to be moved to act by what is moving us. As Chastity Chandler argues, 'to be vulnerable is to be alive'.[20]

And what could we want of a world, if we do not demand to be fully present.

The Bravado of Books

Tabish Khair

IN HIS AUTOBIOGRAPHY, *Les Mots* (1964), Jean-Paul Sartre recalls the time when his mother started reading stories out to him. She had already been telling him stories, often similar ones. He used to love those stories, with their 'half-completed sentences', 'slow-to-come words', and 'brusque confidence, quickly defeated and put to rout, which disappeared with a pleasant fraying sound, and then re-established itself after a silence'. But when she began to *read out* the stories, something strange happened. This is how Sartre recalls it:

> Anne-Marie made me sit down in front of her, on my little chair; she leant over, lowered her eyelids and went to sleep. From this mask-like face issued a plaster voice. I grew bewildered: who was talking? About what? And to whom? My mother had disappeared: not a smile or trace of complicity. I was an exile. And then I did not recognise the language. Where did she get her confidence? After a moment, I realized: it was the book that was talking.[1]

From a writer who displays an almost Proustian ability to circle around the same event or statement and reveal it as slightly different with each shift of perspective, Sartre's account is salutary—at least for 'creative authors'. For creative writers like to believe, sometimes with good reason, that the pen is mightier than the sword.

The sword—unlike the pen—can only cut and slice. The pen can form words, pluck them from thick air. These words can cut and slice too, of course, as anyone who has had a relationship go sour usually discovers. But unlike the sword—which exists only as a sword, for its past is smelted metal and its future, if different, can only be smelted metal again—the word has a past and a future as a word. In that sense, a word is the exact version of how religious people like to imagine themselves. The sword has no soul: it exists only in its present. It does not survive its own smelting. The word has a soul: its present is always linked to a past and a future *as a word*.

I am not just talking of the fact that the same word can be used in different ways by different sections of a linguistic community or in different ages: that is a fairly obvious point. I am not talking only of the imagination or etymology. What I am saying is this: at the moment when we pen down a word, we pluck it from air and pin it on to paper. Let's say paper for the time being; I will move on to iPads and computers later on.

This word that is pinned down on paper is not the same as the word that was plucked out of thick air, and yet it is the same. Unlike the sword, which turns from molten metal into a sword, the word was a word before and remains a word now. And yet, what a change has taken place!

In literature we can trace this change in so many ways.

The age when words used to exist in air is almost a separate planet from the age when words started getting pinned down on parchment and paper. We look back from our age to the previous one, and we think that we can still breathe in their words, partly because some—*The Odyssey*, *The Mahabharata*, etc—have survived (or so it seems) and partly because some 'tribes' with little or (at least until some decades ago) no writing still exist.

But, alas, the words deceive us. Or they deceive us because we wish to be deceived. Because all those ancient 'untexts' contain glaring clues about their difference. We ignore the clues in those 'untexts'. We attribute them to authors, we squabble to turn them authoritative, we annotate them as texts. We forget that the moment an 'oral text'—an oxymoron—is put down on paper, its words become something else. Even if we imitate the structure of an 'oral text' in writing, we use words differently. Compare the Australian poet Les Murray's excellent 'The Buladelah-Taree Holiday Song Cycle' to the Aboriginal 'songs' it builds upon. Even though these songs, once written down, have already become something other than simply oral, they still differ from Murray's poem in significant ways. For instance, Murray can replicate their repetitiveness and circularity—essential for mnemonic purposes in oral compositions—but he cannot make his song contain the information and work directions that aboriginal song cycles do. You do not need Murray's poem to have even a holiday—itself a concept worth examining—but the aboriginal song-cycles were needed to specify routes, record ancestries, even erect shelters.

This is not Murray's fault. Something happens when the word is plucked from thick air and pinned on paper: 'Literature'—with a capital L—comes into being. The author—who can now be authoritatively discussed—can choose to collect information and 'facts', or do something else with words. In due course, we inevitably talk of medical literature and Literature, though in recent decades the capital L of the latter has been vigorously demolished—a once-brave necessity that has turned into cowardly fashion.

To some extent, the young Sartre noticed this difference between the stories his mother told and the stories she read out to him. For the word has changed—turned flesh, if you wish—not only at the moment of its being written down; it is a change that percolates down to the reading. It is the same word, and entirely different—and we are not even talking of changes in meaning because of time or space! The book that talks through the mouth of Sartre's mother speaks another language. Every book turns its reader into an exile—and books of 'Literature' use this too.

The huge planetary distance between orality and literacy, between 'untexts' and texts—which we largely ignore— haunts even our reading of 'texts'. And yet it is a different kind of haunting—and it comes with many advantages. For one, to interpose from Sartre, we learn to speak in tongues!

Who is reading? Sartre wonders when he hears his mother read. Who is speaking? we wonder when we read a book. Any book, even a book of physics equations or chemical formulae. Of course, with such books, we usually look up the name and details of the author. If we are advanced readers, we might look up more—in order to ascertain what slant this particular author, given his or her institutional location, might have on a scientific presentation.

But Literature—with a capital L, I insist—poses greater problems. The authorship of Literature is deceptive; its readership is disruptive: this is largely due to the connected and separate acts of plucking words from thick air and putting them down on paper and, in another year or space, releasing them from paper into thin air. One always reads Literature in one's own voice and someone else's voice. The young Sartre is yet to learn that.

Words that have existed before they were set down on paper are then released into the air again—in a different time and/or place. This happens for all kinds of words— whether of medical literature or of Literature. But Literature is not—as Murray discovered—about passing on useful facts to other individuals. The 'untext'—when it existed before writing became prevalent—had to do so. It had to combine the emotive, imaginative, formal and other skills of what we call Literature today to record and convey useful mundane facts: lineages, routes, hunting lore, foundational myths, building techniques, pairing rituals, etc. But the very fact of words becoming flesh—on paper—has split them, slowly at first, and with greater acceleration later on as writing spread and became easier to reproduce. Now there are words that give us facts and information, and…and what?

And there are similar words, the same words, often exactly identical words, that refuse to be pinned down. The words of Literature are not different from the words of medical and other literatures, which is why there was once the need to demolish the capital L of Literature. And, of course, all these words are not different from the words that hover in the air all around us, the words of our speech, breath-words.

We have penned down the words, but we have not really pinned them down. If the text can never be the untext, there are things that the text can do which were not possible for the untext: it can split up words. Or, maybe we should say, words in a text can split themselves up. So, there are the words in the book read by Sartre's mother; there are the words released by Sartre's mother into thin air; and there are the words heard by Sartre. And, actually, for this accounts for the difference Sartre notices, there are the words Sartre has heard elsewhere or earlier. They are all the same words, and they are not the same words.

The young Sartre cannot read yet. Later on in the autobiography, he learns to read. And he learns to read like all of us do—what he feels he should read, what he has to read, and what he likes to read. More than that, he reads in texts what his grandfather or his mother does not read in them. This is an ability of the text that the untext could not have to the same degree, for the untext had only one enunciation in the present. In that sense, it was like the sword.

The fact that there are so many different versions of oral untexts like the earlier stories of the *Mahabharata* often fools us—textual paragons that we are—into assuming that the untext contained multiple meanings. This is misleading. The untext did not have a text against which it could be compared, and hence it could change across time and space. But because it did not have an authoritative text, it needed to be enacted and learnt by heart—so that, in any specific social context, its words were fixed and unchanging. The untext could have only one rendition at a time—and its speaker and hearer were joined by common socio-cultural bonds.

The text—by trapping words—also frees them. Academics frequently make bright careers out of this basic fact: intentional fallacy, death of the author, reader response theories, distant reading, etc. But the fact is rudimentary: the word, plucked out of thick air, and made flesh on paper, will one day be read, and released into thin air. More interestingly, unlike the untext, the text will be read a hundred kilometres away or 50 years later 'as it is'—and its words again released into thin air. One understands where the religious might have got their hopes from: the spirit is made flesh in the text, and then it is released again and again into all eternity. Except that each release is different, it changes eternity, it changes the word made flesh, and it changes the spirit behind it all. And yet, unlike the sword, the word remains a word.

Reading a word is not the same as speaking it; it never was and never will be. Reading doesn't just do something to you; it also does something to the word. Literature knows it, and literature knows it too. Literature (with a capital L) is sometimes frightened of it—hence, for instance the Liberal Humanist insistence that Literature is only about what is constant and permanent in human nature across time and space—and literature is frightened of it too. But while there are reasons for literature to be frightened of it—it wants to communicate facts, information etc with the minimum of confusion, contradiction, noise—there are no real reasons for Literature to be frightened of it. Hence, literature does its best to contain the words it uses. It doesn't always succeed; some of the words, sooner or later, rip themselves away, change into something else, turn into noise, or lapse into silence. But literature does its best, as it should. It plugs the gaps and goes on: alchemy becomes chemistry, Newton shrinks to accommodate Einstein, natural selection is buttressed with genetic mutations.

But, ah, Literature learns—or at least its handful of real practitioners do, despite what its publicists, agents and editors might choose to promote—Literature learns to live with brave (new and old) words. More than that, it learns that the capital L in its name is solely and entirely due to this one characteristic: the fact that it can live with words becoming flesh and turning into ghosts, with words in thick (or thin) air and on paper, with words speaking in voices unknown to the author and the reader, with words tapering into silence or escalating into noise, with words being too much or not enough for this world (and the next).

The bravery of words is also the bravado of books. This exists on the page before it comes to exist elsewhere. Something has changed not just when the untext became a text; something also changes when the word is pinned to a page. To say that it dies would be a mistake. It changes, just as, for the religious, the soul does not die when it is imprisoned in flesh for the duration of a lifetime. The word that existed in the air—in the age of the 'untext' or of the text—was always the same word. Its utterance, as Valentin Voloshinov or Mikhail Bakhtin might have put it, determined its meaning. This meaning, as Bakhtin suggested, was monological—fixed by the context. I could shout 'idiot' to a rash driver, and it would be a word of hatred and aggression.[2] I could say 'idiot,' smiling and softly, to my gambolling child, and it would be a word of love and approbation. In either context, it has only one meaning. That, however, is not the case when the word 'idiot' is written on paper and left lying about. What are its meanings? Does it have any meaning? What noise does it create? What blank silence envelops it?

The word made flesh on paper is trapped in the context of other words: phrase, line, sentence, paragraph, stanza, chapter, book. But something has happened to this word. The context of the text is not the context of the untext. The latter always has a speaker who is present; the latter has an author who is absent. The much-touted death of the author is one way of noticing this absence. The passage of the book across time and space releases various meanings—and adds various meanings—to the word. The passage of the book from hand to hand releases also the silence and noise that, actually or potentially, wrap every word that is written down. Literature, with a capital L, is the kind of literature that is fully aware of this, and uses it differently than literature: it is the necessary endeavour of literature to do its best to turn the molten spirit of the word into a singular sword of meaning, desperately, and always with partial success, fighting against its eventual metamorphosis into something slightly different when it is read and released back into air in another space or time. But Literature is the kind of literature that accepts both the changes and provides for them on the page.

The author of Literature, who, in this sense is never truly dead as long as the text is read (though always entirely absent, even if she does the reading herself), frames the word in the context of its possible meanings and meaninglessness, its noise and silence. She frames the word in the context of its excess and inadequacy. She frames the word as insufficient and necessary, misleading and superbly accurate. It is not that she knows all the meanings of the word, past, present or future, but that she knows the meanings will accrue— along with silence, noise, gap, contradiction, etc—and hence Literature does not use words as sufficient. It also uses the limitations of words, even their failures; it uses silence, and noise, gaps and contradictions, paradox and irony. These are essential to a kind of communication that will not be considered communication by literature, and one of the tragedies of Literature is that when it is *studied*, as it inevitably needs to be, by scholars and academics, it can only be pronounced upon in terms of literature. That is why, finally, the capital L of Literature remains so unpopular: the need to score that fact that the words of Literature and literature are no different has been taken over by the disciplinary need of a kind of literature to explain, communicate, typify, regulate, keep the molten spirit of words shaped into the singular meaning of a sword.

In other words, reading Literature is an act that is at least different in quantity, if not in quality, from reading literature. But even if it is just a difference of quantity, it is enough for us. For, as old Marxists used to say, a sufficient difference of quantity translates into a difference of quality. Reading Literature requires a kind of concentration and space that, until now, only the book has fully enabled. Here, as the reader is aware, the scope of Literature has already expanded to include some kinds of literature, ranging from philosophy to, perhaps, some texts of theoretical physics.

The Korean-German philosopher Byung-Chul Han points out that contemplation or deep attention defines human activities. Culture demands deep attention, writes Han. He adds that, in our age, such immersive attention is being displaced by an accelerated and disjointed form of attention: 'hyperattention'. He goes on to argue that a hectic rush into activity and a low tolerance threshold for 'boredom' are not conducive to culture, just as multitasking is not progress but a regress. Animals have always 'multitasked', for instance, by eating, grooming and keeping a watch for other predators at the same time. 'Multitasking,' Han suggests, is the common plight of all animals, including humans, in a hostile environment. What humans had partly achieved, and are now gradually losing, is the space and capacity for contemplation. It is impossible to contemplate on computers. This is not just because, as Han suggests, computing as an activity is opposed to contemplation. Computers, iPads and other such screen-reading devices are structured to split our attention; the internet forces us to 'multitask', as all those pop-ups indicate at the simplest. All this might change in the future, with digital options perhaps adapting to the cultural and intellectual needs of human beings, but that will only happen if these needs are registered and recognised.[3]

Is that happening today? Are we aware of the fact that the word on paper enabled a kind of close attention which the word on a digital screen does not? Are we aware of the fact that, when a word is plucked out of thick air and set down on paper, something happens to it—in the present and the future of its release by a reader into thin air again—which is different at least in quantity, if not quality, from what happens to it when it is digitally trapped? The word of writing was brave, I have argued, because it went where no word had gone before. And, having gone there, it inserted the change of reader, space, time, context into the very soul of the word's meanings. Imagine it, if you will, as a door flung open to welcome otherness, again and again. All this required (and requires) deep concentration—both on the part of the writer of Literature and on the part of its readers. It required a perennial openness to the multiplicity and malleability of meanings, which went, ironically, with a desire to make meaning. It was a complicity of concentration—not just 'interpretation'—between author and reader. That is why reading texts—even religious ones—as Literature is anathema to all religious fundamentalists.

Let us not underestimate the bravado of the book. Imagine a singer in an oral society composing a song of strong dissent. A Boris Pasternak, a George Orwell of orality. What would happen to her? What would happen to her song? Would she be allowed to sing it? Would anyone in that society—full of people who disagreed with her—want to learn it by heart, so that it could be passed on to the next generation? For dissent to survive—if not exist—oral communities would require large segments of support. Individual dissent might exist but would never be recorded in purely oral societies. You need writing for it; you need a book. The bravado of books allows the bravery of words.

You might say that digitalised reproduction makes it easier to circulate and preserve words. Yes, and no. Because mere preservation is not enough, mere circulation is not enough, even mere information, as Han notes, is not enough. A kind of concentration—deep attention—is required. Reading words in books enabled this kind of concentration—not only on the contextual meaning of the word, but also on the shifts in its meaning across contexts. Reading words in Literature books enabled a similar concentration—not only on the shifting meanings of the word, but also on the silences, noise, gaps and contradictions that enabled those meanings to shift in many cases. I will put it bluntly: the word pinned down on paper has a different afterlife than the word that is digitally recorded.

The bravery of the word is not just the bravery of the individual who uses it. For the individual has too short a life. She can mutter, under her breath, *e pur si muove*, but breath is short and fragile, inquisitions are long and powerful. The bravery of the word is enabled by the medium. To move unthinkingly to another kind of medium might enable other kinds of bravery—or cowardice.

Because, finally, the pen is not mightier than the sword. Authors love to fool themselves into thinking so, particularly authors of Literature. Some of it has to do with the author's deep investment in Literature, and Literature's deep investment in life. '*Ragon mein daurate phirne ke hum nahi qayal / jab ankh hi se na tapka to phir lahu kya hai,*' wrote the great Urdu poet, Mirza Ghalib in the early nineteenth century ('I don't believe in its running about in one's veins, / If it doesn't drip from the eyes, it is not blood'). He was expressing a view of Literature as bearing witness (eyes: ankh) to the atrocities of the human psyche, the human heart. '*Maata-e-loh-o-qalam chhin gayi to kya ghum hai / ke khoon-e-dil mein dubo li hain ungliyan maine*' wrote the revolutionary twentieth-century poet, Faiz Ahmad Faiz ('Why sorrow because my tablet and pen have been snatched away / I have dipped my fingers in the blood of my heart'). He was expressing a view of Literature as bearing witness to the atrocities of human society. Around the same time, of course, WH Auden, in his eulogy to WB Yeats, appeared to have fewer expectations from Literature:

> For poetry makes nothing happen: it survives
> In the valley of its making where executives
> Would never want to tamper, flows on south
> From ranches of isolation and the busy griefs,
> Raw towns that we believe and die in; it survives,
> A way of happening, a mouth.[4]

But Auden is still talking of Literature's need to bear witness. This is the ability of the word—trapped on paper—to be murdered and released every time it is read here or there, now and then.

No, the pen is not mightier than the sword. But it is much more slippery. The bravery of words—new, old, new again—is not primarily the bravery of the pen, despite the blood with which many have been stained. It is the bravery of the molten word that assumed flesh, and becomes molten again—changing every time, and changing as flesh too, but never, to plagiarise the religious, losing its soul. It is bravery enabled by the book, and the pen of Literature knows that words in a book are not hard, singular and unchanging as swords. They have a past and they will have a future because of this. Unlike literature, Literature uses words with this knowledge. For the pen might not be mightier than the sword, but the word can be.

Out Loud: the experience of literature in the digital space

Marina Warner

IN THE PRESENT CLIMATE of discouragement that threatens all of us who hold the Humanities dear, one of the worst threats, or so it seems, has been the dumbing down consequent on digital media and the rise of hate speech on digital platforms. I want to offer some countervailing reflections and hopes, and explore the activity and the potential of the www as a forum for literature; in spite of the instinctive recoil and bristling horror I feel for social media as currently used, it is possible to consider and reframe the question of reading on the web. Doing so leads to the questions, what is literature? And can literature be found beyond the printed book? It is my contention—perhaps my Candide-like hope—that the internet is spurring writers on to creating things with words that are not primarily aimed at silent readers, but at an audience that is listening and viewing and feeling, and maybe also reading all at the same time, participating in word-events channelled through electronic media.

The internet and mobile phones can muster vast crowds behind a slogan or a cause; for the most part, we have seen damaging consequences. Yet I think—I hope—that it is a mistake to take the current products of the web for ineluctable consequences. Indeed, the metaphor of the web is itself misleading, because the internet is more of a loom than a net or a web; it is a tool and its products can take myriad forms: many varieties of fabric—and fabrication. The hubbub of the internet—as we know in our deepest anxieties—swallows up individuals in fanatical elective affinities and magnetises many to sectarian and extreme causes. However, to think it must lead only to Trump, Cambridge Analytica, trolling and hate speech is to mistake the artefact for the tool, the irrigation system for the water that flows through it and for the loaf of bread grown from the field of corn it watered.

'The medium is the message,' Marshall McLuhan's historic aphorism, expresses an ideological *parti pris*, and accepting it now, in changed circumstances of communications, offers a counsel of despair.[1] Digital media are open doors—so far. They invite entry to all comers. At the beginning of the era of the www, the Catalan philosopher Eugenio Trías noticed the interconnection of digital media with the rise of large, symbolic communal events, from political demonstrations to flash dances when a crowd suddenly comes together for no reason other than wild, wilful, mischievous joy. Such actions, he argues, have taken over from inward prayer and private acts of faith, and become the dominant means of fashioning the sacred today.[2] This realm of the sacred is not exclusively religious, but also forms to create new commemorative and symbolic rituals which have their roots in shared histories; this consensus takes shape through writing—it emerges in fiction, poetry, and history itself.

Trías's perceptions about the transformations of religious and public uses of symbolism allude to currently thriving forms of assembly; these range widely in form, but his thinking anticipates current developments which rely on striking visuals and slogans spreading on Twitter and Instagram, such as the Occupy movement, the mass sit-ins in Tahrir Square and popular commemorative acts—including nationwide recitals of the names of the dead after recent massacres and disasters.[3] Texts, often embedded in visual signs, are key to these acts of self-definition and utopian dreaming. As Toni Morrison has observed, 'Language (saying, listening, reading) can encourage, even mandate, surrender, the breach of distances among us...' She then turns to visual media and warns, 'Image increasingly rules the realm of shaping, sometimes becoming, sometimes contaminating knowledge... These two godlings, language and image, feed and form experience.'[4]

Multiplicity, archival capacity, speed of retrieval, and multi-media communication across distances and cultural boundaries, such as linguistic difference: these are the fundamental properties of the internet relating to the diffusion of ideas and their literary and visual expression. In a recent essay about contemporary cosmopolitanism, the comparatist scholar Bruce Robbins looks forward to the communities which, I believe, these conditions can nourish: 'The desire for justice is also normal within a global tradition of storytelling that's much larger than realism.' He continues: 'Narrative as such poses the broader question of what circle of readers can recognise themselves at any given moment as a political collectivity or community of fate, whether in any given narrative enough guests have been invited'[5] The concept of 'communities of fate' defines a possibility of imaginative co-existence, a way of dwelling in fractured space and interrupted time. Robbins continues: 'But I would also like to think that there exists a narrative, or a possibility of narrative, within "world literature", a narrative in which the emergence of the category of "world literature" would constitute a significant event. Contemplating a seemingly endless series of atrocities receding into the depths of time, atrocities that no longer seem easily divided between modern and ancient, it may seem that meaningful history has become impossible and that literature itself, taken as existing outside of time, is the best refuge from the centuries and centuries and centuries of meaninglessness.'[6]

In this essay I ask: can the internet's reach and capaciousness help build a community of fate, 'a country of words' where the humanities can flourish? And, at a time of high tension in the world, flourish beyond the borders of nation and language and economic interests? How does the www work as a vehicle for literature? What forms does literature take in this global communications system, this virtual infinite library, as if the encyclopaedic fantasy of Jorge Luis Borges's story, 'Tlön Uqbar Orbis Tertius' were a prophecy?[7]

The process whereby a story, such as the adventures of Gilgamesh, moves from the song, the recitation, the performance and the scene of storytelling into the precious manuscript and the sanctum of the library, has been fascinatingly explored by the classical scholar Florence Dupont in her study *The Invention of Literature* (1999). She proposes a different model from the straightforward contrast between the written and the oral, demonstrating that some of the greatest works of human imagination were created not as written literature, but as texts to be performed, to be heard. Voicing was an art of living creators, who took a piece of writing and worked with it as singers or players work with a score, or, perhaps, even more closely, as jazz soloists take up a tune and improvise on it. The voice of the storyteller was multiple, and the stories created were all different and the same at one and the same time. Immutable inscription—writing—was used for tallies, the law and other reckonings intended to be solid and permanent. But narration belonged to the different order of time—flowing time, mutability... chromatic harmony. Every listener became—and becomes—a potential new storyteller. Early literature, she declares, was composed of play scripts and prompt books, storytellers' scrolls, pattern books. She writes, of *The Golden Ass*, 'The book that moderns have mistakenly called a novel seems in truth to have constituted an intermediary between two kinds of orality.'[8]

Literature was a speech act performed by living voices present to their audiences, as in many art events today (this might go some way to explaining the ever-growing popularity of literary festivals). Writing, according to Dupont's reading, represented an attempt to capture those voices—the book was a kind of early phonograph, which would preserve the dead and bring them back, living and audible, into time present. When books established canonical, fixed texts, they turned into death masks, entombing the once living beings that made the sounds of the words. In the absence of those bodies, Dupont writes, literature, when enclosed in a book, was fated to draw attention endlessly to that absence.

The digital age is also seeing a vigorous renewal of Performance and 'Spoken Word', and innovative work is being done on this development, for example by Haun Saussy in his bold and incisive manifesto, *The Ethnography of Rhythm*.[9] Saussy, like Dupont, invokes voice rather than script in reviewing the history of literary expression and the communication of stories, poetry and, sometimes, history. Oral embodiment—rhythm, rhyme, metre, beat—transmits words more memorably: pictures punctuate the recitation or performance. The work of the rhapsode in Greek culture is returning, the role of the bard is being self-consciously re-occupied by poets—from the poise and enraptured quality of Alice Oswald's recitations to the rap commentary on the world of Hollie McNish, writers are performing their work by heart as if they were born digital, and publishing the text later, as the cast sheaths of the live creature they filled literally with their breath during the performance.[10] In the lacerating narrative poems of Kate Tempest, written 'to be read aloud', rock music meets Ovid, and both Samuel Beckett and Kathy Acker are remembered. The potential for communicating such recitations and artefacts has grown beyond all previous imaginings: nobody expected the popularity of podcasts, for example. In cultures of the Middle East and the Caribbean and the continent of Africa, historical traditions are being reclaimed: the Palestinian-Egyptian Tamim al-Barghouti is purposefully reoccupying the role of the *rawaii* or reciter, and the ancient Arabic bardic tradition, with impassioned, agile—and often caustic— variations on ancient prosody.

By a sharp paradox, the immaterial internet has become the vehicle of record for creations with words which are attempting to overthrow the medium's lack of tactile, sensuous qualities, the way its smooth screens and their uniformity of presence fail to hook its contents into the mind: I have found that when I read a work of literature on a kindle or on the screen it slips from memory as if the ink were instantly dissolving in water, or indeed, the words were written in invisible ink. To exemplify resistance to the glabrous lack of purchase to sense and senses that web-based literature suffers, I will bring in here the work of the writer-artist-performer Caroline Bergvall and especially her book and installation entitled *Drift* (2014), a remarkable art-and-sound essay-poem. Bergvall creates mixed-media publications to communicate her work; her performances are live, enacted in the moment with a ritualistic emphasis on unique presence, but they are also filmed and recorded for webcasting. The need to agglomerate all these different descriptions of what these creatives do—and many others like her—demonstrates how the multiplicity and connectivity of digital media gives scope for hybridities and grafts between genres and forms of creative expression.

The book of the work is one impression of it, the *YouTube* or online *vimeo* an archival memory, a brass rubbing off the acoustic track of the performance. Several of these performer-writers, these new rhapsodes, have audiences online that run to the millions, beyond the wildest dreams of the most famous print poets in the world. When publishers like Picador begin to publish them in print, the passage from the web to the page replicates the appearance of print editions of bards and skalds in the past. The book version becomes a record, not the primary state of the work. These contemporary poets' voices and/or their texts blur the generic boundaries between pop music, rap, entertainment, film and even dance, on occasion.

The 2018 music video 'This is America', which Childish Gambino made, epitomises the generic multiplicity of such word-events: it was an incendiary thing—a danced poem on digital film online. Platforms for such work, such as UbuWeb,

Button Poetry, Asymptote and www.archiveofthenow.org provide showcases for poets whose popularity equals rock stars, and sometimes also for writers of fiction, essayists (bloggers) and dramatists.

Some of the poets especially have come under enemy fire from those who pride themselves on keeping up a literary tradition: in the pages of *PN Review*, the poet Rebecca Watts lashed into Hollie McNish, Warsan Shire, et al (stars of the spoken-word circuit) for their 'crass verse'.[12] But attacks of this kind, setting out to resist 'dumbing down' and amateurishness, fail to take account of the vigour that a convincing oral performance can bring to the page and how necessary this demotic energy is to the life of language. For example, Kei Miller in both his novel *The Last Warner Woman* (2010) and his poetry, in the collection *The Cartographer Tries to Map a Way to Zion* (2014), tunes the reader's ear to his characters' voices, even when they lie silent in type on the page, by the sheer virtuoso ventriloquism of his diction.

It is entirely in keeping with this strong, and in my view, enriching trend in cultural taste that in 2017 the Nobel committee chose the singer/songwriter Bob Dylan. This last property of the internet—its symbiosis with oracy—renders it hospitable to independent, web-based literary creativity.

1 Multiplicity

In a memorable series of lectures just before his death in 1985, Italo Calvino defines Multiplicity as one of the qualities he most desires from literature, alongside Quickness and Lightness, among others.[13] He mentions many branching works, such as Ovid's *Metamorphoses* and the *One Thousand and One Nights*. He died before the era of the internet, but digital media might have been a natural playground for his Oulipian games with aleatory structures and chance sequences, as in his novels *Invisible Cities* (1974) and *If on a Winter's Night, a Traveller* (1979). The web's multiplicity matches the polymorphous forms of literature, mostly classic works which exist in multiple versions, through variations, editions and translations: Virgil's revisioning of Homer; Racine's reworking of Euripides; and, in our own times, such memorable revisionings as Philip Pullman's recasting of *Paradise Lost*, in the trilogy *His Dark Materials* (2005); Naomi Alderman's *The Liars' Gospel* (2012); Colm Toibin's *The Testament of Mary* (2012); and an extreme instance of heterodox retooling in the shape of JM Coetzee's own Gospel stories, *The Childhood of Jesus* (2013) and *The Schooldays of Jesus* (2016). These fictions take place within complex genealogies, and represent encounters with and responses to works which in their origins were voiced: either because they claim to set down words which were once recited and spoken—Homer, or part of the Gospels—or because they are written to be performed, and indeed benefit from being read out loud, as in the case of Racine and Milton.

Works of literature that are multiple in structure and—to some extent—authorship, include many of the most well-travelled stories, their journeys tracking audiences and cultures where the stories have been welcomed and often told again, with differences. These transformations of tellings and retellings take oral form as well as written form. Many works of such travelling literature are myths and fairy tales, intrinsically filled with magical and imaginary elements. But many such narratives are not works of literature in the prevalent sense of the genre: like the funeral laments the artist Taryn Simon collected in *An Occupation of Loss* (discussed below), they have several authors or

Anon—think of the multiple branches of the Trojan War, of Arthur and Roland/Orlando and other tales of chivalry and crusades, or of the myth of Oedipus. Prime travelling texts include animal fables which are known in Europe as *Aesop's Fables* and in Arab countries as *Kalila wa Dimna* and the Babylonian *Epic of Gilgamesh*, with echoes in the *One Thousand and One Nights*.

Literature is migratory: if it can, it will travel, and move across languages and cultures; as texts translocate, they change, but still retain recognisable features.

Works such as these suffuse cultures rather than define free-standing landmarks: they are like rivers, fed by tributaries and fanning out in deltas. Many of them are not even well-written in the conventional sense (as CS Lewis pointed out, for example).[14] The principal reason for reading the four gospels is not their value as literary artefacts of late Greek/Aramaic; at least that is not the principal reason. The New Testament flows through international culture in translations carried in the bloodstream of story, maybe inspiring a masterpiece now and then, such as Pier Paolo Pasolini's *The Gospel according to St Matthew* (1967). The same can be said of other works, which are likely to have originated in verbal form, but which circulated in images and other media down the centuries and have gained wider circulation in digital media today.

We are living now in a new Tower of Babel before it fell—not because we share an ideal Adamic unity of language, but because we are increasingly familiar with a common narrative lexicon: from Troy to *Game of Thrones*, from Jerusalem to *Stranger Things*. An understanding of collective cross-pollination, of grafting and splicing, reshaping, recovery and rediscovery, excavation, retrieval and reassembly has been growing strongly.

One of the impulses behind the shift to fabulism is a fresh consciousness that fiction can be a forum for exchange, a cosmopolitan arena. Translations are growing in number into English, and the value of the translator's work has been brought into the limelight and applauded far more than in the past, when his or her name sometimes did not appear anywhere in the book.[15] Reworking inherited stories has strikingly become the pursuit of many contemporaries—at the popular level, the GDP of New Zealand surged after *The Lord of the Rings*, and since authors such as Neil Gaiman (*The Norse Gods*, 2018) and Maria Dahvana Headley (*The Mere Wife*, 2018) are increasingly turning to the Norse sagas and Anglo-Saxon epics such as *Beowulf*, blockbuster films dramatising the Icelandic sagas have significantly swelled the numbers of tourists to Iceland. All these record-breaking artefacts are the offspring of old stories, conjugated in different patterns.

The multiplicity marks the sheer abundance of material flowing through the web. We are seeing on the one hand a worldwide dissolution of boundaries and enclosures around global networks of culture—music, literature, knowledge, money, and nation states—and, at the same time, furious, countervailing oppositional forces (Brexit, Trump's wall, the Israeli wall surrounding Palestine, the miles of barbed wire rolled out throughout Europe, the detention centres and refugee camps that aim to contain these flows and prevent further movement of people). I see this as a contest between a classical geometry of Euclidian forms—the cube, the pyramid,which are defined containers that include some and exclude others—and a modern, fluid topology, as embodied by arabesque tiling patterns that keep generating and branching, endlessly dynamic and embracing, proliferating with exuberant variations and flipping figure and ground so that exclusion or inclusion need to be redefined.

The internet at its most fertile can be placed under the sign of such branching systems as the structure of the Arabian Nights, the generative arabesque of Arab ornament and the constellated *maqarnas* of Moorish architecture. As Marshall McLuhan noted some time ago: 'Electric circuitry is Orientalising the West. The contained, the distinct, the separate—our Western legacy—is being replaced by the flowing, the unified, the fused.'[16] Its social effects can be understood in this light. Its potential for connectivity generates clusters, rather in the same way as a tray of shapeless piles of sand or grit will, when its receptacle is shaken or vibrated, gradually settle into coherent and even beautiful patterns and relations. The messiness of the web can crystallise into sets of collectibles for the surfers of eBay, into groups of like-minded connoisseurs and hobbyists, of desirous specialists in taste for this or that, and Facebook friends. And one sphere of activity that can grow, through this efflorescing property of the internet, is narrative: the web is a sea of stories, where flowing streams of creative imagination meet and memories and fantasies intermingle.

2 Archival capacity and speed of retrieval

No matter how distant geographically or how abstruse the topic, the internet makes and will continue to make research accessible to a degree we could never before imagine. With the expanding digitisation of archives, as well as books, it is possible to land with quicksilver speed and a simple click or swipe on an item that would previously have taken a distant journey, and long days' trawling through dusty boxes.

The web offers genealogies of archival deposits at a previously unimaginable swiftness and breadth. But you must have the means to judge the quality of the information and to grasp its relations: the internet's vast hangars do not teach or train this use of the tool, and it is indeed crucial to its commercial operations that you don't know how to discriminate but only to crave more.

The capacity of the web gives users unprecedented access to literary material in archival forms, to manuscripts and to photography and other visual ephemera, while the British Library Sound Archive has built—and continues to build—a remarkable collection of writers' recordings. You can hear Alfred Tennyson reciting his poetry, his thin quaver making him feel much closer to our time than his pictures. The remarkable website UbuWeb continues to accrue an ever-growing anthology of avant-garde texts in several languages; on Asymptote and Library of Babel, compendia of works in translation are judiciously selected and presented, introducing visitors to literature from distant points on the globe, difficult to obtain or know about. It is telling that Asymptote's editor is based in Taiwan.

Andrea Brady, herself a fine innovative poet, has established *The Archive of the Now* on the web, a vast anthology of poets performing their work, sometimes specially for the site itself, and at other times during appearances at festivals. The collection spans a huge variety of voices and styles.[17] Brady's editorial interests do not lie with spoken-word poets as such, nor do the recordings attempt to be artefacts made for digital broadcasting, like music videos. *The Archive of the Now* is not as much a phenomenon of the times as several other platforms which do specialise in spoken word, such as Button Poetry. Button Poetry is based in America and its stars, for example Neil Hilborn and the British-born Suli Breaks, reach—literally—millions of views, followed by a terrific rise in book sales for the writers involved.

3 Proximity and connectedness

The internet also interacts symbiotically with the mass movements of peoples, including those fleeing war zones, as it can keep them in touch retrospectively with their dispersed relatives, their abandoned mother tongues and, prospectively, with their longed-for destinations elsewhere. The powers of the mobile phone with its camera and its recorder are both lifesavers and catalysts for all the people swept up in the huge dislocations convulsing the world. Young refugees in Sicily, who have landed there after risking the terrible passage across the Mediterranean, hold on to their mobiles when all else has gone. When they have no papers or possessions, they will keep a sealed waterproof pouch around their necks to hold the device. If they lose their phone at sea, it is one of the first things the authorities try to provide for them, or they choose to acquire: earphones dangling their white cables are a symbol of their human citizenship of the world. The new arrivals in Europe are extremely adept at using them, at Instagram and Facebook, WhatsApp and Snapchat: for example, if they are played a word or phrase in a foreign language they have software to find its equivalent in a language the refugee understands.

As Virginia Heffernan points out, in *Magic and Loss: The Internet As Art*, it is the poor and disadvantaged who desire and need this kind of connectivity, but that is not a reason to despise it.[18] Immense distances, social and physical, have shrunk through telecommunications; clusters of individuals and even large proportions of some populations are regrouping in different patterns in other places, as their conversations across space bring them closer. This new proximity shrinks the world and also flattens it; as horizons grow nearer, the sense of time also changes: the past feels closer, the future more graspable.

These powerful, productive qualities of internet reading and writing—agility, speed, range, accumulation, connectivity, acceleration and proximity—have immensely fertile potential. When words are sounded and accompanied by images, such sensory effects can help overcome the fugitive character of digital communication and imprint the poem or work more deeply on memory and its processes. The web mimics the branching and firing of the brain in many ways, or at least it appears to offer a dazzling mirror of thought itself, its aleatory quickness of association and retrieval. But this effect of replication, of the software acting as a quasi-organic prosthesis for the mind, is misleading, and this delusion, and the damaging effects that are consequent upon it, need some attention and redress through other channels of inquiry. For one of the sharpest problems of digital technology and literature arises from the data's immateriality, which leads to sensory deprivation and the attenuation of haptic knowledge.

The chief drawback of internet reading arises from the absence of the full sensorium, and this lack can't be fixed by adding scratch-and-sniff patches to the screen—a whiff of lime blossom or a salt breeze—or embedding them in virtual-reality headsets, as no doubt will happen. The *mémoire involontaire* Proust tapped into required acts in space and time (stubbing his toe, dunking the madeleine in the tea) to activate the connections; his novel then retrieves and reorganises the co-ordinated senses and feelings involved in acts of memory—and in acts of imagination as memories are re-membered, resurrected and reimagined. We all know how memories of someone or of a story can come back to mind by reorienting oneself in space, to where one was at the time; the neuroscientists tell us this returns us to our beginnings as hunters and our needs to sense where we were in relation to others—to helpers, to prey, to dangers. Similar ancient capacities form our sense of smell.

In many epic moments—in Homer, in Virgil—the writer will hand over the story to a speaker—a bard or a storyteller inside the narrative—and describe how the recitation has an overwhelmingly moving and disturbing effect on the audience. We are invited to read into the story the sound, the voice and the body of the narrator-performer, and we hear the performance couched in the ongoing flow of the verse and its metre; these suggestions tighten the screw on our emotions, too, as well as on Penelope, Helen, Dido or Desdemona, who are standing in here for the inflamed reader. Haun Saussy calls this 'oral embodiment', which literally enfleshes the text by projecting it through a narrator. The summonses to such figments helps cancel out the fictive qualities—the necessarily phantom-like nature of a written text when read silently to oneself. 'Rhythm is the technology of oral inscription, and the human body with brain and muscle...has been for ages its material base,' as Olga Soloviev comments.[19] Delivering words on the vibrations of the voice helps overcome the fugitive character of words on a screen, especially because the timbre, the accent, the musicality of the reciter all inflect the words with meaning, in the same way as a pianist will enrich a piece in a new performance, even when it is familiar.

4 Acoustic redress

After a brief spell of silent reading from the page—an era that lasted, roughly speaking, from mass printing and mass literacy to the invention of radio and the wireless technologies that followed—literature is returning to its ancient habit of performed events, orally communicated. The web has made possible new forms of acoustic and oral performance—records of everything from elegies to stand-up comedy. It has become a forum for innovatory literary work, although, when we consider literature on the web, ambiguity wraps the very nature of literature itself.

The artist Taryn Simon recently created, in a subterranean panopticon in Islington, an installation called *An Occupation of Loss*.[20] In the cells arranged around the central courtyard of this disturbing bunker small groups stood or sat: men and women, usually swathed in black, sometimes in white, they came from twenty different cultures. After a single voice was raised in lamentation, they all began singing—or rather keening, for they were all mourners by profession, who had come from Japan, Albania, Ghana, Azerbaijan, Korea and elsewhere, and are employed at funeral rites to help the dead person to leave this existence and pass over into the next world, to commemorate the deeds and character of the deceased, and to console the bereaved, weeping and crying out on their behalf.

I had misgivings about Simon's piece, because it does not seem to honour the distinctiveness of each mourner's tradition, but merges them together to express meanings of her own. However, the relevant question to pose here, in relation to literature and digital media, arises from the oral quality of the laments: is this literature at all? It is verbal, it has been committed to memory from a long time ago, remembered over unfathomable distances of time in several cases, and, as far as the audience knows, it only exists as voiced by the professionals whose chosen role requires them to know the words by heart, and in some cases, to embroider them to fit the occasion and the circumstances of the dead person's life and character—be it a child, a man or a woman.

If the laments were written down, most of us, it is fair to say, would include them in the annals of literature: when Wordsworth and Coleridge called their collection *Lyrical Ballads*, they were consecrating a spring of inspiration: popular anonymous poems written by culture itself as it were:

> … will no one tell me what she sings
> Perhaps the plaintive numbers flow
> for old unhappy far off things
> and battles long ago.[21]

The Albanian writer Ismail Kadaré, in a thoughtful essay about the origins of tragedy, independently evokes the lamentations of his country's culture in relation to literary innovation. He takes an anthropological view, stressing the communal character of the impulse to create, and its social function—to testify, grieve for the dead and redeem the crimes of the past in order to safeguard the future. He writes: 'Just as the man who after rain falls on him unexpectedly remembers the crimes of his youth, so the conscience of the Greeks was surprisingly awoken, and in its age of maturity the Greek nation remembered a crime it had committed in its childhood. Eight hundred years ago the Greeks had suffocated the Trojans in their sleep… If you were to take out the rotting corpse of Troy from Greek literature, the canon would be diminished by at least half.'[22]

He senses an intimate connection with his own culture's rituals of mourning—and situates the first stirrings of art in funeral chants and their joyful counterpart, marriage songs or epithalamia—which still continue, he points out, all over the Balkans, as in many parts of the world.

The United Nations has started to respond to the immaterial needs of displaced peoples and stated that cultural heritage—connectedness and belonging established through memory and imagination—should be considered a human right. Such compass points are formed, often, not by material goods, but by intangible artefacts: by words spoken, recited, performed, sung and remembered. They may travel by ethereal conduits, especially in the age of the internet when they are at one and the same time vigorous and fragile. They may inhere in things, containers of memories and history. In 2003, UNESCO declared protection for intangible cultural heritage, but the dominant implication was that this applied principally to the culture of unlettered peoples—to orature. This needs adjusting: highly literate civilisations also flourish through oral—performed, played—channels of transmission.

The traffic in mobile myths is rising with the strong and omnipresent return of acoustics to communication—we have entered a hybrid era, in which the oral is no longer placed in opposition to the literate. When Jorge Luis Borges once commented that he had always 'imagined Paradise will be a kind of library', it is interesting to remember that the great writer was himself blind for a great part of his life, and was read to—books for him were *sounded*.[23]

The web is a performance space, a kind of electronic theatre, which gives poets and writers of other genres a medium that includes sound, gesture and image accompanying the word. 'Spoken word' performances in live venues differ fundamentally from web-based artefacts, but they can then be transferred, archivally perpetuated, in digital form on to the web where they remain, capturing moments in time, however distant, as if they were happening here and now. The symbiosis between these two manifestations replicates the movement between Demodocus' live recitation of the epic he knows by heart and sings and the record of his song in Homer's epic which has reached us in a manuscript made at some point long after the events evoked in the poem, after the scene of their recitation, and after the creation by the figure or figures we know as Homer. The poem we know is a transcription, and in some profound way its immateriality shares a kinship with the immateriality of the new medium, the internet. In both media the originary performance counteracts this phantom-like unreality—it feeds the ghosts, if you like.

5 Sonic mapping

For the writer and artist Caroline Bergvall the acoustics of writing matter as much as its semantic message. She has currently undertaken to redraw the linguistic map and create a new, inclusive 'sonic atlas'. To this end, she has been collecting *aubades*, or dawn songs, from all over the world, in small languages beginning with Provençal where these poems of lovers parting at dawn are often thought to originate—as well as Breton, Maltese, Icelandic, Welsh, Cornish and other tongues, some threatened with extinction. I heard a performance at the 2017 Poetry Festival in London: she recited her text, quoting some of the poems, and was accompanied by trombone and electronic music. Her interest in languages focuses on their acoustic character, and she listens in to the music of the words, as what they say cannot and should not be attended to as distinct or separate from their meaning. It is very striking, for example, that when you look up a poem on the web, the explanation of what it is saying often appears alongside it as helpful teaching notes, but this denatures the original, missing altogether the reasons for the poem's beauty and effectiveness. In an early work, *Alyson Singes*, Bergvall speaks in the voice of the Wife of Bath, creating a babel-like cascade of words, which she calls 'glottic profusion'.[24] In more recent works, *Meddle English* (2011) and the most recent, remarkable composition, *Drift* (2014), she experiments with multi-channel, multimedia expression to produce a tormented text of testimony that turns outwards to events in the world and inwards to her own specific conditions of identity.[25]

Norwegian on her father's side and French on her mother's, Bergvall has adopted English as her language and London as her home and explores her own chosen *dépaysement* through mapping territories of language and sounds in her work. She presses hard on her own English, which she speaks with an unplaceable accent, strikes harmonics off other cultures and their linguistic expressions, and revels in those parts of speech that might elude, one might imagine, robotic recognition software: 'the materiality of voice, its tics, spit, accent, errors'.[26]

The acoustic maps she creates are absorptive and ritualistic enactments, which deliberately oppose themselves to the losses and fissures that are reducing linguistic richness and attenuating collective belonging in the riven circumstances of global war and disasters. Bergvall is conscious that the music of a language sets ringing political reverberations, and has been concerned with the intersection between language and ethnic cleansing since her early 2001 piece *Say Parsley*. Here, she explores the ever-present threat that 'How you speak will be used against you' through an historical incidence of hostilities that took place in 1937 in the Dominican Republic, when *perejil*, the word for parsley in Spanish, became the brutal test: if you could not pronounce the 'r' Spanish style, you were murdered.[27]

Drift, a rich and multi-layered work on the page, has also been staged as an immersive installation of great power. It tells the story of a boat full of refugees who in 2011 set out from Libya; they were abandoned by the traffickers without fuel or water to drift in the Mediterranean and they were given no help by anyone, including many who noticed them, until everybody on board died of thirst or drowned. It gives an account of this contemporary event—a matter for horror and shame—on many levels of language and visuals: frantic repetitive Cy Twombly-like drawings, aerial reconnaissance photographs of the doomed *gommone* or rubber boat, charts and log of the boat's terrible lost wanderings on the open sea, reports of the coastguards as they tracked its drift, and the accounts of sightings and failures to come to the passengers' rescue. These elements, now starkly registered and documented in official jargons, now scrambled in anguish, wrap around the core of the book, a reworking of the medieval Anglo-Saxon poem *The Seafarer*, an epic narrative of heroic sea voyaging; these sections consist of archaically spelt blocks of sounds and unfamiliar words that force you as a reader to sound them in your mouth to get at the sense. She jumbles and scatters and cuts up what she is making so that meaning leaks out of the gaps, according to William Burroughs' principle that 'When you cut into the present the future leaks out'.

Besides *The Seafarer*, the Vinland sagas, the epics of Erik the Red and the poetic Edda all flow into this work. She invokes sea drifters of the Christian past, Saints Brendan and Cuthbert; she has dropped anchor in the marine wildernesses of her Norse ancestry: she is enthralled by ice. But she has also performed a truly harrowing act of witness as she sounds out anonymous writings from the past and other bearers of memory.

Displacement brings with it encounters with unfamiliar tongues. Bergvall is very alive to the difficulties of acquiring a foreign tongue and inhabiting it: her own adoption of English 'also showed', she has written, 'the extent of the negative and destructive hold language can have on us. And this, of course, applies to all sorts of majoritarian or segregational histories. So it is crucial and really exciting to me that a writer's language can both release these and also create new linguistic connections and emotional fields. Renewed worlds.'[28]

6 Voices

The internet is amassing a global, digital archive of great richness, conserving the artefacts of artist-writers like Bergvall. However, this is not the only way the www is changing the ways we encounter literature now. At a more radical level, the digital potential of the web has been changing the modes of literature itself, the ways writers put it out for their public. Recording and storing work, even performance and spoken word differs from creating poetry and stories for dissemination by digital media, combining sound, gesture and image with the words.

The poet Warsan Shire is Somali-British; she was born in Kenya, probably in the huge refugee camp Daabad, and was the first ever Young Poet Laureate for London in 2013. In Shire's poetry, her irregular diction and take-it-or-leave-it line breaks intentionally sound like someone talking; the poems flaunt their orality. They could be tweets or text messages strung together, provoking adverse critics to rail at the flouting of formal poetic rules.[29]

I first came across her when a friend sent me a postcard, which proclaimed: 'I'M WRITING TO YOU FROM THE FUTURE TO TELL YOU THAT EVERYTHING WILL BE OKAY.'

The words are printed on crinkly gold sweet paper, like the wrapper of a mackintosh toffee, and I was very struck by them: the gentle but incisive irony of their reassurance, the way Shire was taking up occupation of the prophetic role.

Warsan Shire might have languished in the corners of poetry festivals, but her work was noticed by Beyoncé, the world star and singer, lately turned feminist champion, and she invited her to California where she worked adapting some of her poems to Beyoncé's music video, *Lemonade*. The album-film is named in honour of her husband Jay-Z's grandmother Hattie White, who had a saying: 'I was served lemons but I made lemonade.'[30] Grandmothers feature prominently, lovingly, mythically, in the work of many of these writers on the web; they figure tradition and, above all, orality: old wives' tales, proverbial wisdom, down-home knowledge.

Among Shire's poems, 'Anger' and 'For women who are difficult to love…' inspired Beyoncé's reworkings. Here is the former: nin.tl/Anger And here the latter: nin.tl/Difficult

Shire's most powerful and rightly celebrated poem, 'Home', with audience figures in their tens of thousands on the web, is directed towards rising racism against refugees

and immigrants. It's a witness statement, truthful, angry—
in one recording her voice breaks with feeling that sounds
true.[31]

It opens:

> no one leaves home unless
> home is the mouth of a shark
> you only run for the border
> when you see the whole city running as well

and towards the middle includes this unforgettable sentence:

> that no one puts their children in a boat
> unless the water is safer than the land...[32]

The voice is Shire's, but its tone sounds all over the web: it
transmits defiance, protest, testimony. These forms of direct
address and declaratory rhetoric suit the medium, for it
shares in the historic character of the agora, the forum, the
soapbox and the pulpit.

Such writers have assumed the role of porte-parole for
society's conscience, the ancient part of the memory-keeper,
the skald, the bard, though these labels have a kind of fustian
timbre, from which we flinch today. They are speaking of
things they have heard—the susurrations of the tribe—or
things they have only sensed, the task being to catch them
on the go. Writing does often involve private writers in
public lamenting—and less often in jubilating, too. Susannah
Herbert, the Director of the Forward Poetry Foundation has
noted that there is a distinct audience today for spoken-word
performances—it is much larger than the usual audience
for poetry readings. It is made up, she says, of 'an informal
community', engaged in 'a participatory activity'; the places

where it gathers are closer to music venues.[33] The poems respond to the moment, are usually in the first person and frequently draw on personal experience: the witness statement and the lyric are the grounds of its flowerings and are created to be performed instantly—immediacy is of the essence. Often, such poems are only recited once, but then their life continues on the web, as they are uploaded to YouTube by fans, and supplemented with a montage of images and drawings which respond to the material.

As Herbert also notes, these are 'communities of affirmation'; several of its orators have religious backgrounds in childhood and have even been child preachers. Techno-orality asks for works with a speaking quality—not prose or poetry mouthed silently to oneself when reading or absorbed quickly by sight alone. The medium favours cries and groans, what Samuel Beckett calls, referring to Lucky's railing, *vociferations*. Its grandfather is Allen Ginsberg, the author of *Howl*, its family the Beats in general. It is close to prose that imitates music, jiving, scat, free-form jazz—Kerouac's *On the Road*. The lineage offers itself to cultures where books are expensive and lending libraries poorly served: the continent of Africa has a flourishing literature online—performed, to sound and gesture. The BBC made two very well-researched programmes with a Johannesburg poet, Thabiso Moare: the first called *Another Kind of Stage*, the second *Breaking the Window with a Poem*, which were broadcast on 17 and 24 March 2018, but are sadly no longer available on iPlayer. This is truly a shame, as Moare interviewed and discussed the work of poet-performers from Kenya, Nigeria and South Africa, unlikely to find their way into print there or anywhere; not because of the quality of their writing, but because it was composed for this medium, the internet, and because poetry publishing struggles everywhere.

These performers in words have taken up the instruments of the griots, the storytellers and mourners of west Africa, and their work could be assigned to the category of protest song or lyric, to slam and rap and doing the dozens, or jousting with words. But, in my view, these practices are literary. Think of flyting (a contest or dispute in verse form) in Scotland, or of those poetic duels at which the poets of the Abbasid court had to excel when they were pitted against one another by their masters; for these writers—and they were writers, prized for their exquisite calligraphy as well as their wit—were bought and sold as slaves.[34]

This voice has a proud tradition in cultures once perceived as subaltern, and it expresses the impulse to defy that perception and for individuals to speak in their own voice. But it would be a mistake to think the technotext that flourishes online is an especially postcolonial literature.

The most versatile of these new bardic voices encountered during my own browsing is Hollie McNish. She was brought up in Luton and has a light, young and ardent voice. Her range is wide, her material endlessly inventive, as she rises to occasion after occasion, creating love songs of real charm and tenderness as well as anthems of rage, such as the blazing litany, 'A British National Breakfast', inspired by Brexit, and one of the most eloquent testimonials to the contract with imperialist assumptions that Brexit battens on and feeds.[35] Aiming many deadly shafts at those who remain wilfully blind to the interdependency of the British on other peoples, she closes:

Claiming that 'foreigners' have ruined their lives. Finish their day with a cup of hot cocoa. Beans made in Kenya.

Profits to Tesco. Complaining in bed about closing sea
borders, They don't learn Spanish and Retire to Majorca

Conclusion

The links between custom, ritual and literary culture are
becoming tighter, I believe, through the connectivity of the
internet, which can gather participants together and form
a 'community of fate'. Is Morrison right when she calls
language and image 'mere godlings'? I respect both more,
and I fear them. Literature on the web deploys both language
and image, and establishes, through its imagery and vision,
another form of secular assembly, distinct from the political
demo or the mourning ritual for the dead, but no less potent;
the web acts as their powerful transmitter. Language and
image are principles of energy, close to light and gravity, as
they pulse and fire across the world; literature is their most
powerful vehicle, and it can now be ridden on the waves of
the internet.

Acknowledgements

A BOOK LIKE THIS always derives from the vision, ideas and assistance of many. First and foremost I must thank my colleagues in the *Wasafiri* office and my colleagues at Queen Mary, University of London, who have helped me deliver this project in numerous ways—especially Rukhsana Yasmin, who helped build the proposal, shared my enthusiasm for the book and participated in some of the initial commissioning, Matthew Lecznar who managed the administration and supported the copy-editing throughout, Sana Goyal, Emily Mercer, Pauline Walker and Malachi McIntosh.

Thanks too to all the wonderful staff at Myriad Editions, who have patiently nurtured the book's not-always-smooth evolution, bringing it to fruition. It was definitely the energy and commitment of Candida Lacey who picked up on the book's significance and importance that fired me to do it; since then, Chris Brazier has been an eagle-eyed copy editor as well as much more than this; thanks too to Emma Dowson and the rest of the Myriad team for supporting its promotion.

My long-suffering family have had to endure the coming to a head of three big projects this year and have supported me in every possible way. Apart from providing regular meals, insisting I get away from my desk and being good listeners, they have also been most valuable readers and editors, especially Maya Caspari, my daughter.

Looking back at the content of past issues of *Wasafiri*, the many editorials I have written over the years and my academic publications, I realise that the concept I chose for this book was already present, if only in embryonic form, over twenty years ago. Its concept is of course central to the mission of the magazine but its pertinence to the contemporary political moment has grown out of many conversations I have had and which are still ongoing with colleagues and writer friends.

Last but certainly not least I must thank all the writers who have so generously contributed their often most personal reflections and words, sharing their personal libraries, experiences and vision. I know all of you gave up valuable time to do this, mostly when it was not convenient and were fast to respond to editorial queries; especially Githa Hariharan and Mukoma Wa Ngugi who were swift to join the project with little notice due to unexpected editorial changes. Thanks are due also to: *World Literature Today*, where a version of Githa Hariharan's essay was published online (*World Literature Today* 91, no 2, March 2017, worldlit.org); the University of Michigan Press, which published an earlier version of Mukoma Wa Ngugi's piece on the Politics of African Writing, in *The Rise of the African Novel: Politics of Language, Politics and Ownership* (University of Michigan Press, Ann Arbor, 2018); and to the Freud Museum, which published part of Eva Hoffman's 'Seeking the Tree of Life' in *Lost Childhood and the Language of Exile* (Freud Museum, London, 2007)

Finally my thanks to Caryl Phillips for agreeing to write the preface to the book and also for his vision in the opening essay to *Colour Me English* (Harvill Secker, London, 2011). It was this reflection on the personal that moves outwards, flagging the vital space which the room of literature can provide for dialogue and debate, which partly inspired the frame for this anthology.

Susheila Nasta

Endnotes

Introduction

1 In 2019, Shonibare's installation was rehoused at Tate Modern in London. As is now evident from the room housing the 'library', it not only continues to be capacious, but the depth of the stories it tells are further weighted by a series of digital and media archives, which provide detail on the viewpoints and perspectives of individual authors.

2 *Wasafiri* developed out of the activities of ATCAL (the Association for the Teaching of African, Caribbean and Associated Literatures), founded at the University of Kent in 1978.

3 In his review, 'Orwell v Huxley: whose dystopia are we living in today?' (*Financial Times*, 18 January 2019) John Lanchester makes the point that since Donald Trump's election in the US, George Orwell's *Nineteen Eighty-Four* has soared to the top of the bestseller lists worldwide. See also:
www.ft.com/content/aa8ac620-1818-11e9-b93e-f4351a53f1c3

4 Salman Rushdie, *Imaginary Homelands* (Granta Books, London, 1991), pp 393-429.

5 Margaret Atwood, 'Everybody is Happy Now', *The Guardian*, 17 November 2007.

6 In 2004, a spectacular protest against oppression was held at the Kangla Fort by 12 naked Indian women. See: https://frontline.thehindu.com/static/html/fl2117/stories/20040827002903700.htm

7 Caryl Phillips, *Colour Me English* (Harvill Secker, London, 2011), p 16.

'Call Yourself English?'

1 Octavio Paz, *The Other Voice* (Carcanet, 1992), p 88.

2 James Kelman, *Some Recent Attacks: Essays Cultural and Political* (AK Press, 1992), p 9.

3 Salman Rushdie, 'A General Election', in *Imaginary Homelands* (Vintage, 2010), pp 159-162.

4 Ibid, p 162.

5 Octavio Paz, *op cit*, pp 77-98.

The Good Brown Girl: questioning obedience in Indo-Caribbean women

1 Shivanee Ramlochan, *Everyone Knows I Am a Haunting* (Peepal Tree Press, Leeds, 2017).

2 Gaiutra Bahadur, *Coolie Woman: The Odyssey of Indenture* (Hurst & Co, London, 2013), pp 106-7.

The Tablet: a modern séance with Aldous Huxley
1 Aldous Huxley, *Brave New World Revisited* (Triad Panther, 1983), p 41.
2 Ibid, pp 92-93
3 Sources: Aldous Huxley, Speech at UC Berkeley, 'The Ultimate Revolution', 1962 (YouTube); 'The Wallace Interview,' 1958 (YouTube); 'Speaking Personally,' Huxley on CD, Artifact Music.

Seeking the Tree of Life
1 Benedict Anderson, *Imagined Communities: Reflections on the Origin and Spread of Nationalism* (Verso, London/New York, 1983/2006).
2 WH Auden, *The Dyer's Hand and Other Essays* (Random House, New York, 1982, Faber & Faber, 1983).
3 James Wood, 'On Not Going Home', *London Review of Books*, 20 February 2014.

The Minds of Writers
1 This essay was first delivered in 1923 and published in 1924 by the Hogarth Press, London.
2 The full text of this essay is available in *Selected Essays: Virginia Woolf* (Oxford University Press, 2008).
3 Erna Brodber, *Myal* (Waveland Press, 2014, p 106).
4 The full statement can be found at http://thetropixs.com/buju-banton-releases-statement-on-boom-bye-bye.
5 Mel Cooke, 'Bye Bye, Boom Bye Bye', *The Gleaner*, 4 June 2015, http://jamaica-gleaner.com/article/entertainment/20150604/bye-bye-boom-bye-bye
6 Mel Cooke, 'Matters Of "It"', *The Gleaner*, 26 June 2015, http://jamaica-gleaner.com/article/entertainment/20150625/matters-it
7 Cooke, 'Bye...' op cit.
8 Ibid.

What a Time to be a (Black) (British) (Womxn) Writer
1 Chidera Eggerue, *What a Time to Be Alone: The Slumflower's Guide to Why You Are Already Enough* (Quadrille Publishing, 2018).
2 Michelle Cliff, 'Caliban's Daughter', *Journal of Caribbean Literatures*, vol 3, no 3, 2003, pp 157–160, p 157.
3 Audre Lorde, *Sister Outsider: Essays and Speeches* (Crossing Press, 1984/2007), p 41.
4 Shabnam Grewal, Jackie Kay, Liliane Landor, Gail Lewis & Pratibha Parmar (editors), *Charting the Journey, Writings by Black and Third World Women* (Sheba Feminist Press, 1988).

The Dinner that Changed My Life
1 All names have been changed.

2 Bantustans or homelands established in South Africa during the apartheid era. The Blacks were forced to move to them to separate them from the Whites.

3 Goy is the Jewish name for a non-Jew

4 'Nakba'—Arabic for catastrophe—is the term used to describe the forced removal in 1948 of some two-thirds of the Palestinians from what became Israel by Jewish forces and later, after the establishment of the state, by the Israeli army.

The Politics of Writing Popular Fiction: challenging the African literary tradition

1 A version of this essay appeared in *The Rise of the African Novel: Politics of Language, Politics and Ownership* (University of Michigan Press, Ann Arbor, 2018).

2 Mukoma Wa Ngugi, *Nairobi Heat* (Melville House, New York, 2010).

3 Terry Barringer, 'Life is a Thriller: Investigating African crime fiction: selected papers from the 9th International Janheinz Jahn Symposium', Mainz 2008.

4 Frantz Fanon, *The Wretched of the Earth*, translated by Constance Farrington (Penguin, London, 1967), p 27 and p 74.

5 Ibid, p 217. See Fanon's chapter, 'Concerning Violence.'

6 Frantz Fanon, op cit.

7 Chinua Achebe, *Hopes and Impediments: Selected Essays* (Anchor Books, Doubleday, New York, 1989), p 67.

When Bodies Speak: the politics of rewriting Draupadi

1 Gayatri Chakravorty Spivak's translation of this appeared in *Critical Inquiry*, vol 8, No 2, Winter, 1981, pp 381-402.

2 Manipur is a state in Northeast India, bordering with Myanmar.

3 Armed Forces (Special Powers) Acts are Acts of the Parliament of India that grant special powers to the Indian Armed Forces in 'disturbed areas'. Accusations and justifications like these are common in Manipur. The AFSPA was introduced by the British in 1942 in response to the anti-colonial Quit India Movement. The later Partition of India in 1947 left the majority of princely states with an undecided future; Manipur only became part of the Indian Union in 1972.

4 See nin.tl/Draupadi

The Myth of Integration: continuing racisms and inequalities in the Global North

1 Lu Xun was considered the father of modern Chinese literature whose works were widely known as a powerful critique of the establishment. He was also one of founding members of the May Fourth Movement of 1919.

2 The term 'migrant' refers to someone who leaves home and moves to another place, whether within their own country or crossing national borders, regardless of what causes them to migrate and for what aims.
3 Pierre Tevanian, with afterword by Said Bouamama), *La mécanique raciste* (Editions La Découverte, Paris, 2017).

Art and the Lower Orders

1 The author's *How Late It Was, How Late* (Secker & Warburg, London, 1994).
2 The writer Trevor Royle for the Scottish Arts Council and the poet Stewart Conn for BBC Radio Scotland.
3 The play was based on the execution of the weavers Andrew Hardie and John Baird in 1820 for their part in the Scottish Insurrection.
4 Writer-in-Residence to the Renfrew District Libraries Service.
5 *The Busconductor Hines* (Polygon Press, 1984).
6 Alick Buchanan-Smith.
7 Tangerine Press.

All the Feels: vulnerability as political vision

1 Audre Lorde, *Conversations with Audre Lorde*, edited by Joan Wylie Hall (University Press of Mississippi, Jackson, 2004), p 91.
2 Gaylene Gould, Facebook discussion reproduced with permission. Personal Facebook account, 28 March 2019.
3 I am paraphrasing her points here as it was not a public post. I do have permission to reference the discussion.
4 Gaylene Gould, op cit.
5 'The Uses of Anger' is published in *Women's Studies Quarterly,* Vol 25, No 1 / 2. Reproduced in *Looking Back, Moving Forward: 25 Years of Women's Studies History*, (Feminist Press, New York, 1997), pp 278-285.
6 Mona Eltahawy, 'What Would The World Look Like If We Taught Girls To Rage', *NBC News*, 1 February 2018, nin.tl/Eltahawy
7 Mona Eltahawy, 'I Swear To Make Patriarchy Uncomfortable', *NBC News*, 6 May 2018, nin.tl/Eltahawy2
8 Audre Lorde, 'The Uses of Anger', p 280.
9 I want to make a clear distinction between what I have tried to outline above in terms of a culture that only rejects without offering a position, and calling out injustice consistently.
10 I am aware that not all encounters with fictional worlds and characters can be followed with political action, nor need it. I am purposely phrasing it in this manner to highlight that everything we do is political and there is, in this sense, no difference between political and non-political fiction.
11 Sara Ahmed, *The Cultural Politics of Emotion* (Routledge, New York, 2007), p 6.

12 Deborah Gould, 'On Affect and Protest', *Political Emotions*, edited by
    Janet Staiger, Ann Cvetkovich & Ann Reynolds (Routledge, New York,
    2010), pp 18-45.
13 Jasmine Syedullah, 'Radicalizing Dharma Dreams', *Radical Dharma:
    Talking Race, Love and Liberation*, co-authors Rev angel Kyodo williams,
    Lama Rod Owens (North Atlantic Books, Berkeley, 2016), p 84.
14 Deborah Gould, op cit, p 26.
15 Ibid, p 32.
16 Phoebe Boswell, tweet published on 25 March 2019. Reproduced with
    permission. Twitter handle @PhoebeBoswell.
17 Rianna Jade Parker, 'How Artist Phoebe Boswell Teaches Us to Heal
    Our Wounds'. *Frieze Magazine*, 4 February 2019, nin.tl/Frieze
18 Deborah Gould, op cit, p 24.
19 Sara Ahmed has written at length about how speaking up can be
    used, even among feminists, to blame the one raising concerns for
    creating the 'upset', the tension of/in a situation. Her call to be feminist
    killjoys is to be aware of these dynamics and to not let them silence
    us. Black and brown bodies often create tension by pure arrival in a
    situation because they are already marked as upsetting the 'happy
    situation', where certain things can be overlooked and do not have to
    be addressed.
20 Chastity Chandler, guest speaker on the *Therapy for Black Girls* Podcast,
    'Session 96: Exploring Vulnerability', 27 February 2019,
    nin.tl/Chandler

The Bravado of Books

1 J-P Sartre, *Words*, translated by Irene Clephane, (Penguin Books,
   London, 1967/2000).
2 MM Bakhtin, *The Dialogic Imagination: Three Essays*, edited by Michael
   Holquist, translated by Caryl Emerson and Michael Holquist (University
   of Texas Press, Austin, 1981).
3 Byung-Chul Han, *The Transparency Society*, translated by Erik Butler,
   (Stanford University Press, 2015).
4 WH Auden, 'In Memory of WB Yeats,' from *Selected Poems*, edited by
   Edward Mendelson (Faber and Faber, London, 1979, pp 80-82).

Out Loud: the experience of literature in the digital space

1 'The medium is the message' is the title of the first chapter in Marshall
   McLuhan, *Understanding Media: The Extensions of Man* (New American
   Library, New York, 1964).
2 Eugenio Trías, 'Thinking Religion: The Symbol and the Sacred', in
   Religion, edited by Jacques Derrida and Gianni Vattimo, translated
   by David Webb (Polity Press, Cambridge, 1998); see p 110, note 6 in
   particular.

3 Paul Cummins and Tom Piper's installation *Blood Swept Lands and Seas of Red*, Tower of London, July–November 2014, was extended in response to huge public demand. This was a commissioned artwork, and an unprecedented ceremony that adapted religious requiems to a secular context. Its aesthetic value was questionable in my view, but its emotional pull undeniable—crowds flocked to take part, planting the ceramic poppies until the huge castle was gradually lapped by a blood-red tide, www.hrp.org.uk/TowerOfLondon/poppies.

4 Toni Morrison, 'Being or Becoming the Stranger' in *The Origin of Others* (Harvard University Press, 2017), pp 35-36.

5 Bruce Robbins, 'Prolepsis and catastrophe', in Paulo Horta and Philip Kennedy, eds, *Reinventing World Literature* (NYU Press, New York), forthcoming.

6 Ibid.

7 The story was first published in the Argentine journal *Sur* in 1940. For the English translation, see *Fictions*, translated by Andrew Hurley (Penguin, London, 2000), pp 7-25.

8 Florence Dupont, *The Invention of Literature: From Greek Intoxication to the Latin Book*, translated by Janet Lloyd (John Hopkins University Press, Baltimore, 1999), p 11.

9 See Haun Saussy, *The Ethnography of Rhythm: Orality and its Technologies* (Fordham University Press, New York, 2016), and Florence Dupont, *The Invention of Literature: From Greek Intoxication to the Latin Book* (Johns Hopkins University Press, Baltimore, 1999).

10 Alice Oswald, William Tillyer, *Nobody* (21 Publishing, London, 2018); Alice Oswald, *Memorial: An Excavation of the Iliad* (Faber & Faber, London, 2012); Alice Oswald, *Falling Awake* (WW Norton & Co, New York, 2018); Alice Oswald, *Nobody* (Jonathan Cape, London, 2019).

11 For a published translation of his poems, see www.amazon.com/Jerusalem-Other-Poems-Written-1997-2017,dp/1566560233

12 Rebecca Watts, 'The Cult of the Noble Amateur', *PN Review* 239 Number 3, January-February 2018, www.pnreview.co.uk/cgi-bin/scribe?item_id=10090 [accessed 7 February 2019].

13 Italo Calvino, *Six Memos for the Next Millennium*, translated by William Weaver (Faber & Faber, London, 1999).

14 Marina Warner, *Once Upon a Time: A Short History of Fairy* Tale (Oxford University Press, 2014). p 45.

15 See Marina Warner 'The Politics of Translation', *London Review of Books*, vol 40 No 19, 11 October 2018, pages 21-24, and Marina Warner's William Matthews Memorial Lecture, June 2015, entitled 'Translumination or Travesty? The Passage into English', also published in *Other Worlds: The Journal for Literary Translators*, Winter 2015, Number 46.

16 Marshall McLuhan quoted in Virginia Heffernan, *Magic and Loss: The Internet as Art* (Simon & Schuster, London, 2017), p 30.

Endnotes

17 See Andrea Brady, *Wildfire: A verse essay on obscurity and illumination* (Krupskaya Books, 2010), and *Mutability: Scripts for Infancy* (University of Chicago, 2012). The archive of authors can be found here: www.archiveofthenow.org/authors [last accessed 28 February 2019].

18 Virginia Heffernan, *Magic and Loss: The Internet as Art* (Simon & Schuster, London, 2017), p 25.

19 See Olga Soloviev's foreword in Haun Sassy, *The Ethnography of Rhythm: Orality and its Technologies* (Fordham University Press, New York, 2016).

20 See www.artangel.org.uk/project/an-occupation-of-loss/ or the catalogue published, Taryn Simon, *An Occupation of Loss* (Hatje Kantz, Berlin, 2017).

21 William Wordsworth, 'The Solitary Reaper', www.poets.org/poetsorg/poem/solitary-reaper [accessed 28 February 2019].

22 Ismail Kadare, 'Aeschylus, the Lost', *Asymptote*, www.asymptotejournal.com/nonfiction/ismail-kadare-aeschylus-the-lost [accessed 7 February 2019].

23 Jorge Luis Borges, *Dreamtigers*, translated by Mildred Boyer and Harold Morland (University of Texas Press, Austin, 1964).

24 Caroline Bergvall, *Drift* (Nightboat Books, Brooklyn and Callicoon, 2014).

25 Ibid.

26 Eva Heisler, 'Caroline Bergvall: Propelled to the Edges of a Language's Freedom, and to the Depths of its Collective Traumas', *Asymptote Journal*, www.asymptotejournal.com/visual/eva-heisler-caroline-bergvall-propelled-to-the-edges-of-a-languages-freedom Accessed 1 April.

27 Ibid.

28 Ibid.

29 Warsan Shire, *Teaching My Mother to Give Birth*, Mouthmark. Find her on twitter@Warsan_shire.

30 See nin.tl/realblackgrandmothers accessed 1 March 2019.

31 Warsan Shire, 'Home', *The Rights Angle* nin.tl/Home (Video by Garrett Mogge) [accessed 28 February 2019]

32 Ibid.

33 Interview summer 2018. I am very grateful to her for discussing these questions with me.

34 Ibn al-Sai, *Consorts of the Caliphs: Women and the Court of Baghad*, edited by Shawkat M Toorawa, translated by The Editors of the Library of Arabic Literature, introduction by Julia Bray, foreword by Marina Warner, New York University Press, 2015.

35 See for example 'A British National Breakfast', nin.tl/Breakfast 'Mathematics', nin.tl/Mathematics or 'Language Learning' nin.tl/LanguageLearning

About the contributors

Bernardine Evaristo is a British-Nigerian writer who has authored eight award-winning books, including: *The Emperor's Babe* (2001), a *Times* 'Book of the Decade'; *Blonde Roots* (2008); and *Mr Loverman* (2013), winner of the Jerwood Fiction Uncovered Prize and several other awards. Her latest novel is *Girl, Woman, Other* (Penguin 2019). She has written numerous other published and produced works that span the genres of novels, poetry, verse fiction, short fiction, essays, literary criticism, and radio and theatre drama. She is Vice Chair of the Royal Society of Literature, Professor of Creative Writing at Brunel University London and she received an MBE in 2009 in the Queen's Birthday Honours List.

Romesh Gunesekera is a Sri-Lankan-born writer who has published eight books of fiction, including the highly acclaimed novels *Reef* (1994), a finalist for the Booker Prize and the Guardian Fiction Prize, *The Sandglass* (1998), awarded the inaugural BBC Asia Award for Achievement in Writing & Literature, and the cricket-inspired *The Match* (2006). His *Noontide Toll* (2014) captures a vital moment in the aftermath of the war in Sri Lanka through interwoven stories of individual lives. He is also the joint author (with AL Kennedy) of *The Writers' and Artists' Companion to Novel*

Writing. His new novel *Suncatcher* will be published in November 2019 by Bloomsbury.

Githa Hariharan is the author of several acclaimed books, including the novels *The Thousand Faces of Night* (which won the Commonwealth Writers' Prize for Best First Book in 1993), *The Ghosts of Vasu Master* (1994), *When Dreams Travel* (1999), *In Times of Siege* (2003), *Fugitive Histories* (2009) and *I Have Become the Tide* (2019); the short-story collection *The Art of Dying* (1993); and the collection of essays *Almost Home, Cities and Other Places* (2014). She has also edited an anthology of translated short fiction, *A Southern Harvest* (1993), and the collections *From India to Palestine: Essays in Solidarity* (2014) and *Battling for India: A Citizen's Reader* (2019).

Eva Hoffman grew up in Cracow, Poland, before emigrating in her teens to Canada and then the United States. After receiving her PhD in literature from Harvard University, she worked as senior editor and literary critic at the *New York Times*, and has taught at various British and American universities. Her books, which have been translated widely, include *Lost in Translation* (1989), *Exit Into History* (1993), *After Such Knowledge* (2004) and *Time* (2009), as well as two novels, *The Secret* (2002) and *Illuminations* (2009). She has written and presented numerous programmes for BBC Radio and has lectured internationally on subjects of exile, historical memory, cross-cultural relations, political transitions, and other contemporary issues. Her awards include the Guggenheim Fellowship, Whiting Award for Writing, an award from the American Academy of Arts and Letters and Prix Italia for Radio. She is a Fellow of the Royal

Society of Literature, and holds an honorary doctorate from Warwick University. She lives in London.

James Kelman is a citizen of Glasgow, Scotland. His story collections include *Greyhound for Breakfast* (1998), *The Good Times* (1998) and most recently *If it is your life* (2010). His novel *How Late It Was, How Late* won the 1994 Booker Prize; his other novels include *Translated Accounts* (2001), *You Have to be Careful in the Land of the Free* (2004), and *Kieron Smith, boy* (2008). In 2009 he was shortlisted for the Man Booker International Prize. In 2012 he won the Saltire Book of the Year award for *Mo Said She was Quirky*. Also author of several essays, his most recent novel *Dirt Road* was published in 2017 by Canongate Books.

James Kelman writes:

In his essay Blake Morrison refers to the horrible blunder I made in mistaken identity. It derived from a talk I gave in 1989 where I named him as 'prejudiced'. This followed a review of a work by Chinua Achebe where Achebe 'described Joseph Conrad as a thoroughgoing racist.' The reviewer defends Conrad and attacks Achebe. I attributed this review to Blake Morrison. I was utterly wrong. The review was by Craig Raine (*London Review of Books*, June 1989). It was an appalling mistake. Blake was wronged and I was responsible for it. Nor did I discover the truth until twenty years later, when it was pointed out to me by Blake himself, in the most magnanimous manner. I contacted the publisher (AK Press) and they withdrew the collection with immediate effect. The book has been out-of-print ever since. I have amended the essay for future reference, in the event it is ever republished. I thank Blake for his great generosity.

Tabish Khair was born in 1966 and educated in Gaya, a small town in Bihar, India. He is the author of various acclaimed books, including the novels *The Bus Stopped* (2004), *Filming: A Love Story* (2007), *The Thing About Thugs* (2010), *How to Fight Islamist Terror from the Missionary Position* (2012), *Just Another Jihadi Jane* (2016) and the poetry collections *Where Parallel Lines Meet* (2000) and *Man of Glass* (2010). His studies include: *Babu Fictions: Alienation in Contemporary Indian English Novels* (2001); *The Gothic, Postcolonialism and Otherness* (2009); and *The New Xenophobia* (2016). Winner of the All India Poetry Prize in 1995, his novels have been shortlisted for more than a dozen major prizes, including the Man Asian, the DSC Prize and the Encore. An Associate Professor at Aarhus University, Denmark, he has been a Leverhulme Guest Professor at Leeds University, UK, and has also been awarded guest professorships or honorary fellowships at JNU, Delhi University, Jamia Millia Islamia University and IIT-Bhubaneshwar (India), Hong Kong City University and Hong Kong Baptist University (China), York University (UK), and Churchill College, Cambridge University, UK. In 2018, he published the novel *Night of Happiness*.

Kei Miller is a writer who grew up in Kingston, Jamaica. His books include *The Cartographer Tries To Map A Way To Zion* (2014) shortlisted for a Costa Prize and winner of the 2014 Forward Prize for Poetry, and the novel *Augustown* (2016), winner of the OGM Bocas Prize for Caribbean Literature, the Prix Carbet de la Caraïbe et du Tout-Monde, and the Prix Les Afriques. He is the author of seven additional books that range between fiction, nonfiction and poetry. He is currently Professor of Creative Writing at the University of Exeter and has been an Ida Beam Distinguished Visiting Professor at the University of Iowa.

Blake Morrison was born in Skipton, Yorkshire, and has written fiction, poetry, journalism, literary criticism and libretti, as well as adapting plays for the stage. Among his best-known works are his two memoirs, *And When Did You Last See Your Father?* (1993) and *Things My Mother Never Told Me* (2002). He is a Fellow of the Royal Society of Literature, former Chair of the Poetry Book Society and Vice-Chair of PEN. He is also Professor of Creative and Life Writing at Goldsmiths College. His latest book is a novel with poems, *The Executor* (2018).

Mukoma Wa Ngugi was born in 1971 in Illinois, USA, but raised in Kenya, before returning to the United States. A literary activist, scholar and writer, his novels include *Mrs Shaw* (2015), *Black Star Nairobi* (2013) and *Nairobi Heat* (2011). He has two published books of poetry, *Hurling Words at Consciousness* (2006) and *Logotherapy* (2016). He is the co-founder of the Mabati-Cornell Kiswahili Prize for African Literature and co-director of the Global South Project – Cornell. He is Associate Professor of English at Cornell University.

Hsiao-Hung Pai is a journalist and is the author of the books *Chinese Whispers: The Story Behind Britain's Hidden Army of Labour* (2008), shortlisted for the 2009 Orwell Prize; *Scattered Sand: The Story of China's Rural Migrants* (2012), winner of the 2013 Bread and Roses Award; *Invisible* (2013); *Angry White People* (2016); and *Bordered Lives* (2018). She has written for *The Guardian* and many Chinese publications worldwide.

Caryl Phillips was born in St Kitts and came to Britain at the age of four months. He grew up in Leeds, and studied English Literature at Oxford University. He began writing for the theatre and his plays include *Strange Fruit* (1980), *Where There is Darkness* (1982) and *The Shelter* (1983). His novels are: *The Final Passage* (1985), *A State of Independence* (1986), *Higher Ground* (1989), *Cambridge* (1991), *Crossing the River* (1993), *The Nature of Blood* (1997), *A Distant Shore* (2003), *Dancing in the Dark* (2005), *Foreigners* (2007), *In the Falling Snow* (2009), *The Lost Child* (2015), and *A View of the Empire at Sunset* (2018). His non-fiction titles are: *The European Tribe* (1987), *The Atlantic Sound* (2000), *A New World Order* (2001), and *Colour Me English* (2011). He is the editor of two anthologies: *Extravagant Strangers: A Literature of Belonging* (1997) and *The Right Set: An Anthology of Writing on Tennis* (1999). His work has been translated into over a dozen languages. He is a Fellow of the Royal Society of Literature and the Royal Society of the Arts, and recipient of the 2013 Anthony N Sabga Caribbean Award for Excellence. Formerly Henry R Luce Professor of Migration and Social Order at Columbia University, he is presently Professor of English at Yale University.

Olumide Popoola is a London-based Nigerian-German writer and speaker who presents internationally. Her novella *this is not about sadness* (2010) was published by Unrast Verlag. Her play *Also by Mail* (2013) was published by Witnessed and the short-story collection *breach* (2016), which she co-authored with Annie Holmes, by Peirene Press. Her novel *When We Speak of Nothing* (2017) was published in the UK, Nigeria and the USA (2018) by Cassava Republic Press. She holds a PhD in creative writing.

Shivanee Ramlochan is a Trinidadian poet, arts reporter and book blogger. Her first collection of poems, *Everyone Knows I Am a Haunting* (Peepal Tree Press, 2017) was shortlisted for the 2018 Felix Dennis Prize for Best First Collection. She is the book-reviews editor for *Caribbean Beat Magazine*, and writes about books for the NGC Bocas Lit Fest, the Anglophone Caribbean's largest literary festival, as well as Paper Based Bookshop, Trinidad and Tobago's oldest independent Caribbean speciality bookseller. Find her online at @novelniche.

Bina Shah is a Karachi-based author of five novels and two collections of short stories. Her novels include the critically acclaimed *A Season for Martyrs* (2014) and the feminist dystopian novel *Before She Sleeps* (2018). She is a regular contributor to the *New York Times*, *Al Jazeera* and the *Huffington Post*, and is a frequent guest on the BBC. She is a graduate of Wellesley College and the Harvard Graduate School of Education, and is an Honorary Fellow in Writing at the University of Iowa. She is currently the president of the Alliance Francaise de Karachi and works on issues of women's rights and female empowerment in Pakistan and across Muslim countries.

Raja Shehadeh is a writer and lawyer who founded the pioneering Palestinian human rights organisation Al-Haq, an affiliate of the International Commission of Jurists. Shehadeh is the author of several books on international law, human rights and the Middle East, including *Occupier's Law* (1985) and *From Occupation to Interim Accords* (1997). His literary works include: *Strangers in the House* (2002); *Occupation Diaries* (2012); *A Rift in Time: Travels with my Ottoman Uncle*

(2010); *Language of War, Language of Peace* (2015); *Where the Line is Drawn: Crossing Boundaries in Occupied Palestine* (2017) and *Palestinian Walks*, which won the 2008 Orwell Prize, Britain's pre-eminent award for political writing. His latest book is *Going Home: A Walk Through Fifty Years of Occupation* (2019). He has written for the *New York Times*, the *New Yorker*, *Granta* and other publications. He lives in Ramallah, Palestine.

Marina Warner is a writer of fiction, criticism and history. Born in London, her works include novels such as the award-winning *The Lost Father* (1988) and *Indigo* (1992); three short-story collections, the most recent being *Fly Away Home* (2015); and studies of art, myths, symbols and fairytales such as *Stranger Magic: Charmed States and the Arabian Nights* (2012) and *Fairy Tale: A Very Short Introduction* (2018). She has been awarded many prestigious prizes and titles. These include the 2012 National Book Critics Circle Award for Criticism and the 2015 Holberg Prize; she was made DBE in the 2015 New Year's Honours for services to higher education and literature. She is President of the Royal Society of Literature. She is currently writing an 'unreliable memoir' about her childhood in Egypt.

About the editors

Susheila Nasta is a literary activist, publisher and distinguished scholar in post-colonial literature. She is founding editor of *Wasafiri*, which she launched in 1984.

Susheila has published widely, especially on the Caribbean, South Asian diaspora and black Britain. Recent books include *Home Truths: Fictions of the South Asian Diaspora in Britain*, *Writing Across Worlds: Contemporary Writers Talk* (editor), *India in Britain* and *Asian Britain: A Photographic History*. She is the co-editor of the forthcoming *The Cambridge History of Black and Asian British Writing*, the first major literary and cultural history of black and Asian British writing. She is completing a group biography, *The Bloomsbury Indians*, which presents an alternative lens on Bloomsbury after the First World War.

She is Professor of Modern and Contemporary Literatures at Queen Mary University of London and Emerita at the Open University. She was appointed MBE in 2011 for her services to black and Asian literature. In 2019 she was elected an Honorary Fellow by the Royal Society of Literature and awarded the Benson Medal for a lifetime of exceptional service.

Rukhsana Yasmin is the former Deputy Editor of *Wasafiri*. She was winner of the 2012 Kim Scott Walwyn Prize for Women in Publishing and in 2014 was named a *Bookseller* Rising Star. She has worked as an editor at Saqi Books, Profile Books, Serpent's Tail, Jacaranda and Commonwealth Writers. She has judged several prizes and spoken at conferences on diversity in publishing, Muslim literature and international fiction.

Index

Index

Index

Sign up to our mailing list at
www.myriadeditions.com
Follow us on Facebook and Twitter